# *Three on a Toothbrush*

*Also by Jack Paar:*

MY SABER IS BENT

I KID YOU NOT

# JACK PAAR

# THREE
# ON A
# TOOTHBRUSH

DOUBLEDAY & COMPANY, INC., GARDEN CITY, NEW YORK

1965

I would like to express my appreciation to the *Reader's Digest* for permission to reprint portions of this material which appeared in that magazine.

Once again, for
Miriam and Randy

# Contents

# *Introduction*

The cultural exchange has now become an important fact of international life, particularly between Russia and the United States. The Soviet Union sent us the Bolshoi Ballet and we sent them Van Cliburn. They sent us violinist David Oistrakh and we responded with Benny Goodman. They sent us the Moiseyev Dancers and we dispatched *Porgy and Bess* to them. Eventually the world was knee-deep in culture and no one was any the worse for it although the suspicious Russians charged that two members of Goodman's band were spies. Apparently they bugged Benny's clarinet.

While all this was going on, no one offered to send me anyplace. It was pretty discouraging since almost everyone I knew was being sent to some foreign country to entertain. U.S. cultural officials sent Louis Armstrong to Africa, Marian Anderson to India, George Jessel to Israel. And Bob Hope was going *everywhere.* "Bob was going to Greenland to entertain the troops at Christmas but they found there was only one sergeant and a private stationed there," Joey Bishop told me. "The Army had to fly ten thousand men up from New Jersey so Bob's feelings wouldn't be hurt."

Meantime, no one asked me to go *anywhere.* Oh, I got a few nibbles. NBC sent me to Hong Kong, at the time the

Asiatic flu epidemic struck this country, but this may have
been simply a coincidence and not an outright exchange.

Since there was no demand for me in a cultural exchange
(even for Dame Edith Sitwell and a left-handed hitting out-
fielder) I decided to conduct my own series of goodwill
tours, and incidentally, to film as we went. That way I could
not only dispense a little culture on my own but have films
to show on my television show. At first the critics greeted
these films of my travels with my wife Miriam and daughter
Randy with hoots of derision, referring to them as "home
movies." "You are the only man who can make home movies," Jack E. Leonard told me, "and win the Academy
Award for intestinal fortitude." They were do-it-yourself
movies, I'll admit, yet Moscow, New Guinea, the Congo,
Tahiti, the Amazon, Zanzibar, and most of the other places I
filmed were a long way from *home*—which is in Westchester
County, New York.

My friend Jack Douglas says that I'm the Typhoid Mary
of travel, and I guess it's true that I'm a carrier of confusion.
Certainly we encountered a variety of perils and misadven-
tures in our travels. In Zanzibar I was struck by a hit-run
rickshaw. In Germany I was accused of creating an incident
at the Berlin Wall and then absolved by a government investigating agency. Our plane nearly crashed on Guadalcanal attempting to take off from a flooded airfield. In
Jordan we *flew* at 1000 feet *below* sea level. Our helicopter
skimmed just over the Dead Sea and it is 1200 feet below sea
level. In Spain I bested a bull in a bullfight. I beat him to the
fence by one jump. In Hong Kong I lost at Russian roulette
to a Chinese tailor. (You get your choice of six suits and one
is your size.) We lost most of our luggage in Africa and
wound up three on a toothbrush.

We braved all these assorted vicissitudes poking my camera into odd corners of the globe and then the critics call my films "home movies." However, the TV public has indicated that films of our trips were perhaps the most interesting feature of my show. Of late even the critics are saying nice things about them, which worries me a little. In view of the warm reception the travel films have had, it occurred to me there might be interest in a book on our travels and the stories and people I've encountered on my trips and on television.

Of course writing another book presented some problems. I had already written two books, *I Kid You Not* and *My Saber Is Bent,* and both had been best sellers. Would another book be successful? I talked the problem over with my friend Jean Kerr who wrote two highly successful books as well as the Broadway comedy hits *Mary, Mary* and *Poor Richard.* She said that a lot of people had asked her whether it was easier to write a second book with one success behind her and that she finally developed a stock answer.

"Writing the first book was like crawling across a deep gorge on a narrow plank," Jean would say. "Writing the second one is like crawling back over the same plank."

One day Jean met a writer whose last book had been a flop.

"Never mind telling me about crawling back over that narrow plank," he muttered. "How do I get out of the gorge?"

Despite the danger of falling into a gorge, I decided to write another book. My friend John Reddy of the *Reader's Digest* assisted me by extricating me from dangling participles, repairing my spelling and removing excess exclamation points.

What I've tried to do in this book is to effect a sudden ca-thexis of the reader's super-ego, which in turn alters the re-actions of the ego. Freud says that's what happens when your risibilities are tickled. I hope it works.

*RUSSIA*

September 1961

I imagine I'm one of the few people who ever escaped *into* Russia. There's been a lot of traffic going the other way, but fleeing *to* Russia gives you a feeling like going up a down escalator.

It all started innocently enough in September of 1961 when I went to Berlin to film our program in that troubled city just after the Soviet puppet East German regime had put up the infamous wall separating East and West Berlin. We filmed one hour of the program at Checkpoint Charlie, showing the ugly, newly built wall and interviewing a few American soldiers. Immediately, the appearance of the GIs being interviewed near the wall set off an uproar that echoed all the way to Washington. Senators and Congressmen rose in Congress to accuse me of causing an "incident." The State Department was in a swivet. The Army took disciplinary action against the two officers who had assisted in arranging the filming. And all of this happened *before* the program in question was even seen. It was triggered by one wire service story making our interview near the wall, which was about as provocative as the small talk at an Elks' picnic, sound like some kind of atomic brinkmanship. When the

tape was finally televised, a few days later, the whole silly
uproar evaporated. The Army reinstated the two officers
"with full apologies to correct an injustice," and the Senators who had raised the ruckus, without ever having seen
what they were denouncing, shut up faster than you can say
Bobby Baker.

However, while all the uproar was going on I decided to
get out of Berlin. We had been planning to go to Russia, and
had our visas, so it seemed the ideal time to light out for
Moscow and leave the rumpus behind. Our little group of
reverse refugees consisted of Miriam, Randy, and myself,
TV writer Paul Keyes and *his* wife Miriam. Since there were
no direct flights from West Berlin to Moscow, we had to fly
to France to get a plane to the Russian capital.

As our Air France Caravelle winged toward Moscow our
first impression was of the vastness of the land below us. The
immensity of Russia is almost overwhelming. The huge land
is more than twice as large as the continental United States,
and larger than all of South America. Eleven of the world's
twenty-four time zones are included in Russia, our stewardess told us, and when it is midnight at one end of the USSR
it is almost noon at the other. Looking down from thirty
thousand feet, we saw flat forests of birch and pine stretching away endlessly as far as the eye could see.

On landing at Moscow we were immediately struck by
the almost eerie stillness. After the bustle and noise of Orly
airport in Paris, the Moscow airport seemed strangely quiet
and empty. I had some qualms about our reception, because
of the hubbub we left behind in Berlin, but we passed
through customs without incident. We were met at the airport by Eleanor Harris and photographer Phil Harrington of
*Look* magazine, come to cover our impulsive expedition,

and by our Intourist guide, a serious, dark-haired girl named Marina, who said she would be our guide throughout our stay.

"You speak very good English," I told her.

"It's not my best language," she said. "Malay is. I also speak French and Italian and can read German." She also told us that five million Russians speak English.

The drive into Moscow, in a black Zim sedan which resembled a twelve-year-old Buick, took about forty-five minutes. There were no garish signs along the way, such as those which clutter up American highways, and the flat country, with its patches of green forests, reminded us of Connecticut. Our first view of Moscow, as we approached, was disappointing. Although it is as large as New York, the Russian capital looked drab and sprawling and it struck me that the national color should be gray and not red. Incidentally, Marina told us the word red means beautiful in Russian—which Moscow certainly is not. It is a city of big, square buildings, depressingly alike. The streets are wide, straight, and clean, the traffic is light and the cars, like the buildings, as uniform as though stamped out by a cookie cutter. There is one nice aspect to all this: no traffic jams and no parking problems. We saw a great deal of construction going on, but it all seemed to be more of the same square, blocklike six- and eight-story apartment houses which sprouted everywhere. Also, the construction seemed shoddy and we noticed that even relatively new buildings had wire netting extending out from the first story like a trampolin to catch falling tiles and masonry.

Our driver deposited us at the National Hotel, an old, rococo building on Red Square. A buxom woman (virtually all the hotel employees were women, and virtually all the

women were buxom) showed us to our suite, two high-
ceilinged rooms looking out on the historic old square where
Ivan the Terrible used to burn his enemies. (Ivan had a per-
sonality problem. He hated *everybody*.) Our suite, Marina
proudly told us, had been occupied by Lenin for several
months just after the 1917 revolution. I was flattered—until
some American friends later told me that the Lenin suite is
bugged and is always given to guests whom the Russians
think might have something to say worth tuning in on.

The décor of our suite was early Charles Addams: red
plush and white lace curtains, knitted doilies on the furniture, and big old paintings of landscapes on the green walls.
There were several curious touches about our rooms. There
was a telephone but no phone book; apparently the whole
country is unlisted. The towels were as thin as tissue paper
but the toilet paper seemed as thick as towels. The plumb-
ing worked but there were no stoppers in the basin or tub.
We used toilet tissue as makeshift stoppers. With surroundings like that I could understand how Lenin turned on capitalism.

Trying to get room service at the National was a pro-
tracted negotiation as wearing as an international disarma-
ment conference. I had a suit I wanted to get pressed. I
began a sign language parley with the burly floor matron
who presided over our floor. I held up the suit and made
motions as if I were ironing it. She broke into a knowing
smile and summoned another husky woman with an iron.
She spread out a sheet on the floor, put the suit on the sheet
and began to iron it vigorously. Her technique was different,
but I must say it worked. Not only was my suit neatly
pressed when she got through, but the rug looked a lot better, too.

Trying to telephone from the hotel was another exercise in futility. Since there is no phone book you call the operator and right away you're in trouble. Sign language is not as effective on the telephone. Then there is the Russian system. If you want to call long distance you estimate in advance how long you want to talk . . . a neat trick whether you're in Moscow or Ashtabula, Ohio. Then you buy coupons (what else?) for the length call you *think* you're going to make. If you want to talk longer than you estimated, or if someone hangs up on you, that's your problem.

Randy had a separate room on another floor but we didn't feel at ease about the arrangement so she moved in with us. Miriam and I pushed our beds together and the three of us slept in our makeshift king-size bed. While we were unpacking, Randy suddenly asked, "Where are the mikes?" A quick search failed to disclose any hidden microphones, although there did seem to be a lot of extra wires around. Bugging hotel rooms, we discovered, is practically the national pastime in Russia. Bob Hope told me that whenever he went to bed at night in a Moscow hotel he would face the wall and shout: "That concludes our broadcast for this evening. Be sure and catch the late, late show tomorrow, same time, same room." However, just in case someone really *was* listening, Bob would always add, "Only kidding, Kru!"

We learned that American diplomats have a much more subtle way of coping with Soviet bugging. When they were in a room they thought was wired with hidden microphones, they would drop a hint that a Russian diplomat (preferably one they didn't like) was having an affair with the wife of a high Soviet official, and thus plant a little ill will where it would do the most good.

The food in the dining room at the National was quite

good, although they were stingy with menus. One to a table.
Incidentally, they had the same menu for breakfast, lunch,
and dinner. They featured a wide selection of dishes—most
of which they were just out of. However, the caviar, vodka,
sturgeon, grouse, and chicken Kiev were excellent and in
good supply. Our first dinner at the hotel was typical: caviar,
borscht, beef Stroganoff and a dessert called "Intourist Surprise": two scoops of ice cream topped by two grapes. Ice
cream, we discovered, is a national mania. It is served everywhere in Moscow: on the streets, in theaters, even at
cocktail parties. It's nice to be able to get ice cream at cocktail parties, because you usually *can't* get cocktails. The Russians invented the Molotov cocktail—a gasoline-filled bottle
handy for blowing up enemy tanks. The Molotov cocktail is
out of style now, what with peaceful co-existence, but I had
a couple of straight vodkas that might be just as effective
blowing up tanks. The Russians also have good wine and
passable beer. There is no Bourbon, Scotch, or gin—except
at a few places like the U.S. Embassy.

During our stay we were able to go anywhere we wished
(although we couldn't get far without our Russian-speaking
guide) and to film anything we liked. We toured the Grand
Kremlin Palace, former residence of the Czars, visited the
Children's World, a four-story department store that sells
only children's clothes and toys and rode the gleaming,
modern subway, with its ornate chandeliers and artistic murals, where you can absorb culture while getting your foot
stepped on. The Moscow subway is something! It carries
over three million passengers a day, and the fare is just six
cents. We also visited the USSR's permanent Agricultural
and Industrial Exhibitions, went through towering Moscow

University on the windswept Lenin hills and toured the outskirts of the city where old Russian log or plank cottages, with gaily painted shutters, nestled amid the blue, white and green prefabricated housing blocks. Although we saw much poor workmanship in the buildings, we could not help but be impressed by the Russians' eagerness to learn. We saw them reading everywhere—in buses and automobiles, in elevators and even walking along the streets. When one of us used a word an English-speaking Russian didn't understand they would ask us to repeat the word and explain it. Then they would eagerly whip out notebooks and jot down the new word.

One thing that impressed us in exploring the city was its cleanliness; it is far cleaner than most big American cities. The hotels and apartment buildings are heated by steam piped in from plants on the outskirts of the city, so the air is free of the smog that besets many American cities. Then, too, there are the legions of elderly women, many of them war widows, patiently sweeping the streets with short brooms. They invented the broom—but had not yet discovered handles. Also, of course, there are less cars adding their exhaust fumes to the city's air. Cleanliness and order, we found, are a national mania like ice cream, drinking vodka, and red tape. There are a hundred and fifty traffic laws, Marina told us, including one making it compulsory to keep your car washed. We noticed the police stop and warn drivers about a dirty windshield or dented fender. The taxis, which are owned by the state, whipped around as recklessly as taxis everywhere, often zipping sixty or seventy miles an hour. The Russians boast there is very little crime in the Soviet Union, yet we observed that when they parked their cars they carefully removed the windshield wipers so they couldn't be stolen. As long as it was raining the windshield wipers would be busily swishing away, but as soon as the rain stopped the Russians would quickly remove them and lock them in the trunk. When it began raining the process was reversed. They would stop the car, get the wiper out of the trunk and install it on the windshield. Spare parts are hard to come by. We saw only one dog in Moscow—a little mongrel—and it was being petted almost to death by passers-by. In contrast to the shortage of dogs and cats were the pigeons we saw everywhere. The city has many fenced-off areas where the pigeons, considered such a nuisance in American cities, are fed and tended by uniformed women.

Our most striking impression of Moscow was the almost unbelievable gap between the Russians' amazing achievements in space and the drabness and inefficiency of their everyday lives. It is a city of startling contrasts and contradictions. New apartments were rising on every hand, yet the tile and masonry was falling off almost as soon as they were put up. We saw gleaming sputniks yet in most stores they computed change with the centuries-old abacus. The cars and trucks were ten years behind ours, but the beautiful, air-conditioned subway, with trains arriving at main stations every ninety seconds, was infinitely better than New York's. They spoke proudly of their new skyscrapers, but Moscow's finest buildings were still the spired and turreted Kremlin, onion-domed St. Basil's, and the Novodevichy Monastery—all built long ago under the Czars. They have gone from the outhouse to outer space with no in-between. The week that Yuri Gagarin orbited the earth Moscow had a meat shortage and no caps for the milk bottles. The Russians we talked to are defensive about these short-

ages and say they are the result of channeling so much of
the country's energies into the space effort. We were told of
the Western diplomat who said to a Soviet woman official,
"You can make sputniks, madam, but how is it you can't
make nylon panties?"

"It's true," the Russian woman said, "but I think it's going
to be a lot easier to go from sputniks to nylon panties than
it will be to go from nylon panties to sputniks."

The most impressive thing about Russia, to us, was the
Russian people. Physically, however, they are not impressive. Perhaps because so many things about Russia are so
huge (there are 220,000,000 Russians of 185 different racial
groups), we were surprised that the people themselves were
not larger. Most of the men and women we saw were short
and stocky. Even the Russian soldiers, whom we sometimes
saw in pairs walking hand in hand, seemed surprisingly
young and small. However, we found the Russian people we
met pleasant and friendly and we liked them immediately.
Despite being subjected to years of anti-American propa-
ganda, the Russians we talked to seemed to like and even
envy Americans. We saw a good many English-speaking
Russians around the National Hotel just waiting for a chance
to practice their English on American or British guests. Several times Russian men and women grabbed Miriam or
Randy on the street and said, "Peace, peace." Children
swarmed around us offering to trade medals for ball-point
pens or "chooin gum," and whenever we filmed in public
places a crowd would gather to watch us with grave curiosity.

For all their friendliness and courtesy to strangers, we
found them quiet and serious, at least in public. We noticed

this particularly the day we stood in line in Red Square to visit the tomb of Lenin and Stalin shortly before Stalin's body was unceremoniously removed from the mausoleum. There were thousands of Russians standing in line and they shuffled along patiently and quietly with no conversation or laughter. Seeing this huge throng, day after day, waiting to gaze on the bodies of Lenin and Stalin, I was reminded of the line said when a huge crowd turned out for the funeral of a much-hated Hollywood tycoon: "Give the public what they want and they'll come." We got at the tail end of the long line. The Russian in front of us asked, "Tourist?" When I nodded he beckoned us to move ahead. We demurred but he insisted so we moved in front of him. This was repeated over and over until we reached the massive red basalt tomb where the bodies of Lenin and Stalin lay enclosed in a glass case under neon lights, guarded by two soldiers. With his slight figure, pointed beard and waxen face, Lenin looked as undistinguished as a jeweler from Toledo, Ohio. It was curious to think that this little man, who had lived and worked in the very rooms we were presently occupying, had so greatly influenced the world we live in. Gazing down at him I was reminded of former NBC Moscow correspondent John Chancellor's definition of the difference between Communism and Capitalism. "Under Communism man exploits man," Chancellor said. "Under Capitalism it's the other way around."

Seeing thousands of Russians in one group we could not help but be struck by the drabness of their appearance. The men, stocky and husky, looked like American Midwestern farmers come to town for a Saturday night. They were dressed in floppy, ill-fitting suits of browns and grays. Some wore hats pulled down over their ears and the bareheaded ones had long, tousled hair. The women, similarly plump and dowdy, looked like losers from a bargain rush at Klein's. They wore shapeless dresses of drab colors and wore babushkas rather than hats. We saw no high heels worn by women and the shoes of both men and women were down at the heels. I filmed the line waiting to enter the tomb and when one role of film was almost used up I pointed the camera at the ground to run out the last few feet of film before replacing the role. I noticed an expression of disapproval on Marina's face. "I've done something you didn't like," I said. "What did I do?"

"You disappoint me," she said. "You were making fun of my shoes."

This was not the only occasion we encountered this feeling of defensive pride by a Russian. Another time I offered some ball-point pens to the guide who had shown us through the Kremlin Palace. The man declined. "Please have some," I insisted. "I have many of them."

"Why do you say you have many?" Marina said, frowning. "Why not just offer him one?"

I did offer him one and he accepted with a smile.

The Russian children were bright, alert, and friendly, although sometimes adults discouraged them in their offers to trade us medals for "chooin gum." The children are strictly raised, we found, and juvenile delinquency is almost unknown in Russia. So great is the pressure to conform that there are no left-handed children in Russia.

Wherever we went we found women working, including doing much heavy work. Women clean the streets. Seventy percent of the doctors, Marina said, are women. Oddly enough, we saw almost no women automobile drivers, although they drive cabs, tractors and trucks. All barbers are

women. I got a haircut and shave from a lady barber for
nineteen cents. The Russians spray on after-shave lotion,
rather than rubbing it on as we do, and my lady barber was
so intent on being courteous to a tourist that she nearly
drowned me in a blast of Essence of Siberia or some such
bracing Russian tonic.

We found the Russians strangely contradictory in their
moral values. They are heavy drinkers, and we saw many
public sobering-up stations, yet they are prudish in their attitude toward sex. From what we gathered there is very
little hanky-panky between the sexes and Russians frown
on low-cut dresses or short skirts. On the other hand, both
men and women wear the briefest of bikinis on the beach
and even undress there publicly without anyone taking any
notice. Russian men never show their admiration for a pretty
girl on the street by whistling, like American males, or
pinching like Italians. They just invite them up to the apartment to look at their etchings—of Lenin.

As we know, the Russians claim to have invented a great
many things from the airplane to baseball. I have always
had some difficulty accepting the theory that our national
pastime was invented by somebody like Rasputin, rather
than Abner Doubleday, but there is no denying that the
Russians are an inventive people. They have invented, or
at least perfected, the food shortage, the apartment shortage, and the shopping queue. We were introduced to some
of these inventions one day when we went shopping at
GUM, the big department store that is the Macy's of Moscow. GUM (the letters are the initials, in Russian, for Government Department Store) is a block-square, three-story,
old stone building across from the Kremlin on Red Square.

It looks like a cross between a Victorian railway station and an American department store, with dozens of small individual shops selling everything from TV sets to toilet paper (which you buy in the stationery department!). The merchandise was shoddy and overpriced, by our standards, yet more than 100,000,000 customers shop there a year, Marina told us. In a country where the average wage is $100 a month, we saw men's shoes for $28 a pair, women's shoes for $55 a pair and a cardigan sweater, which would cost $15 in London, for $35. A candy bar sold for $1.50 and a TV set for $700. There wasn't much appealing but I wanted to buy something so I got a Russian hat to wear at parties. It's funnier than a lampshade.

Although the Russians are ordinarily disciplined and courteous, the crowded department store brought out the worst in them and they were elbowing one another as enthusiastically as the ladies at a Bargain Day at an American discount house. One reason for this is probably the Russian retail selling system, which must have been devised by some enemy of the state. This is how it works: Say you want to buy a cabbage. First you find out if they have any cabbage. Then you stand in line a half hour to pick out the cabbage you want. You are then given a check for the cabbage you chose. You then head for the cashier and stand in line for another fifteen minutes to pay for your cabbage. *Then* you go back and stand in another line with your check to show you paid for your cabbage. Then you get your cabbage— which, by that time, is wilted. It's all very simple. In fact the Russians have a joke about it. "What," they ask, "is fifty yards long and lives on cabbage?" The answer is: "The line in front of a meat counter."

After not buying any cabbage, we set up to film GUM's

fashion show. The store stages a fashion show three times a day, with an orchestra, woman commentator, a dozen models and similar capitalistic frills. The models are plumper than our cadaverous U.S. models, and when they first came out I thought the commentator was introducing the Green Bay Packers. I noticed from the manner in which the well-upholstered Russian girls jounced and jiggled that the Soviets apparently look on girdles and brassieres as tools of decadent capitalism. At any rate, the ample curves of the Russian women are *one* thing that are not controlled by the Kremlin or anything else.

The clothes modeled at the fashion show were not unstylish, but there is a catch. The dresses worn by the models are not for sale. If a Russian woman sees a dress she likes, she can buy a *pattern.* First she gets in line . . .

The Russian people rarely smile—which can make an entertainer rather nervous. Marina told us that they feel that Americans smile too much and consider our ready smiles and laughter rather foolish. We noticed the Russians' unsmiling faces on the streets, but they were particularly apparent at the theater where you expect to see people laughing and smiling.

We attended a performance of Moscow's famous Puppet Theater featuring Sergei Obraztsov, who later had a successful run on Broadway. Although the puppets were the greatest I have ever seen the crowd was curiously silent and laughed very little. We also went to a concert (as they call a variety show) where the master of ceremonies was an attractive young Russian man. He was well-dressed and wore a white handkerchief in his breast pocket, which we hadn't seen any other Russian doing. I nudged Miriam and called her attention to it. When the young man came out to introduce the next act the handkerchief was missing. I never did understand *that*. Perhaps he was offended at my noticing his handkerchief. Or maybe he just had to blow his nose.

During intermission, while we stood around munching salami sandwiches, an English-speaking Russian struck up a conversation with us. He was a slim, dark-haired, outgoing man and proceeded to invite us to his home for dinner. We had been told that Russians almost never invite foreigners to their homes, and we certainly didn't want to go to the home of a total stranger we had just met, but he wouldn't take *nyet* for an answer. "I want you to come for a proper meal," he insisted. "But there are six of us," I objected. "Good," he said. "My car holds six."

Our host, whose name was Victor, drove us to his apartment where we met his attractive English wife and a group of their Russian friends including puppeteer Obraztsov. Although Victor lived in one of the new apartment houses, his four-room apartment was already rather run down. He said the apartment cost $100 a month—very high for Moscow—but there were cracks in the masonry, the doors didn't fit properly and the bathroom ceiling sagged. It had transparent plastic pipes so if you had nothing better to do you could spend an evening watching the plumbing. However, he had fine furniture, expensive modern paintings and two cars. He also offered us Scotch, Bourbon, and even American beer—all extremely rare in Russia.

Victor asked me what I did and I confessed I was a television entertainer. Then, like so many Russians, his next question was, "How much do you make?" For probably the first time in history an actor *understated* his salary. I didn't want Victor to know how much a tool of decadent capitalism makes. He might want me to smuggle him back to America and my luggage was already overweight.

Victor told us he was a translator. He had just translated *My Fair Lady* into Russian, he said, where it came out *Maya Prekrasnaya Lady*. There were a few other little changes, Victor said. For instance, *The Rain in Spain Stays Mainly in the Plain* emerged as *Carl Stole Corals from Cora*. I asked if Russia would pay royalties for the use of the musical in the Soviet Union. I just wish I could get laughs with my monologue like I did with that question. We discussed Russian and American writers, artists, and composers and he inquired about Jackson Pollock, the American painter, who had recently been killed in an automobile crash on Long Island. "Pollock was killed recently, you know," I told him. He puffed reflectively on his long Russian cigarette. "Who did it to him?" he asked.

All during the evening Victor kept the volume of the hi-fi, on which he was playing Louis Armstrong and Nöel Coward records, turned up to a deafening pitch—presumably so our conversation could not be bugged. It was so loud I was finally willing to send in a signed confession rather than hear any more Louis Armstrong turned up to such an ear-splitting pitch. A couple of times I casually turned the volume down myself, but each time our host turned it back up full blast.

At one point in the evening the inevitable Russian toasts began. Victor poured vodka and asked that I propose a toast. "Peace," I said, raising my glass. Obraztsov got up and went to Randy. "Not peace to us," he said, "but peace to this child."

We talked of living conditions in Moscow and the Russians said the government was building apartments feverishly to alleviate the housing shortage. The crowding was severe, they acknowledged, and as a result the people suffered from a lack of privacy. In fact, one of them said, there is not even a word for privacy in the Russian language. They pointed out, however, that there is one bright side to Moscow's overcrowded housing. Fires are very rare, they said, because all apartments are so crowded that it is almost impossible for a blaze to get started unobserved.

Fueled by vodkas, I finally asked the question that was on all our minds: What was their explanation of the gap between the inefficiencies in their everyday lives and their magnificent accomplishments in space. "We didn't walk," said Obraztsov. "We jumped." It was a well-turned phrase. But I still don't understand why their rockets go up and their elevators often don't.

I was pleased to discover in Moscow that the Russians stage the biggest parade in the world every year on my birthday. The fact that my birthday happens to be May 1—a red letter day in the Communist calendar—may have something to do with this. In any event, Moscow's May Day parade is not only the largest but the *shortest* parade of the year. For years I had seen newsreels of the impressive display of Soviet military might in Red Square: the goose-stepping troops, the modern armored vehicles and rockets and the massed civilians carrying banners and pictures of Marx, Lenin, and Stalin, while the Communist hierarchy looked grimly down from atop Lenin's mausoleum. Yet it wasn't until we visited Moscow that I learned that this awesome display of Soviet power marches only *a few blocks*.

A half-million Russians—soldiers and citizens—gather just off Red Square. They march the length of the square—about four blocks. And that's it. They then disband. There are other typical Russian ironies about the parade. One is that the Russian people can't see it—except on TV. Only visiting dignitaries, diplomats, and foreign correspondents are allowed into crowded Red Square to see the march. Another of the curious features of the parade is that the marchers carry pictures of Lenin in the same way that they once paraded with icons of Christ. We did not see pictures and statues of Khrushchev, as we had of other dictators in other countries, but replicas of Lenin were everywhere. We also saw children wearing medals of the infant Lenin the way children in America and elsewhere wear medals of the infant Jesus. Lenin's face was omnipresent, even stamped on the pieces of chocolate served on the Aeroflot planes. For Russia has officially abolished religion only to substitute a religion of the state. Lenin is now the opium of the people, and the whole country is hooked.

When we asked about religion in Russia we were told, "That's for the old people." This does seem true, and most of the churchgoers we saw were older women. Although the press rails constantly against religion, and famous St. Basil's is now an antireligious museum, many older people, particularly women, stubbornly continue going to church. The government grudgingly permits churchgoing, even while scoffing at it. Paul and Miriam Keyes, who are Catholic, were able to attend Mass on Sunday in the small apartment of a priest in an ordinary apartment house. There were six other worshipers, and the Keyes went to confession in the priest's tiny kitchen. Oddly enough, despite the state campaign to abolish religion, and the fact that no one can become a Communist unless he is an avowed atheist, crosses still topped some of the Kremlin towers and we saw some of the most beautiful icons and religious art in the world inside the Kremlin. Sunday is still a special day, but the Russians observe it not by praying but by shopping. They get all dressed up in their Sunday best and head for GUM department store.

The campaign against religion has taken most of the romantic atmosphere out of marriage. We visited the Palace of Weddings where Russians are married rather than in a church. A Commissar of Weddings in a business suit stands at a desk and marries a couple in a brief, one-paragraph statement. Divorce was formerly similarly cut and dried, we were told, although lately it had become more difficult to get. Previously a Russian who had grown a little tired of the little woman simply wrote the government a letter saying, "*I've had it with Natasha.*" A few days later Natasha got a letter telling her she was at liberty.

One of the highlights of our Moscow visit was a lunch at the U.S. Embassy as guests of Ambassador and Mrs. Llewellyn E. Thompson. We were delighted to be so hospitably received as Mrs. Thompson is not particularly familiar with American entertainers or else she enjoys pulling a leg occasionally. When Bob Hope entertained at the Embassy she greeted him with, "Oh, I'm so glad you're here. Did you bring your violin?" This apparent or tongue-in-cheek confusion of Hope with Jack Benny—or Yehudi Menuhin—left Bob speechless for probably the first time in his life.

"I don't know whether she meant it or was just putting me on," Hope said later. "But the hospitality certainly paid for the bruise."

Certainly the Thompsons were most hospitable and the Ambassador a brilliant source of information on Russia. I asked him about the life of a diplomat, which Adlai Stevenson once defined as "protocol, alcohol, and Geritol," particularly in Russia where the Soviets favorite indoor sport is bugging foreign embassies. He told me some of the means U.S. diplomats had devised to thwart Soviet eavesdroppers, one being to hold confidential discussions out of doors. These precautions were well taken as sometime later forty hidden microphones were found in the Embassy—some of them in the very room where we had lunch! It seems to me the Embassy officials should have become suspicious when they found the shower knobs marked "Hot," "Cold," and "Volume Control."

We found Ambassador Thompson to be a witty and resourceful conversationalist, which I imagine are mighty handy qualities in a diplomat—especially in Russia. A conversational skirmish which he engaged in with Khrushchev's son-in-law, Alexei Adzhubei, illustrates Thompson's quick wit. They were both guests at a dinner given by American Moscow correspondents for leading Russian journalists. An American handed Adzhubei a book of matches to light his cigar and the Russian fixed them with a beady eye. Then he rapped for attention. "I have here some American matches," he announced. "Since you continually say that you are a peaceful people, I would like to read what I see here." He glanced around the room and then read: "'Enlist in the U.S. Army.'"

Then he handed the matches to Thompson. The American envoy glanced at them. "I'm afraid you are being a little hasty," Thompson said quietly, "and looking at only one side of the story. If you turn the matches over you will see the other side says, 'Safety First. Prevent Accidents.'"

Even the Russians roared with laughter at Thompson's topper.

Although we enjoyed our stay in Moscow, and the Russians were most hospitable, several little things made us uneasy, perhaps foolishly. One was the circumstance of our coming just at the height of the Berlin crisis and immediately after I had been accused of creating an "incident" at the Berlin Wall and had been called a *provocateur* by the Communist East German press. Also Russia has just exploded a number of nuclear bombs which didn't seem a particularly friendly gesture. Then, too, there were little things that gave us the feeling that we were being watched. One was being put in Lenin's suite which was said to have so many hidden microphones it was like a broadcast studio with beds. Outwardly we had complete freedom to go anywhere we wished, and our Intourist guides were not with us at night. We noticed, though, that Marina always seemed to know what we had done the previous evening even though she was not with us.

One night we attended a variety show to see a particular act. After seeing the act, we left at intermission. The next day Marina asked how we enjoyed the show.

"Oh, we liked it very much," I enthused. "All of us thought it was exceptionally good."

"Why was it then," Marina asked dryly, "that you didn't come back after the intermission?"

Little things like that, indicating that our guides knew what we were doing even when they weren't present, were somewhat disquieting. Then, the night before we were to leave, I got a phone call from New York at two o'clock in the morning. I was so startled I jumped out of bed like a pilot ejecting himself from a jet fighter plane. It was Syd Eiges, a vice-president of NBC, calling.

"Jack, when are you leaving?" he asked abruptly. I told him I planned to leave in the morning.

"I want you to leave as quickly as you can," Eiges said. "Dag Hammarskjold has just been killed."

Then our connection was broken off. I didn't know whether he had hung up or we had been cut off. All sorts of wild thoughts raced through my mind. I envisioned Hammarskjold being shot at the United Nations—and by a Russian. Miriam and Randy had been awakened by the call and since we were all too keyed up to go back to sleep we got up and began packing.

We were relieved when we got to the airport and through customs without incident and began to feel easier when we settled back in our Aeroflot jet for the flight to Prague and Zurich. The plane was about to take off when I was called and an official asked to see our passports. Since I had just shown our passports, I got the panicky feeling that some problem had arisen to prevent our going. I showed the official my passport and Miriam's on which the photo of Randy had been canceled out by an X on a trip to Japan.

"This, this," he said, pointing angrily to the defaced photo.

I explained that it was crossed out in Japan because Randy now had her own passport. He frowned at the photo with the X stamped across Randy's face. "It's inhuman," he snorted, handing back the passport. "You may go."

Our collective sighs of relief generated as much thrust as the jet engines as our TU-104 raced down the runway and took off for Prague. Even when we were airborne, though, we still didn't have a sense of being completely at ease. I reminded the other members of our party that we still had to land at Prague, which was also behind the Iron Curtain, and for everyone to avoid any possible misstep until we arrived in Switzerland. During the layover to change planes at Prague, we were first in line at the gate from which it was announced our plane was leaving. Shortly before departure time, a self-important little man in a black overcoat and Homburg hat pushed by us to take first place in line. I grabbed him by the shoulder, spun him around and pushed him back toward the end of the line. Sputtering something I couldn't understand he stalked furiously into the terminal. A few minutes later he came out and took his place alone at a different gate. Our flight was then announced as leaving from the gate where the angry man stood alone, so the rest of us had to trail him up the ramp into the plane.

"Who was that rude man?" I asked an airline attendant.

"That," said the attendant, "is the Russian Ambassador."

# THE SOUTH PACIFIC
April–May 1962

The big island rose slowly off our starboard bow like a low-flying green cloud on the horizon. "Guadalcanal," grunted the bo'sun, a native attired only in frayed shorts, his ebony skin glistening with sea spray. I looked through the worn binoculars he handed me. The waves breaking on the palm-fringed beaches gave the island a serene, picture-postcard quality, and the sun breaking suddenly through a tropical rain squall, casting a rainbow overhead, heightened the illusion of a South Sea paradise. But I remembered Guadalcanal from the war. I remembered the rains and the malaria and the loneliness. The wartime code name for Guadalcanal was Cactus and it was well named. Like a thousand other GIs, I'd sworn that if I never saw that pestilential island again it would be too soon. Yet now I found myself coming back on a sentimental journey in April of 1962.

Like most Americans who were stationed there, I was on Guadalcanal after the fighting was over. There were still a few Japanese stragglers, and occasional air alerts, but the "Canal" as the GIs called it was being used as a staging base for attacks on enemy-held islands farther north.

I was technical sergeant in a special service company of
the infantry for twenty-eight months in the South Pacific,
mostly on Guadalcanal. My job was to make men laugh in
a place that was one of the least funny places in the world.
With a little group of GI performers I would go wherever
there was a group of men to entertain. I told jokes for Marines weary and haggard from battle; for fliers so horribly
burned they were covered with tissue paper because they
couldn't bear the touch of a sheet. I tried to be funny for
scared and nervous soldiers about to go into combat. We
entertained on ships, on airstrips, in hospitals, on beaches, in
jungles. We played for as few as twenty men and as many
as five thousand. From Guadalcanal we went out to entertain men in the Russells, on Tulagi, on Munda, Espiritu
Santo, Fiji, New Caledonia. In between trying to be funny,
we griped about the rations, the weather, and the loneliness.
Yet now, I found myself drawn back to the South Pacific to
see what the islands I had known in wartime were like after
the passage of two decades.

With two friends, Tom Cochran and John Reddy, I had
chartered the *Kingfisher,* a tired, sixty-foot, old interisland
boat, to revisit some of the places I had been stationed. For
several days we had explored the "Slot," the waters between
the long double row of islands down which the "Tokyo Express," as the Marines called the Japanese Fleet, used to
come to bombard the Marines on Guadalcanal in the early
desperate days of the fighting.

Now we were approaching Guadalcanal. Memories came
flooding back as I watched through the binoculars as the
big island loomed larger as we approached through heavy
swells. As we rounded Cape Esperance, where fierce naval
battles had raged, I could see purple morning glories grow-

ing over the skeletons of Japanese ships rusting in the sun along the shore. So many ships are sunk in those waters that the Americans grimly joking named it Ironbottom Sound. Now Bo'sun Jack Nwame showed me the name on the map.

The changes wrought by time were quickly apparent as the *Kingfisher* rounded Cape Cruz, the scene of much hard fighting in the war, and put into the harbor of Honiara. The men who served on Guadalcanal would never know it now. Even the name Guadalcanal is rarely heard in the Solomons today. People in the islands usually speak of Honiara, the new Solomon Islands capital, built on Guadalcanal after the war. When the war ended the British abandoned the bomb-battered former capital of Tulagi, twenty-five miles away across Ironbottom Sound, to build this new capital from scratch along the beach near Cape Cruz. Honiara (it means "where the wind blows") is a sleepy tropical town of some five hundred Europeans, four hundred Chinese and three thousand natives. On the island where so many Americans served (there were two hundred thousand at one time) we found only one American family. They were the Alvin Blums of Brooklyn. The Blums had a general store in Honiara and Mr. Blum was president of the Chamber of Commerce.

The wife of the British High Commissioner of the Western Pacific, David Trench, was the only other American. Even the American dead are gone. After the war the Army removed them from the Army-Navy Cemetery near Lunga Beach and returned them to their home towns or to the National Cemetery of the Pacific in Honolulu.

Honiara has a hotel of sorts (with cold beer and cold showers), a bank, Masonic Temple, modern schools, a club, and a good Chinese restaurant. In the low green hills, behind the business district near the shore, is a residential district with some attractive California-type homes. It also has such up-to-date touches as a mental hospital, high taxes, Little Theatre group (the Honiara Hams), labor unions, a nine-hole golf course built on a former fighter strip, and a radio station that has a nightly news broadcast in pidgin English.

The town is built on the site of some of the fiercest fighting of the Guadalcanal campaign. In one engagement a Marine group under Major Otho Rogers made a landing behind Japanese lines approximately where the Hotel Mendana now stands. As the Marines pushed into the hills, which is now Honiara's residential section, they were cut off by strong enemy forces. Major Rogers was killed and they suffered heavy casualties before fighting their way back to the beach. Today the beach and hills where this action took place is the very center of the town of Honiara. "I still uncover signs of the fighting all the time," Evan Evans, a young Australian building contractor, told me. "Not long ago I was bulldozing soil for a wharf and I uncovered a pit full of Japanese skeletons just off Mendana Avenue. In 1954, while excavating for a new building, we found a dead Marine right in the middle of Honiara."

Despite the fact that Honiara is built largely with abandoned American equipment and materials, Guadalcanal generally seemed worse off than it was in the latter stages of the war. In those days, when the island was being used as a staging area, the Army kept everything shipshape. Roads were good, drainage excellent, mosquitoes under control. Today, apart from Mendana Avenue, the once fine main road that hugs the coast is rough as a washboard and pitted with pot holes. Ditches are overgrown with weeds. Malarial mosquitoes are back in droves, elusive as Jap Zeroes. Henderson Field, which formerly had a magnificent runway of crushed coral topped by metal Marston matting, is now overgrown with grass which becomes a quagmire in the tropical rains.

When Guadalcanal was used as a staging area it was as if a city the size of Jacksonville, Florida, or Albuquerque, New Mexico, had been dropped into the jungles—largely in one corner of the island. There was a big PX, a radio station, more movie theaters than in New York City. The theaters consisted of seats made of felled coconut logs and a stage of plywood board set on oil drums. A projection booth, about the size of a phone booth, would be set in a clearing among the men. It beamed the film at a white canvas screen made to withstand the rain. When it rained, which was often, the men pulled on ponchos and the movie went right on. Natives would materialize silently from the jungles and sit around the fringes of the GI audiences watching Betty Grable, Clark Gable, and Hedy Lamarr.

Now there is one theater in a former Quonset hut. It shows movies of ancient vintage and Randolph Scott is the most popular star on Guadalcanal. With the ancient movies, the natives, who react with gleeful howls to the violence in Western and gangster movies, get a spate of ads flashed onto the screen to the accompaniment of the rousing strains of "Onward, Christian Soldiers."

Guadalcanal has some beautiful beaches but the whites don't go swimming because there are sharks in the oceans and alligators in some of the rivers. The people in Honiara blame the sharks' ferocity on the Solomon Islanders' habit of burying their dead at sea.

In spite of the sharks, some natives stubbornly persist on going in the ocean and several are taken each year. One native has the marks of a shark's teeth imprinted plainly around his face where the shark seized him by the head. He broke free and was not fazed by the narrow escape. "Shark brother bilong me," he said. (The shark is my brother.)

Highway 50, the American-built road, once choked with trucks, jeeps, and weapon carriers, is now a quiet, tree-shaded street called Mendana Avenue after Alvaro de Mendaña, the Spanish explorer who discovered Guadalcanal back about 1567.

Leaving Honiara along the winding avenue lined by lush casuarina trees we set out eastward along the coast one day to visit the scenes where the various major battles were fought and to try to find again some of the places in the jungles where I had entertained after the fighting had passed on to other islands. Although Guadalcanal is ninety miles long and thirty miles wide, virtually all the land fighting was squeezed into a narrow strip a few miles long around Henderson Field. Rattling along over the now corrugated highway in an English Austin with Eric Lawson, an old island resident, we came to the Matanikau River where some of the hardest fighting of the Guadalcanal campaign took place. Fighting seesawed back and forth across the Matanikau throughout the early months of the struggle for the island.

Today the Matanikau is the eastern boundary of Honiara as well as its Chinatown. The sleepy Chinatown, with some dozen stores, flanks the west bank of the stream. Chinese laundry flaps from an old tumbled-down Army bridge downstream and the highway crosses the river on a newer Bailey

Bridge farther upstream. On the opposite bank of the Matanikau is a neat Fijian Village built by Fiji Islanders imported to work as artisans in the growing Honiara construction business.

It was hard to believe that this peaceful scene was the site of a major Japanese counterattack aimed at taking Henderson Field. The Japanese were thrown back in several days of hard fighting with thirty-five hundred killed. Now Chinese children played along the muddy stream where so much fighting took place, and big, ebony-skinned Fijians peddled past on bicycles.

Going on eastward, past "Sleepless Lagoon," past the coconut groves on the Lunga River, once tattered and blasted by shelling but now tall and stately, we turned off the main highway and followed a winding road to a hallowed landmark: Henderson Field. The big field, about a mile inland from the beach, where Major John Smith and Captain Joe Foss used to rise to battle the Japanese Zeroes against stiff odds, now stood quiet and deserted. Clouds of little yellow butterflies rose from the grass as we walked across the field and a family of quail darted out of our way.

Walking across the field, memories returned of the tales I had heard on Guadalcanal during the war of the desperate days Henderson Field lived through in the early months of fighting. Those were days when a motley handful of doughty Marine, Navy, and Army pilots sometimes took off several times a day to fight off enemy planes that droned down from Rabaul to bomb the field.

Japanese ground forces constantly attacked the thin Marine lines around the field. Enemy air raids sometimes came so thick and fast our pilots napped in their planes between dogfights. At night Japanese warships standing offshore

would bombard the field with devastating broadsides. Sometimes the harried American pilots would have to circle overhead while Seabees and Marines frantically filled bomb
craters so they could land. Yet the Americans finally won the
skies over Guadalcanal.

Now nothing remained but memories. Gone was the old
Japanese pagoda that served as headquarters for Cactus
Air Force—bulldozed away after it was wrecked by Japanese
shelling. The runways, where once the tough Grumman
Wildcats and the swift, twin-tailed Lightnings had taken
off in swirls of pink coral dust, were now overgrown with
grass. The skeleton of the old control tower, etched starkly
against the sky, was the only landmark that served as a reminder of the gallant, outnumbered pilots who fought there.

Now a twin-engined Fokker Friendship flies in once a
week from New Guinea. Every fortnight a four-motored
De Havilland Heron arrives from Fiji.

Off beyond the field I could see the rugged green rise of
Bloody Ridge where the Marines under Colonel Merritt Edson threw back a determined Japanese attack that came
within a hair's breadth of overrunning the beleaguered airfield in the biggest single action of the Guadalcanal campaign.

Now a soft rain was falling and mist shrouded the scarred
ridge where the Marines fought so stubbornly. On a knoll directly overlooking the field, where the headquarters of Com-
AirSoPac had stood when I was on Guadalcanal, there is
now the attractive modern residence of the manager of Lever Brothers' coconut plantations. I tried to find the wartime
theater nearby, where I had often played to hundreds of
officers and enlisted men, but there was no sign of it. On a
slope where it had stood was now a collection of huts where

bare-bosomed native mothers watched over naked young-sters playing happily in the rain.

Across the highway from Henderson Field what once was the Army-Navy Cemetery is now an abandoned field of kunai grass.

From Henderson Field we continued eastward again to-ward Red Beach where the Marines first splashed ashore. Leaving the car we walked through the wet, tassled kunai grass toward the beach. A white cockatoo scolded from a banyan tree as we made our way through a clearing, past a small native copra cooker to the beach. The waves lapped softly on the beach and the only reminder of its history was a rusted American gun pointing mutely out to sea.

Turning back west toward Honiara, we crossed the Te-naru River, a sluggish stream which was the site of Guadal-canal's first major land battle. Now native children splashed in the river, oblivious alike to the threat of alligators or the reminders of fighting that once had raged there. The murky waters of the river swirled silently around a half-submerged American tank.

Leaving the highway near the Tenaru we headed up into the hills to see if we could find the hospital where I had been a patient on Guadalcanal. It was there I met Jack Benny—a happenstance that changed my life. As a result of that chance meeting, he chose me a few years later to re-place him for the summer on his popular radio show. Follow-ing a dirt road we found the old hospital—now St. Joseph's Boy's School conducted by the Catholic Marist Brothers. The school, on the old hospital grounds on a cleared hilltop over-looking the jungle, commands a beautiful view. Brothers Coleman Carroll and Ervan McDonough, two Australian teachers, showed us through the old hospital buildings now converted into teaching facilities. The buildings had been lifted and set on gravestones from the abandoned cemetery to keep them from rotting in the tropical camp. The names were carefully erased from the headstones before they were used to prop up the school—a use that probably would have pleased the dead whose graves they marked. What had once been the hospital operating room was now a chapel, and the convalescent wards, where I had been confined, were now classrooms.

"We have one hundred and forty native boys from all the Solomon Islands," Brother Carroll told us. "We have primary grades through junior high school. The brightest boys receive government scholarships to complete their higher education in Australia or New Zealand."

I heard the entire student body, dressed in red and blue *sulus* (a brief native skirt), sing "Japani Ha Ha," a song in pidgin English composed by natives during the war poking fun at the Japanese.

From the school at Tenaru, we continued west again through Honiara to explore the coastline toward Cape Esperance off which great sea engagements were fought. When I was there during the war the jungles bristled with antiaircraft batteries and many a night I jounced along this same road to do a show for the AA battalions. Then the well-kept road was jammed with Army vehicles. Now it was deserted. We passed a few thatched native villages where boys swung along hand in hand, some smoking pipes and with bright yellow hibiscus in their hair.

At Doma Cove we walked down to the beach and gazed across Ironbottom Sound to tiny, volcanic Savo Island standing like a melancholy monument to the thousands of men who died in the waters around her. Seeing the peaceful waters, sparkling in the sunlight, it was hard to realize that more ships are sunk there than anywhere in the seven seas. Those limpid, blue-green waters, foaming softly at our feet, are the graveyard of more than half a hundred major ships —many of them some of the proudest ships of the U.S. Navy.

Evidences of the sea fighting were still visible along Cape Esperance as we drove along the deserted highway along the cape. Landing barges lay half-sunken in the sand everywhere along the cape. The surf broke over a midget submarine on the beach. Between Aruligo Point and the Bonegi River we saw the wrecks of three large Japanese transports. Ironically, the many other Japanese hulks that once littered the shores of Guadalcanal have been cut up and shipped as scrap metal—back to Japan.

"Two years ago a Japanese firm made a deal with the British Solomon Islands government to buy the wrecked ships for scrap," Eric Lawson told me. "Eighty Japanese set up camp at Doma Beach, cut up the old hulks and shipped them back to Japan. Then the price of scrap dropped and the Japanese left, leaving these ships and barges you still see along the beaches."

New York's Sixth Avenue "L" had gone to Japan again.

Albert Kuper is a lean, dark half-caste with receding black hair. I first met him one night over a Chinese dinner in the gloom of the Kwong Chow Restaurant on the banks of the Matanikau River in Honiara. His father, who served in the German merchant marine, had come to the Solomons before World War I. He settled on Santa Ana Island, one of the most southerly of the Solomons, and married the eldest daughter of the island's chief. Albert Kuper was one of the

children of that marriage. The elder Kuper ran a coconut
plantation, raised his family and enjoyed the solitude of his
remote island. "A man comes all the way out here to get
away from everything," he said, "and then history brings it
all to your door." History was in the form of World War II.
A couple of great naval battles were fought off Santa Ana
Island, and there were frequent air battles overhead. The
Kupers, father and sons, rescued about twenty-five American sailors and fliers during the war. They saved three of
the ten survivors of the U.S. cruiser *Juneau* on which nearly
seven hundred Americans, including the five Sullivan brothers, lost their lives.

It was from Albert Kuper that I first heard the touching
story of a Marine flier killed on Guadalcanal, and his father's heartbreaking search to find his son's grave and bring
his remains back to the United States. Later I heard more
details of the story from Alfred Wright and Joe Foss, fliers
who had served on Guadalcanal, and from the father himself.

Charles "Red" Kendrick was a Marine flier in the first
desperate days on Guadalcanal when Japanese planes
swarmed to attack Henderson Field by day and Japanese
warships bombarded it by night. A lean, carrot-topped San
Franciscan, he was a fighter pilot with Major John Smith's
valiant Squadron 223 and a brilliant young man. He was a
fine musician and knew Latin, Greek, Spanish, German, As-
syrian, and Hebrew. He had been studying law at Harvard
before becoming a Marine flier. Kendrick was wing man
for Major Smith and had five Japanese planes to his credit.
The day before he was killed he was decorated by Admiral
Chester Nimitz with the Distinguished Flying Cross. But he
was best known among the pilots for his irreverent song

parodies. Later, when I was on Guadalcanal, I heard pilots
sing one of his parodies to the tune of *On the Road to Man-*
*dalay*.

> Hit the road to Gizo Bay,
> Where the Jap fleet spends the day.
> You can hear the bombs a chunkin',
> From Rabaul to Lunga Quay.
> Pack a load to Gizo Bay,
> Where the float plane Zeroes play,
> And the bombs come down like thunder,
> On the natives cross the way.

The day after he was decorated Kendrick was ill and
grounded by the flight surgeon. But when Japanese planes
attacked the field he ran for his plane and took off. Eleven
Jap Zeroes came out of the sun and pounced on him before
he could gain altitude. His plane crashed in the hills. Some
Marines fought their way up to where he crashed. The plane
lay upside down in a clearing, riddled with bullet holes.
Kendrick was dead, his body hanging from his safety straps.
The Marines buried him alongside the wrecked plane and
then fought their way back to their perimeter around Henderson Field.

About a month later a friend of Kendrick's family, who
was commanding an Army transport, came to Guadalcanal.
On learning that the young flier had been killed he took a
photographer into the hills to photograph the grave. It was
on a hilltop clearing near a jungle-choked ravine into which
the Marines had pushed the smashed plane. The photographer took pictures of the grave and the friend sent them to
Kendrick's parents in San Francisco.

Two years after the war, Kendrick's father turned up on

Guadalcanal with the picture. He wanted to find the grave and take his son's body home. He was then over seventy years old but tall and straight as a ramrod. He had served in the battles of Saint-Mihiel and the Meuse-Argonne offense in World War I and had won the Silver Star and Purple Heart. The only Americans left on the island were a few soldiers guarding the mass of war matériel rapidly being reclaimed by the jungle. The GIs felt sorry for the old man and let him share their mess and stay in an abandoned shack. From dawn to dusk, by jeep and on foot, he searched for his son's grave. He had nothing but the old photos to guide him. For eight days, in suffocating heat, he searched the hills and jungles around Henderson Field. He was almost at the point of collapse from exhaustion. On the ninth day, when his search seemed hopeless, he met an Australian miner named Bob Symes.

Symes told the senior Kendrick that the natives had amazing memories and, if shown the photograph, might recall the spot in the hills where the flier had crashed. They asked among the natives and finally Albert Kuper said he felt he could lead them to where the grave was.

Together they drove in an old jeep into the hills behind Henderson Field. Kuper stopped at a spot where the contour of the land and jungle seemed to match that of the photograph. However, the hilltop clearing was covered with coarse, saw-toothed grass higher than a man's head. Symes touched a match to the grass and burned it away. They continued searching. Then one of the natives, who had been searching the ravine near the clearing, came running up shouting, "Him plane, him plane!" He had discovered the crashed F4F-3 in the ravine. But there was no sign of the grave.

British officials assigned about thirty natives to help lo-
cate the grave, Kuper told me. They dug shallow ditches
three feet apart in the area where bits of wreckage indicated
the plane had crashed. But there was no sign of the body.
Finally, British officials kindly tried to prevail upon the father to give up the seemingly hopeless search. The flier's
body must surely have been moved to the cemetery, they
said sympathetically, and buried among the unknown dead.
Yet the father stubbornly refused to give up.

"A few of us stayed with him," Kuper told me. "We
started digging more trenches intersecting those we had
already dug. Finally we found the body. It was heartbreaking to see the old man as we uncovered his son. He was
buried wrapped in his rubber life raft."

The senior Kendrick removed his son's body to Henderson Field. There was a little chapel there and a Requiem
Mass was held with a choir of native children singing the
hymns. Then the father took his son's remains back to rest
in his home town of San Francisco.

"Would you like to see where we found him?" Kuper said.

Touched by the story of the father's devotion, I said I
would. In an old truck, with three of Kuper's shy, dark-eyed
sons hanging precariously on the back, we set off to find
where the flier's grave had been. East of Henderson Field
we turned off on a winding, muddy road that climbed up
into the green rolling hills. Some miles back in the hills the
truck jolted to a stop. "This is the place," Kuper said.

We walked through the wet kunai grass looking for where
the plane had crashed. Even twenty years later it was still
littered with the debris of battle. Finally we came to a spot
where scraps of wreckage and chunks of metal showed
where the plane had crashed.

"This is where the grave was," Kuper said, indicating indentations in the earth where they had dug the trenches to find it. "The plane was over there," he added, pointing to the ravine. We looked into the dark depths of the jungle but the dense growth shut away any sight of the plane.

The three little boys looked solemnly at the damp earth where the American flier had been buried. Around us the waving grass stretched away to the impenetrable jungle. Even the sky was gray and forbidding. I thought of that lonely scene months later when I talked with Mr. Kendrick about his sad search. "As long as my son was lying alone in that forgotten grave on that lonely island," he said, "I could never be at peace. I have always been impressed by Maeterlinck's passage in *The Blue Bird* that 'the dead are happy when we remember them and speak well and fondly of them.'"

On the porch of his residence, on a hill overlooking Honiara, I heard from Bishop Dan Stuyvenberg, the Catholic Bishop of the Solomons, the story of how he rescued Joe Foss, the leading American ace of Guadalcanal. The bishop's cathedral is a former American Quonset hut. In front of it stands a white marble statue of the Virgin Mary. The Virgin's left sleeve is missing, shot away in a naval bombardment. Below and beyond us lay the waters of Ironbottom Sound. Across the shimmering waters Florida Island seemed to slumber in the sun. Over a cold beer the bishop, a genial, ruddy-faced Dutchman, who has spent a quarter century in the islands, chuckled about how he saved the cigar-puffing U.S. pilot who gunned down twenty-six enemy planes.

"I was a priest then at the mission station of Buma on the

big island of Malaita," he said, pointing across the water. "Malaita is about fifty-eight miles across there. It has about twenty-five thousand natives, far more than any of the other Solomon Islands including Guadalcanal. It was never occupied by either the Japanese or Americans. But we used to see some of the big air and naval battles. One night, just as it was getting dark, we heard a plane come over the mission. We could tell from the sound of the motor it was in trouble. But in the dusk we couldn't tell if it was American or Japanese.

"A few minutes later we heard the plane crash in the sea. Some of the native boys paddled me out to try and find it. But it was pitch dark by then and we couldn't see anything. We paddled around in the darkness for a while but didn't find anything and were about to give up. Suddenly a man's head popped up right alongside my canoe. He said: 'I hear you speaking English. I'm an American.'

"It was Joe Foss. We hauled him into the canoe and paddled ashore. He was tangled in his parachute and sick from swallowing sea water. We got him to the mission and the first thing he asked for was a cigar. We gave him some twist tobacco and some dry clothes. In fact I never did get my pants back. We talked until late that night. He told us he had shot down three Japanese planes that day before his own Grumman Wildcat was so badly shot up he had to ditch in the sea. We became good friends. He is a wonderful man. Later he was elected Governor of South Dakota. Now he's head of the pro American Football League.

"The next morning we were eating breakfast when we heard a plane. 'That's the patrol,' he yelled. We all ran out and spread his parachute on the beach. It was an American plane all right. The pilot saw us waving from the beach

and they sent a Catalina Flying Boat to get Joe. He left us
his parachute. It was white silk, the finest. We used it to
line the tabernacle of our altar.

"A few days later we heard a big roar. We ran out to see
an American fighter squadron heading straight for us. It was
Foss' squadron. They swept down and buzzed the mission.
Then they peeled off one by one and each pilot dropped a
gift. They dropped chocolate and cigarettes and flour. Then
they swept over the mission once more and roared away
across the water back to Guadalcanal."

Although thousands of men fought on Guadalcanal, and
in the skies and seas around her, today there are only a tiny
handful who took part in the fighting still on the island.
None of them are Americans. They are either Australians or
New Zealanders, who served as coastwatchers, or native
Solomon Islanders who served as scouts and guerrillas.

The Solomon Islanders were valiant allies. They killed
hundreds of Japanese and rescued many American fliers and
seamen from sunken U.S. ships. There is no record of any
Solomon Islander betraying any member of the Allies to the
Japanese. The most famous native hero is a scout named
Vouza. Before the war Vouza had been a sergeant major
in the island constabulary.

A few days after the Marines landed, Vouza and some
other natives appeared at the American lines and offered
their services. Later he appeared to report that a large Japanese force was gathering farther east along the coast for an
assault on Marine lines. A few days later he gave dramatic
conformation of his warning when he stumbled into the Marine lines more dead than alive. He had been caught by the
Japanese in a native village with a flag the Marines had

given him. The Japanese questioned him about the Americans. When he refused to talk the Japanese tied him to a tree, bayoneted him repeatedly and left him for dead. Vouza somehow gnawed through his bonds and made his way twenty miles through enemy-held jungles to reach the Marine perimeter around Henderson Field. The most vivid account of Vouza's exploit is his own written report of it:

"Well, I was caughted by the Japs and one of the Japanese officers questioned me but I was refuse to answer & I was bayoneted by a long sword twice on my chest, through my throat, a cutted the side of my tongue and I was got up from the enemies & walked through the American front line. They took me to the hospital at Lunga and there they done the treatment & the wounded was healthed up. After I was discharged from the Hospital I wad do my fighting with the Japs and paid back all what they have done with me & now, here I'm I, still alive."

For his courage Vouza was awarded the American Silver Star and Britain's George Medal. In 1953 he was invited to London for the Coronation of Queen Elizabeth and presented to Her Majesty. He is now a magistrate at the village of Roroni on Guadalcanal.

"How can I meet him?" I asked.

"You radio the Leprosarium at Tetere," I was told. "Sister Mary Joseph will send a leper for him."

I called and it was arranged that the nun at the Leprosarium would send a truck for Vouza to bring him to the coast. I arranged to send a boat to pick him up there. I was on the dock at Honiara as the boat rounded Point Cruz and entered the harbor where scores of beaming, dark-skinned natives lined the wharf to witness the excitement. My eyes grew misty as Vouza, now an old man, stepped from the boat. He was erect and unsmiling with the proud bearing of an Indian chief. He was barefooted but wore his old white sergeant major's uniform with a row of gleaming medals.

We talked for a while about his wartime experiences and he showed me the ugly scar where the Japanese sword had pierced his throat. Looking at the scar I remembered that an American Army doctor had reported that as soon as they had sewed up Vouza's throat he had asked for something to eat.

I asked Eric Lawson, an old friend of Vouza's, what gesture I could make to show my appreciation for the old scout's coming to see me.

"What Vouza needs more than anything else," Eric said, "is a new pair of teeth."

It seemed that a new set of teeth for Vouza was a matter of some civic concern in Honiara. The sturdy teeth, with which he had gnawed through the Japanese bonds, were mostly gone now and he needed a pair of false dentures which he could not afford. Her Majesty's government had been considering the problem but the wheels of officialdom sometimes grind slowly in remote British islands and nothing had been done. I said that I would consider it a pleasure to donate a new set of teeth.

However, the question of new dentures is not a simple matter on Guadalcanal, I discovered. The dental technician who makes them, it developed, doubles as the proprietor of the Kwong Chow Restaurant in Chinatown. I sought him out there and found him busily mixing drinks behind the bar. He was a stocky, affable man named Arthur Foy.

I suggested rather dubiously that I had heard he made false teeth and that I was interested in a pair for Vouza.

"That's right," Foy said cheerfully. "I'll show you some."

With that he rummaged around among the array of bottles behind the bar and produced two sets of false plates.

"These are for a lady here in Honiara," he announced, proudly displaying a gleaming set of artificial teeth. Convinced of his qualifications I completed arrangements for a set of teeth for Vouza.

Then we all drank a toast to the gallant old scout.

Just recently I heard from Eric Lawson in Honiara. He enclosed photographs of a beaming Vouza proudly displaying his new store teeth.

Whenever you talk today of the fighting on Guadalcanal, whether to British, Australians, or natives, they invariably speak proudly of the coastwatchers. The story of the coastwatchers is one of the fascinating and largely unknown stories of the war. During the fighting the Allies never even admitted the existence of such an organization. Yet this comparative handful of men, mostly past middle-age, hiding out on Japanese-held islands and radioing warnings to the Americans of approaching Japanese ships and planes, was of incalculable value. General Alexander Vandegrift, who led the invasion of Guadalcanal, saluted them in his final Order of the Day. "The coastwatchers saved Guadalcanal," said Admiral William Halsey, "and Guadalcanal saved the South Pacific."

When the Japanese struck Pearl Harbor, and began overrunning the South Pacific Islands, an Australian Naval commander, Eric Feldt, began building up the coastwatchers. The code name of the operation was Ferdinand for the storybook bull who was reluctant to fight. Their job was to observe, not fight. Feldt recruited men who knew the islands: planters, prospectors, government administrators.

Some retired to the hills when the enemy invaded. Others were slipped ashore by submarine or canoe on Japanese-held islands. Many were killed. Yet before long this little band of men, perched on jungle mountain tops, with only a teleradio, sidearms and the help of a few friendly natives, formed an uncanny intelligence network that blanketed more than a half-million miles of islands and ocean. From their precarious hideouts, surrounded by Japanese, they radioed word when the "Tokyo Express" was on the prowl or when Japanese bombers were heading for Guadalcanal.

When the Marines landed at Tulagi it was coastwatchers who led them ashore. It was coastwatcher Paul Mason on Bougainville who radioed that twenty-four enemy torpedo bombers were en route to make the first attack against our landing force on Guadalcanal. With more than two hours' warning our carrier aircraft were waiting at high altitudes to pounce when the Japanese planes came over the invasion fleet. Only one of the twenty-four planes escaped.

One of the well-known coastwatchers was Kenneth Houston Dalrymple-Hay. Hay is a huge man, weighing nearly 300 pounds. He resembles the late Sydney Greenstreet, the actor. Today he is the proprietor of Honiara's Hotel Mendana, the only hostelry between New Guinea and Fiji. The Mendana is a cluster of light green frame buildings with corrugated metal roofs. It has Guadalcanal's only swimming pool, a piece of ocean front fenced off to keep out the sharks. Hay also owns the only movie theater on Guadalcanal, a converted Quonset hut.

Sitting in the late afternoons, in the lobby of his hotel looking out over the sea, Hay told me of his wartime adventures as a coastwatcher. Before the war he managed a rubber plantation on Guadalcanal. When the Japanese invaded he took to the hills with a couple of natives, two dogs, a teleradio, twenty cases of gin, twenty-two cases of vermouth, and twenty cases of Scotch. He hid the liquor in a cache. Some natives found it and poured it out to use the bottles to carry water—a memory that still pains him after twenty years. "It was a sacrilege," he growls.

Hay set up an observation post in an abandoned miner's house at Goldridge, twenty-eight hundred feet up in the mountains behind Lunga Beach. There he was joined by another coastwatcher, Lieutenant D. S. Macfarlan, and A. M. Andressen, a miner. Before long the Japanese began building an airfield directly below them. Hay radioed the information to the Americans. The Americans waited until the field was nearly finished. Then they invaded Guadalcanal and captured the field.

When the Marines invaded Guadalcanal the landing took place directly beneath Hay's mountain hideout. "I had a grandstand seat at the Battle of Guadalcanal," he said. "The main land fighting was right below us, and the air fighting directly overhead. In one nine-day period I counted sixty-nine Zeroes and twenty-two Jap bombers shot down, against ten American fighters. One Jap bomber crashed almost on top of us."

Hay gradually accumulated a force of natives. The natives hunted down Japanese stragglers in the hills and brought them in bound in vines. In between hunting stragglers they cultivated sweet potatoes and mined alluvial gold.

One day a party of natives arrived with an elderly French nun who had escaped death at the hands of the Japanese by fleeing into the jungle.

"She told me the terrible story of how her four companion missionaries were murdered by the Japanese," Hay said.

"The Japanese came to the Catholic mission at Ruavatu where they found two priests and three nuns. One of the priests was an American from Massachusetts. All the others were Europeans. They ordered the two priests to go to the American lines at Tenaru and say the Japanese had landed twenty thousand men with tanks and the Americans would be wiped out unless they surrendered. The priests refused to go. The Japanese threatened them and then confined them to the mission village. One morning they came and marched the two priests and two of the nuns away. The other nun, a French woman named Sister Edmée, was in another hut with a seven-year-old native orphan girl. When she saw her companions led away she slipped into the jungle with the little girl. The natives brought them to me. How they made it through the jungles I don't know. The nun was sixty-five years old and emaciated from hunger and malaria. The other nuns and priests were bayoneted to death."

Hay said he doctored the sister with quinine and got a native woman to care for her and the little native orphan. The nun spoke only French and some pidgin. During air battles overhead she and the orphan girl named Cecilia, would watch fascinated from a slit trench.

"I tried to send her through to the American lines with an armed guard of natives," Hay said, "but they had a skirmish with a Japanese patrol and had to come back. Eventually an Australian colonel with a native patrol got through to us to take her out. "There was a touching farewell with the little orphan she had raised from an infant. However, the little girl was adopted by my native houseboy."

A month later the Americans sent word to Hay that his work was accomplished and he could come down from the hills. He started down but found that he was so worn out he couldn't negotiate the rugged jungle terrain. He sent the Americans a message saying: *"Cannot move any further. I am knocked up."* (An Australian expression meaning exhausted.)

A short time later a jeep arrived with an American captain and four soldiers. As Hay shook hands he noticed they were studying his ample girth.

"My God," said the officer. "I think it's true."

Another leading coastwatcher was a New Zealander, Major Donald C. Kennedy, who was stationed at Segi Point on southern New Georgia Island. Kennedy, a slight, taciturn man, had been a district officer in the islands before the war. When the Japanese seized Tulagi, across from Guadalcanal, he radioed word to the Americans. The Americans sent carrier-based planes to plaster Tulagi harbor sinking nine Japanese ships. Later he set up a hideout at an abandoned plantation at Segi Point 160 miles northwest of Henderson Field. He had two schooners, the *Waiai* and the *Dadavata* in which he and his native crews played hide-and-seek with Japanese warships. Kennedy and his force of natives saved many downed American fliers and killed hundreds of Japanese.

Kennedy's chief native scout was Billy Bennett, the announcer who broadcasts the news in pidgin on the Honiara radio station each night. Bennett's father was a New Zealander who died fighting with the British Eighth Army in Italy. His mother was a native Solomon Islander. Billy is a chunky, smiling father of six children. His name, William Billy Bennett, is tattooed on his right forearm. He has a winning grin, speaks beautiful English and must be the most cheerful man who ever slit an enemy throat.

One night over a Chinese dinner at the Kwong Chow Restaurant in Honiara's Chinatown he told me of his experiences with Kennedy. "Major Kennedy was an amazing man," he said. "We started with two rifles, two pistols, and a few natives. Before long he had a regular guerrilla army. His main purpose was to radio information on enemy activities but he started killing Japanese in self-defense and never stopped. There was lots of air fighting over New Georgia and we saved quite a few American pilots who parachuted into the jungles or the sea. Kennedy would give a can of meat and a bag of rice for any flier the natives brought in, American or Japanese. We picked up eighteen American pilots and twenty Japanese. We would radio Guadalcanal and a PBY with a fighter escort would come to pick up the Americans. The Japanese usually resisted capture. When they did we killed them."

Kennedy's hideout was a strong defensive position, Billy said. The waters were full of uncharted reefs so it was difficult to approach by sea. There were thick jungles behind it, and anyone approaching along the beach could be easily observed.

"Our orders were not to fight unless we had to," Billy said, "but we had to when Japanese patrols approached. We knew we would be wiped out if they caught us. Several times Japanese barges approached. We ambushed them and killed everyone aboard. Once a barge filled with Japs surprised us aboard the fourteen-ton schooner *Waiai*. Machinegun fire sank the *Waiai* but we dived overboard and escaped. Another time we spotted a whaleboat with about a dozen Japs approaching through Marovo Lagoon. We went out to meet them in the ten-ton schooner *Dadavata*. It was night but we could see the whaleboat clearly in the bright moonlight. They opened up with machine-gun fire and we were firing rifles. Major Kennedy and I were both wounded, but we rammed the whaleboat and sank her with all aboard."

Once Billy was visiting a native village when two armed Japanese soldiers arrived. He was unarmed so he pretended to be one of the villagers. The Japanese called the natives together. They said the Japanese were occupying the island and the villagers should cooperate with them and avoid the Americans. To impress the villagers the Japanese showed them their weapons. The natives expressed wonder at the modern arms and one Japanese passed his pistol among them. The natives handed it around gingerly with exclamations of admiration and respect. Finally it was passed to Billy. He, too, accepted it with an expression of curiosity and awe. Then he shot the two Japanese dead.

With A. R. Evans, a wartime Australian coastwatcher, I journeyed by plane and boat through the Solomons, visiting some of the islands where the coastwatchers had served so ably. Reg Evans, a slim, wiry man, with an air of quiet authority, is the kind of man you would want to go into the jungles with. Today he is an accountant in Sydney. Before the war he was a supercargo on a trading ship plying the Solomons. When war broke out he enlisted in the coastwatchers and was sent back to the islands he knew so well. Together we explored some of the islands of the "Slot" where the coastwatchers used to play their deadly game of hide-and-seek with the Japanese. We flew over Vella Lavella, Choiseul, and Bougainville while Reg pointed out points where coastwatchers had hidden.

"Most of the Japanese air strikes at Guadalcanal originated at Rabaul or Bougainville," he said. "If they left Bougainville Paul Mason or Jack Read would radio word on the number and type of planes. As they flew south coastwatchers on Choiseul or Vella Lavella would usually spot them. I'd generally pick them up as they passed over Kolombangara. South of me Major Kennedy on New Georgia or Dick Horton on Rendova would see them. Then radar at Henderson Field would pick them up as they neared Guadalcanal. As the enemy planes flew back we would get another count on them, which gave us an accurate score on their losses. We reported Japanese naval movements the same way."

At Munda on New Georgia Island we took a small, interisland boat, to visit Kolombangara where Reg had been stationed. As our boat, with its crew of natives, threaded its way among the lush, green islands, amid treacherous coral reefs, Reg told me one of the most remarkable stories of the amazing coastwatcher operation.

"I landed on Kolombangara in February of 1943," he related. "I traveled to the island by canoe from New Georgia with a native boy named James Malasa. We hid in the daytime and paddled at night. We passed so close to Munda that we could hear the Japanese trucks working on the airstrip."

On Kolombangara, Evans said, friendly natives built him a bamboo hut on a hill overlooking the jungles and ocean. He had a radio, revolver, tommy gun, telescope, and binoculars. "These are the same binoculars," he said, handing me the worn glasses. "Take a look."

Peering through the binoculars I could get a good view of Kolombangara, a dark green pyramid-shaped mountainous volcanic island.

"The Japanese were building an airstrip there on one of

the few level places on the island," Evans said, pointing to the near tip of the island. "I was on the second knob there. It's called Hipera. I had a wonderful view of the sea and the airfield."

I expressed amazement that his hiding place was so close to where the Japanese were.

"It wasn't as dangerous as it looks," he smiled. "The jungles there are so thick that even the natives build their villages on the coast and rarely go inland. I would have natives perched in the trees on sentry duty night and day. They would report anything they saw and I would radio Guadalcanal. Japanese barges moved around those waters a lot under cover of darkness and the American PT boats would hunt them down."

I asked Reg if he hadn't minded the loneliness.

"Not so much," he mused, rolling a cigarette. "You get used to it. Malasa was a mission boy and spoke English. After a time they sent me a young American corporal named Frank Nash. He was a farm boy from Colorado, a big fellow. He had been in communications on Guadalcanal and we used to talk on the radio. He asked to be transferred to the coastwatchers and they sent him to me. As far as I know he was the only American who ever became one."

It wasn't the danger or loneliness he minded, Evans said, so much as the frustration. "Our island seemed to be jinxed," he said. "Inexperienced American fliers would bomb and strafe our friendly natives by mistake. Because Kolombangara was a Japanese-held island the American fliers weren't too particular who they strafed and bombed there. It was probably a combination of green pilots and poor briefing. Our work was dependent on native help and these air attacks were devastating to the morale of my scouts.

"Things got more and more discouraging and I began to feel I was in a backwater of the fighting which was moving farther west toward New Guinea. The coastwatchers on neighboring islands did so much, but the main action seemed to pass us by. On Vella Lavella and New Georgia, on either side of us, they saved many American fliers and survivors of sunken U.S. ships. But on Kolombangara I didn't save one. My native scouts rescued seven American fliers but I wasn't personally involved in saving a single American. It was just the fortunes of war, I guess."

Finally, Evans told me, he decided to leave his Kolombangara hilltop and move to Gomu, a tiny island a few miles off the coast. On the new island he thought he would be closer to the action.

"Just before I left we got a report that a PT boat had been sunk in Blackett Strait," Reg said. "I studied the strait through my big telescope. I could see some sort of floating object but couldn't tell what it was. There was no sign of any survivors. Later my scouts found three torpedoes on the beach that might have come from the sunken boat. I radioed this word along. When nothing more turned up I decided to go through with my plan to move.

"I notified my scouts and radioed headquarters of my plan. Malasa and I slipped down to the coast at night and paddled across to Gomu. When we landed I heard a sudden sound. I raised my tommy gun but it was one of my native scouts. He reported that natives had found eleven Americans on an island near Gizo. I radioed this good news to headquarters. Then several more natives arrived, all smiles over the news.

"The next morning I wrote a message to the senior officer of the stranded Americans and gave it to the natives to take

to him. I advised him to return to Gomu with the natives
so we could work out means of rescuing his party. Then
seven natives, led by Benjamin Kevu, paddled away toward
the island where the Americans were. All day Malasa and
I scanned the ocean impatiently waiting sight of their return. Late in the afternoon we saw the canoe coming back.
We could see only the natives who were paddling but Ben
Kevu was wreathed in smiles. As they glided up to the
beach an American Navy lieutenant crawled out from under the palm fronds in the bottom of the canoe. He looked
like a scarecrow. He was bearded and wearing nothing but
skivvies. He was very young. His thin half-naked body was
sunburned and splotched with infected coral lacerations.

"'Man, am I glad to see you,' he said.

"'I'm bloody glad to see you, too,' I told him.

"I said that I had radioed headquarters where he and his
men were. I suggested the natives paddle him back to his
base while boats from the base picked up his men. He
wanted to pick up the men himself. Finally it was arranged
that our natives would paddle him to Patparan Island. There
boats from his base would pick him up and he would lead
them to the island where his men were. I gave him a pair
of my coveralls and a Jap rifle and sent him off in the canoe
with Ben and the natives. The next day I got word from
headquarters that he met the boats according to plan. His
men were taken off the island and returned safely to their
base at Rendova."

Evans told me all this while our boat cruised the very
waters where all this had happened. With Ben Kevu we
went ashore on Gomu Island where the meeting with the
young lieutenant had taken place. "The old shack where I
lived used to stand right here," Evans said. "There's nothing

left." The clearing around the house was now choked with palm and casuarina trees. The air was filled with a sweet odor from dead leaves of the naqi naqi tree.

"It was strange," Evans said, standing on the beach where the natives had brought the lieutenant. "That lieutenant was the only man I saved in all that time as a coastwatcher. He told me his name at the time but I forgot it. Not long ago I read a story in the *Reader's Digest* about a naval incident in the war. Suddenly I recognized the circumstances. It was the story of the rescue of the young lieutenant. The man I had saved was your President Kennedy."

Benjamin Kevu, the scout who played the leading role in the rescue of Lieutenant John F. Kennedy and his crew, is a frail, dark native of Wana Wana Island in the New Georgia group of the Western Solomons. When I first encountered him, aboard the *Kingfisher,* he was wearing a sports shirt, frayed shorts, and was barefooted. His slight frame, bare legs, and silver-rimmed spectacles gave him an appearance not unlike that of Mahatma Gandhi. His thick, kinky black hair was streaked with a reddish tinge from being dyed with lime juice and his shy smile, when we were introduced, revealed a few missing teeth. His large, expressive eyes seemed to be permanently bloodshot. Certainly he scarcely looked the part of a hero. Yet he was the leader of the group of natives who, with Reg Evans, rescued Lieutenant Kennedy and his crew when their PT boat was sliced in two by the Japanese destroyer *Amagiri* the night of August 1, 1943.

It was now April of 1962 when I arrived in the Solomons to retrace that fateful last mission of Lieutenant Kennedy and his crew. The wartime incident had received much attention since Mr. Kennedy's election as President, and I felt the television audience would be interested in seeing films of the actual places where the incident occurred and some of the people who played leading roles in the event. As the many thousands of Americans who served there during World War II can attest, the Solomon Islands are one of the most remote places on the face of the globe and remain almost as inaccessible today as before the war.

After flying to Australia to pick up Reg Evans in Sydney, we took off by Trans-Australia Airlines for the Solomons. We left Sydney at nine o'clock at night in a DC-6 and flew most of the night, passing over the Great Barrier Reef and the Coral Sea, to land at Port Moresby, New Guinea, at 6:10 the following morning. There we changed to a plump-bodied, two-motored Fokker Friendship for the remainder of the flight to Munda.

The weather in New Guinea was oppressively humid, with a soft, warm rain falling, and the flight from there on was exceptionally turbulent. We passed through broken clouds and sudden rain squalls and our plane lurched and dipped alarmingly as we flew across the mist-shrouded Owen Stanley Mountains to Lae. At each stop the airport facilities became more primitive. At Port Moresby, the capital of the Territory of Papua and New Guinea, the airfield boasted a modern terminal building. At Lae, from which Amelia Earhart took off on her fatal flight, the terminal was a small, cottagelike building. At volcano-fringed Rabaul, on the island of New Britain, the terminal was a small shed with privies in back. At Buka, across a narrow passage from jungle-choked Bougainville, the only facility was a shed with a corrugated metal roof. As we flew over the islands the clouds gradually dispersed and we could see patches of blue-green water and green islands clearly in the tropic sun.

Evans, who knew the islands and surrounding waters inti-
mately, identified the islands of musical names but bloody
memory as we passed over them: Vella Lavella, Wana
Wana, Kolombangara, Rendova.

The sun seemed to burn away the clouds as we neared
the island of New Georgia and it was blazing hot when our
plane set down on the deserted looking airstrip at Munda,
the scene of much fierce fighting during the war. In a small,
shedlike building, that seemed to double as post office and
terminal, we waited in the stifling heat for what seemed like
an eternity while native custom officials, in khaki uniforms
with red piping, studied our passports as intently as though
they were trying to decipher hieroglyphics. Flies buzzed
around the uncomfortable little room and about a dozen natives, men, women and children, watched the formalities
solemnly and silently. Finished at last, Reg Evans led us
through the little native village to where the *Kingfisher* was
waiting.

Hot and tired from a night and most of a day of flying, we
were glad when Jack Nwame, the native bo'sun, put out
from the dock and headed through Kula Gulf and Diamond
Narrows for Blackett Strait where PT-109 was sunk. It was
then, while the 60 foot *Kingfisher* threaded its way through
the calm waters of Diamond Narrows, that I first got to
know Ben Kevu. I was reading Robert Donovan's excellent
book, *PT-109*, to familiarize myself with the details of the
story we planned to film, and decided to brief the native
crew on our project. Several of them were sitting on the
fo'c'sle so I decided to try to get acquainted by talking
with them and explaining our objective.

I showed them the book, with its picture of the thin,

boyish Lieutenant Kennedy on the dust jacket, and undertook to explain what we planned to do. Some of the crew
nodded tentatively but I had the feeling I wasn't exactly
getting through. I dropped into my best Hollywood Tarzan
talk, pointed at the picture of Kennedy, and said: "Him
President. You understand? Like chief." They smiled in a
friendly way but I had the feeling I still wasn't making myself clear. Since the Solomons are a British protectorate, I
decided to try a more British tack. "Him like Queen," I suggested, pointing again at the picture of the young naval officer. There were more rather mystified smiles.

Then Ben took the book from my hands and leafed
through it. "Him, me," he said shyly, pointing at a photograph in the book. Sure enough, it was Ben, but looking not
nearly so fierce in person as he did in the photograph in the
book. From then on he became a fast friend as well as an
invaluable guide to the scenes we wished to film. He had
been educated at a Methodist mission school and spoke and
wrote quite good English, although he was shy and spoke
only rarely. He had worked in the post office at the village of
Gizo and told me proudly that he was a "retired civil serv-
ant." He knew the surrounding island-studded waters inti-
mately, having traversed them all his life, usually by native
canoe. Although he looked frail, he was strong and wiry and
could walk the decks of the *Kingfisher* in heavy weather as
gracefully as a cat, or row a canoe swiftly and tirelessly. He
shaved with an old safety razor, without benefit of either
lather or water, patiently whittling off his gray stubble as
he walked the deck.

As the *Kingfisher* retraced the course of PT-109, through
Blackett Strait and past Kolombangara, I heard firsthand the

story of how Reg Evans, Ben, and some other natives had
saved Lieutenant Kennedy and eleven of his men after their
boat was sunk with the loss of two crewmen. Ben was a sort
of silent partner to Reg's account of the incident. He sat by,
showing his betel-nut-stained teeth in a shy grin, as Evans
described the rescue. Occasionally Ben would add some
comment, rolling his bloodshot eyes excitedly.

For several days we cruised the waters of the Western
Solomons rowing ashore and filming the three islands on
which Kennedy and his crew had taken refuge. Since the
waters of the "Slot" are filled with treacherous reefs, we
would anchor at nightfall and sit on deck in the soft tropic
night listening to the news in pidgin English from Guadalcanal. The islands were breathtakingly beautiful, the lush
foliage a brilliant green, the sand white and the water slate-
blue in the open channels but greenish over the submerged
reefs. Sometimes there would be a sudden rain squall, and
the sun breaking through would paint shimmering rainbows
in the sky. It seemed almost impossible to imagine these
hushed waters and vast skies, with no visible sign of life,
as the scene of the terrible air and naval battles that had
raged through them. Now their peace was broken only by
a soft breeze or a sudden tropical rainstorm. Occasionally
we would pass a long native canoe, powered by an outboard motor and jammed with natives and produce, headed
for the market at Gizo or Munda.

We had heard stories that the natives still sang a song
about "Captain Kennedy" and his PT boat being sunk during
the war. I was skeptical about the reports but Reg made
inquiries of natives we met and finally reported it might be
worthwhile to go ashore on Kolombangara to try to track
down the song. Reg and Ben rowed ashore in the *Kingfisher's*

dinghy. They landed at a point called Dulo Cove and disappeared into the jungle. An hour went by with no sign of them. The sun beat down fiercely and clouds of bugs assailed us. Another hour passed with still no sign of them. The sun grew hotter and the bugs more voracious. Since I doubted the story of the song about "Captain Kennedy" anyway, I began to mutter about my stupidity in sending Reg on this fool's errand while we sweated at anchor. Suddenly we saw a strange procession emerging from the jungle at the water's edge. It was a half-dozen natives and some of them seemed to be carrying musical instruments. As the crowded dinghy approached we saw they *were* musical instruments! The strange musical group which climbed on deck consisted of six young frizzy-haired natives and a stooped, gray-bearded elder supporting himself with a cane. One of the young natives carried a guitar and another a ukulele. Their leader was a husky young man with the resounding name of Shakespeare Teusinihite and more hair than Van Cliburn. We asked about the song about "Captain Kennedy" and they flashed white teeth in a smile of recognition. I set our portable recorder to spinning and they sat on the deck and swung into a number, singing in English with a beat that would have done credit to Louis Armstrong. They sang of a young "Navy Captain," and an incident that sounded like the PT boat sinking, but the song did not mention "Captain Kennedy" by name. (Of course, when PT-109 was sunk, the natives didn't know the identity of the men involved.) After recording the song, I played it back to the natives and their eyes widened in astonishment at hearing their own voices replayed instantaneously from a little roll of tape. Shakespeare Teusinihite and his sweetest music this side of Gizo never sounded better and

I had to promise to send them all records even though there was no phonograph on the island. After they paddled back to the island, we decided to head for Rendova Island to see if we could find anything left of the PT boat headquarters from which PT-109 had set out on its last mission.

We had talked of filming the view from the peak on Kolombangara, from which Reg had first sighted the hulk of the wrecked PT boat, but on further reflection it seemed impractical. Reg estimated it would take about a day to climb through thick jungle to the peak of Hipera where he had hidden out on the Japanese-held island during the war. Since a filmed shot from the peak would only give a panoramic sweep of sky and sea, which would mean little on a 21-inch TV screen, we decided to push on to Rendova. But not Reg.

"I think I'll climb the peak anyway," he announced. "I've thought about that mountain for twenty years."

He had always wanted to climb Hipera once more, he said, and he meant to do it whether we wanted to film or not. It was agreed that we would drop Reg and Ben at Munda, and we would continue to Rendova while Reg went back by canoe to climb his mountain and Ben returned to his native village of Wana Wana. We waved goodbye to them from the deck of the *Kingfisher*, two slight figures standing side by side on the dock at Munda, slowly receding from view in the long, shimmering shadows, cast by the palm trees along the shore.

When we waved goodbye, in the shadow of Evans's mountain peak on Kolombangara, I never expected to see either the doughty coastwatcher or his native scout again. Yet as the date of the television show about PT-109 grew near I began to think it would be exciting to bring them both to New York and reunite them with the crew members they had helped save. This proved no problem with Evans, a seasoned traveler, but it loomed as a major undertaking in the case of Ben Kevu who had never been anywhere outside the Western Solomons and had never seen any evidences of civilization except, ironically, warships and planes engaged in bloody battles in which he had rescued several Americans in addition to Lieutenant Kennedy. He had, for instance, never seen a train, a building of more than one story, an elevator, a restaurant, or even any animals other than the common domesticated variety. (There are no wild animals in the Solomons.) As far as I knew he had never worn clothes other than the tattered shirt and shorts which were standard masculine attire in the Solomons. I never saw him with shoes on. What would happen when he was whisked off his island and deposited by jet plane in New York? It took a bit of doing, and some help from the British Commissioner of the Western Solomons in Gizo, but it was finally arranged for Ben to come to New York. He went by canoe from Wana Wana Lagoon to Munda where he caught the weekly plane for New Guinea and Australia. There he was met by Evans and together they flew via Fiji, Honolulu, and Los Angeles to New York.

As I awaited Reg and Ben at New York's International Airport it was hard for me to envision how Ben would look and how he would react to the maelstrom of sight and sound that is New York and which has been known to bewilder outlanders from no farther away than Boston or Philadelphia. What would he be wearing, I wondered, and how would he cope with such confusing features of Manhattan

life as traffic lights, escalators, and subways? Would he know
how to use a telephone or a shower bath or how to tie a
necktie? He was beaming as always, his bloodshot eyes wide
with excitement, as he stepped off the plane with Evans.
His wardrobe was an assortment of clothes to which I suspect the whole village of Rarumana had contributed. He had
on a jacket of brown over a gray pullover sweater, with un-
pressed trousers of a darker shade of gray. He also wore un-
comfortable-looking mustard-colored shoes.

Ben took in the bewildering scene that is the International
Airport—the ultramodern buildings, the maze of roads, the
planes of scores of different countries ceaselessly taking off
and landing. "Number One," he pronounced cheerfully. The
expression "Number One" seemed to be the Solomon Islands
equivalent of "great" or "terrific," and Ben used it frequently.
After our limousine had deposited us at a midtown hotel
I set out on foot with Ben to initiate him into the sights of
Manhattan. We walked down Fifth Avenue in the bright
September sun through thick crowds that thronged the sidewalks. A walk of a few blocks brought us to Rockefeller
Center, the towering complex of buildings which marks the
very heart of midtown New York and where, I explained,
the program about PT-109 would be televised. Ben gazed
raptly at the group of gray skyscrapers, centered on the
seventy-story RCA Building, and the spires of St. Patrick's
Cathedral across the street. He was silent for perhaps a minute. Then he beamed again and said, "Number One." Then
I remembered the nearby Associated Press Building with its
teletype machine chattering away in the window. Certainly
this would be something strange and wonderful for Benny
to see. He watched intently as the machine clicked out its
news dispatches at sixty words a minute.

"This is a teletype machine," I explained. "The same story that you see being printed here is being printed simultaneously in other cities like Los Angeles where you landed on your way here."

Ben nodded, fascinated. Then I looked at the story being hammered out in the window. It began: "A third Negro church was burned today in Georgia . . ."

Ben liked to walk around midtown and enjoyed watching the crowds of people rushing about in a way quite unknown in his native Solomons. The thing that seemed to please him most was the sight of a policeman. Perhaps they were one thing he could relate to because they have uniformed constables in the Solomons and certainly there is little else in midtown Manhattan that one is apt to find on Guadalcanal or New Georgia. In any event, whenever he would spot a policeman he would tug at my arm and eagerly exclaim, "Police!" A few minutes later he would spot another officer and with undiminished enthusiasm again exclaim, "Police!" He was absolutely enthralled by the mounted and motorcycle police.

Perhaps the greatest revelation of all was the Central Park Zoo. Since there are no wild animals in the Solomons, except a few lean wild pigs, Ben had never seen any animal other than mongrel dogs and cats and perhaps an occasional cow. Suddenly he was introduced to elephants, lions, bears, hippos, gorillas, and seals, and all in fine form! The seals gamboled playfully about the murky waters of their pool, a hippo opened its cavernous mouth for Ben to chuck Crackerjack in and the gorillas performed dazzling feats of aerial acrobatics. Ben was entranced. He pronounced it all Number One.

Even wilder than the zoo was a visit to one of New York's large discount houses. Ben had announced he wanted to buy some odds and ends including, for some unknown reason, a heavy wool sweater. I asked him what he meant to do with a heavy wool sweater in the tropical Solomons and he smiled mysteriously and said, "fishing." So we introduced him to another uniquely American institution: the bargain rush. With Reg Evans and myself running interference, we plunged into the crowded store. Ben put aside his usual shyness and entered into the fray with relish. He squeezed into jammed elevators and held his own with pushy matrons twice his size in wedging up to crowded counters. This must be some American game, he apparently reasoned, and no more strange or amazing than other wonders he saw on every hand—although certainly more wearing. Exhausted but triumphant we emerged with all the things he wanted including new luggage and a pair of binoculars. We also outfitted him, at a less strenuous but more genteel men's clothing store, with a complete new outfit in which he cut quite a distinguished figure.

Ben also attended the show at the Radio City Music Hall as I wanted him to see the famed Rockettes. Tom Cochran, who had been with us in the Solomons, accompanied him. Since the thirty-six beautiful precision-kicking dancers are the featured attraction, Tom didn't want to take time to see the accompanying movie as Benny had seen movies before. Therefore he arranged for Benny and himself to take seats just as the stage show featuring the Rockettes began. As the elaborate stage show ended, in a flourish of high-kicking Rockettes, Tom got up and told Benny the performance was over and it was time to leave. Benny was not taken in.

He eyed Cochran innocently and asked, "No talking picture?"

Cochran had to sit grimly through two hours of a deadly movie, but Ben enthusiastically pronounced it "Number One." "Personally," grumbled Cochran, "I would call it about 'Number Nine'."

The closest Ben came to any South Sea atmosphere amid the concrete canyons of New York, was a party we had for the PT boat crew at Trader Vic's, a gilded Polynesian establishment with air-conditioned trade winds. The exotic rum drinks were flowing freely when we arrived, and there was much back-slapping and hugging when the crew met Reg and Benny again. They were embraced and pummeled by Pat McMahon, the badly burned crewman whom Lieutenant Kennedy had towed to safety, George (Barney) Ross, the handsome, strapping lieutenant who had gone along for the ride on that fateful night, and all the others.

The evening was a merry one, full of boozy reminiscences, raucous stories, and ribald speeches, and at times I got the feeling that some of the former fighting men might end up in a small war among themselves. They all spoke with obvious fondness of the President whom they referred to by his wartime nickname of "Shafty." Benny sat quietly through all this cheerful confusion, saying little but grinning shyly at the speech and sallies. Because of this shyness, I had decided not to embarrass him by calling on him to speak, especially amid such rowdy surroundings. However, as the evening and the frozen daiquiris progressed, I felt Ben tug at my elbow.

"Aren't you going have me make speech?" he asked softly. Surprised but delighted, I introduced Ben. He made a brief but charming speech. His syntax was somewhat tangled but his warmheartedness was so apparent that you could have heard a guest drop—and I think a couple did. He said he was glad to be in America and to see his old friends again. I'm not sure what else he said, but by that time it didn't matter much. He got a rousing round of applause from the surviving celebrants.

Ben's speech at dinner prompted me to suggest he might like to say a few words on the television program and he readily agreed. Although he had never seen television, much less appeared on it, Benny showed no concern about appearing before a national audience of an estimated 30,000,000 people, live and, as NBC says, in living color. He apparently was resigned to the fact that America was full of mysterious and complicated inventions, and faced going before the cameras and an audience with less trepidation than going up on an escalator (the only thing that *did* throw him).

After we had shown films on the program of our trip through the Solomons, retracing the last mission of PT-109, I brought Reg and Benny on stage for a few words. My heart constricted as the crew, seated together in the audience, rose to give them a standing ovation. Reg chatted away with all the homey, hearty assurance you might expect of a man who hid out on a Japanese-held island, and Ben showed equal aplomb though in a quieter vein.

He looked small and very frail as he stood center stage in the TV studio with the powerful lights beating down hotter than any Solomon Island sun. He stood hesitantly a moment and then began to speak. He talked softly and shyly, in his curious involved but appealing way, his eyes darting about eagerly. His little speech was simple and at times he groped for words I feared he might not find, but he found

them and spoke them with a gentle sincerity that made itself felt in the studio and, I'm sure, to viewers across the
country.

Ben's television appearance, which the august New York
*Times* found "absorbing," was not, however, the climax of
his American visit. The next day in his hotel room he got a
telephone call. It was the White House calling. "Ben," President Kennedy said, "I heard you were here. I'd like to see
you." After chatting a couple of minutes, Mr. Kennedy asked
Ben to visit him in Washington. George Ross, who had been
on PT-109, and who knew Ben, would meet him and make
arrangements for his Washington visit, the President said.

If he was impressed by this invitation, Benny gave no
sign of it. "I welcome chance to visit Washington City," he
said, with his shy smile. Ben was a decided hit in "Washington City," as he called it. Ross, who was a member of the
President's Committee on Youth Delinquency, had him as
his guest at his suburban home where he was a favorite of
the neighborhood children, who besieged him for his autograph. With Ross as his guide he took in all the usual sights,
the Washington Monument, Smithsonian Institution, Lin-
coln Memorial. He visited the Pentagon where he talked
with Undersecretary of the Navy Paul B. Fay and was given
a photograph taken from a satellite. He also called at the
Justice Department where he met Attorney General Robert F. Kennedy. On Sunday he attended Episcopal church
services with the Ross family. They also took him to services at a Methodist church, his own denomination. Benny
was quick to notice Washington's large Negro population.

"I think," he told Ross, "that Washington City has more
natives than New York."

Ben developed into quite a social lion during his Washington stay. Ross took him to several parties and he was a hit at each. He learned to play charades and was very good at them. He would also stand up and recite a little poem called "The Seed" which he had learned at the mission school in the Solomons. He became a television devotee and would sit before the Rosses' set for hours, shucking his uncomfortable shoes and rubbing his feet as he watched the action on the screen. When they watched the program on which he appeared, which had been videotaped a few days earlier, Ben buried his face in his hands and giggled.

The highlight of his Washington trip was his visit with President Kennedy. Mr. Kennedy greeted him warmly, showed him to a couch in his office and seated himself in his rocking chair to reminisce about their fortuitous wartime meeting. The President went into an outer office and returned with the note, now framed, which Evans had written and Ben had taken to Kennedy on Olasana Island. The President also showed him the coconut, encased in a plastic case on his desk, on which he had scratched an appeal for help and entrusted to two other natives. Mr. Kennedy asked Ben whether he had any children, and Ben told him that he had six.

The President then gave him some gold PT boat tie clasps and asked Ben to give them to his children and the other native scouts who had assisted in the rescue. Perhaps the best account of his meeting with the President was written me later by Ben himself.

"I met the President at the White House and shook hands with him," he reported with characteristic brevity. "Lieu-

tenant Ross arrange the program and we went at the same
time the program were—

"1. Prince from Vietnam, 1000 hours, White House
 2. B. Kevu, 1015 hours
 3. Mr. Menzies, Prime Minister of Australia, 1100 hours."

"This is what I would do," he added, "to learn more experience and to know the life of the people in other countries and is very much interest to me."

I last heard from Ben from his native village of Raramana.
On lined tablet paper he wrote: *"The message came through
the air local news that the great friend J.F. Kennedy at the
White House has get shot. It was a sad news . . . I feel
deeply sorrow for his death."*

The voyage through the Solomons had many memorable
moments. There were grave and poignant moments, re-
visiting the scenes of the battles on Guadalcanal and the
waters where President Kennedy's PT boat and so many
other American ships, large and small, were sunk. Yet there
were lighter moments, too. Most of these had to do with
getting to and from that remote corner of the globe where
transportation remains perhaps the most primitive on earth.
The *Kingfisher,* the venerable vessel in which we began our
trip through the islands, had only one class travel—steerage.
The cabin could accommodate only two persons and since
there were four in our party we drew straws for it. The losers
had to sleep there.

I had prepared for the possibility of cockroaches, or so I
thought, by buying a big aerosol bug bomb in Sydney, but
this secret weapon backfired. When we noticed the advance
guard of cockroaches in the cabin, I sprayed it thoroughly,

thinking to rout the bugs. However, the spraying had the opposite effect of bringing a legion of them swarming from cracks and crevices around the bunks. We retired in confusion leaving them in possession of the cabin while we slept on deck.

The bo'sun ran a tight ship—the crew drank beer all day. The crew consisted of six villainous-looking natives only one of whom spoke pidgin English. The rest spoke only pidgin *pidgin*. The service, however, was excellent. We could eat any time of day—whenever *we* felt like cooking. The galley was a telephone-booth-sized cubicle with a balky one-plate Primus stove that defied lighting. The best means of cooking, we finally figured out, was to put the meat on deck and let it tan a little.

Eventually we coped with these trying culinary conditions by settling down to a diet of beef stew and beer. The stew was usually cold (because we couldn't get the stove going) but this was compensated for by the fact that the beer was warm (because we had no refrigerator). After two days of this kind of do-it-yourself cooking we took down our pin-up pictures of Brigitte Bardot and substituted some of Betty Crocker. Other features of the *Kingfisher* were equally challenging. The shower was a pipe with three perforations which emitted a bare drizzle of water. I spent two hours trying to fix the slow drip before I discovered it was a shower and not a leaky pipe.

Such was cruising on the *Kingfisher*—on good days. When the weather turned bad it got *really* uncomfortable. This happened on the last stage of our voyage from Rendova to Guadalcanal. We left Rendova Island in late afternoon with breath-taking cloud formations overhead. However, the spectacular cloud masses grew swiftly dark and the sea became rough as Rendova receded into the distance and the *Kingfisher* began butting through open seas. It began raining heavily as darkness fell and the seas grew rougher. After listening to the latest news in pidgin English from Guadal-canal (those soccer scores really grab you) we settled down to a night of tossing and turning with no effort on our part. The *Kingfisher* did it all for us. There were just three of our party left: Tom Cochran, John Reddy, and myself. Since no one wanted to sleep in the bug-infested cabin—even in a storm—all three of us bedded down on deck. Cochran curled up in a pretzel position in the stern while Reddy and I took up precarious positions on the hatch cover amidships. The ship was now pitching and rolling so badly in the heavy seas that we lay on our sides clinging to the hatch cover so as not to be dumped three feet to the deck. All night long the *Kingfisher* labored through the heavy swells, showering us with spray as she dipped her bow into the big waves.

We were afraid to try to walk even to the head as the rain-lashed deck was so slippery and the boat was rolling so badly we were afraid we might be thrown overboard. The railing was only waist-high and it was apparent that if one of us was hurled suddenly against it he might be pitched into the sea. We were concerned about Cochran, alone in the stern, but it was impossible to get back to him because of the hazardous footing. Later we found that he had tried to reach us with some life jackets but was unable to get up forward on the spray-swept deck. So all night we lay soaked and wide awake, clinging for dear life to the hatch cover and with the depressing prospect of having to sing *Nearer, My God, to Thee* with no orchestral accompaniment if the boat sank.

The coming of day brought only a slight lessening in the heavy seas and we still had to cling grimly to the hatch cover throughout the morning. The sea grew less rough when we reached the lee side of the island of Pavuvu and I was finally able to stagger back to the stern to find Cochran soaked and wobbly from lack of sleep. After a conference with Bo'sun Nwame we decided to put in at Banika, in the Russell Islands, which I remembered from the war, to pull ourselves together and await better weather. The storm gradually abated and the sun beat down hotly as we neared Yandina. The village of Yandina on Banika is the headquarters of Lever Brothers' coconut plantations in the Solomons, and we saw scores of natives working in big wooden sheds as we tied up at the wharf there. Cochran, Reddy, and I straggled up through the village exhausted, bleary-eyed, and hungry, with visions of a hot meal or cold beer as Nwame had told us we might find a club or restaurant. We asked several natives if there was a club or restaurant and were greeted with a variety of uncomprehending shrugs. Finally we spotted a group of small neat buildings which proved to be a Lever Brothers' office, a small branch bank and—happy days!—a little club. Alas, the club was deserted and locked tight. We went next door to the one-room bank where two proper Englishmen, immaculate in white shirts and shorts, greeted us as coolly as if we'd come for a loan.

"We're American," I said, "and we've been through a terrible ordeal. We've been eating our own cooking. We wondered if we could eat at the club?"

It was obvious the bank wasn't the Chase Manhattan where you have a friend. The Englishmen said that the club was reserved for the few English families of Yandina. Despite their cool manner, however, they must have taken pity on our bedraggled appearance as one of them opened the club and gave us a couple of cold beers which seemed heaven sent. We thanked them and were about to head back for the *Kingfisher* when another Englishman stuck his head in and said, "The Lever Brothers' managing director would like to see you in his office next door."

The Lever Brothers' representative proved to be a distinguished-looking man with the impressive name of Waldegrave Ungless. He greeted us as suspiciously as if we were salesmen from Procter and Gamble bent on introducing deodorants to the island (which mightn't be a bad idea). I explained that we were going through the islands filming for an American television show. "Oh, yes, the telly," he said with a lack of enthusiasm that told me I had a very low Nielsen rating on Yandina. We chatted for a few moments and then he abruptly said, "Well, I must get back to work now."

This curt dismissal, after he had asked to see us, surprised and annoyed us. We were further surprised when one of the Englishmen followed us out and said, "Mr. Ungless would like to have you as his guests at dinner." I was tempted to suggest what Mr. Ungless could do with all his coconuts, but in the interests of Anglo-American amity I merely said we didn't want to impose. We were walking back down the road to the wharf when a small British car overtook us and Ungless greeted us as if he were from the Welcome Wagon. "I say, have I offended you chaps?" he asked. "I'd like to have you for dinner." Still irked at our reception I said again that we didn't want to intrude. "Mrs. Ungless and I would love to have you," he insisted.

"You could probably do with a hot shower and some civilized food."

The promise of hot showers did it. We capitulated and climbed into his car. Ungless drove us along a winding road to his home—a beautiful modern residence on a hill surrounded by coconut groves with a sweeping view of the harbor of Yandina.

After our fifth-class accommodations on the *Kingfisher*, topped off by the storm, the Ungless home and hospitality were pure luxury. In that remote tropical backwater, we suddenly found ourselves amid pleasant company, good books, a shortwave radio and hi-fi and, almost unbelievably, air conditioning and hot showers!

After we had luxuriated in the showers, the Unglesses took us on a tour of the island to try to find some of the places where I had entertained during the war. Then the lovely island had been a huge military camp, the coconut groves crowded with Quonset huts, and I found it hard to orient myself in the almost cathedral-like hush of the deserted groves, stretching away for miles without a sign of a human being. We drove for miles along a coral road built by Seabees during the war, through tall palm trees where the remains of U.S. installations rotted in the lush foliage. Here and there we saw native huts built on the foundations of the abandoned American Quonset huts. Once we got out of the car and walked through a grove to an old well choked with vines. A rusting plaque identified it as Clawson's Well, named for a sailor killed on the island. Continuing our drive we came to the site of the hospital at Lingatu where I had entertained. Now only debris marked the place where the wartime hospital had stood, and cows and horses grazed peacefully among the surrounding palms.

Later, after a bountiful dinner served by a barefooted native houseboy, Ungless' British reserve began to thaw a bit and soon we would have been on a first name basis if I could pronounce Waldegrave. Ungless admitted that when he first met us he suspected we were labor organizers come to stir up the natives. In my anxiety to establish our respectability, I told them I had my own television show in America. This announcement elicited a deafening silence. It was apparent that the Unglesses didn't know me from Captain Kangaroo in the realm of television. As we talked, I silently racked my brain for some way to establish a better image with our hosts. Suddenly my eye lighted on a stack of magazines including some American publications. I remembered there had been a story in a recent issue of *Time* magazine in connection with my leaving the *Tonight* show on NBC after five years. If I could find that I could demonstrate to Ungless that I was a TV entertainer and not to be confused with Jimmy Hoffa or Harry Bridges. Shuffling through the pile of magazines I was delighted to find the issue I was looking for. "Here's a little story about me," I said modestly, handing it to Ungless. Unfortunately, I had forgotten what *Time* said about me. Therefore, I was a bit startled as Ungless began reading aloud the magazine's description of me, "*'Though at times he blew foul or fraudulent . . .'*"

That, as my friend Jean Kerr once said, is known as the nick of *Time*.

Refreshed but deflated from our pleasant interlude with the Unglesses, we finally made it to Guadalcanal. Yet getting there was a breeze (or rather a hurricane), compared with getting *out* of Guadalcanal. It seems we arrived during

the rainy season—which lasts twelve months—and it poured
most the time we were there. It was still raining buckets
the day we were scheduled to leave for Fiji from where we
would catch a jet for Hawaii and home. We were routed
out of bed at 5 A.M. for an early take-off on the long overwater flight. The reason for leaving at this ungodly hour,
someone explained, was that the flight, with a stop at the
island of Espiritu Santo, took twelve hours and the Fiji air-
liner did not have proper equipment for night landings.

At Henderson Field, which was dotted with pools of water, we had our introduction to Fiji Airways—the last of the
wood-burning airlines.

Our plane—a four-engined De Havilland Heron—was sitting in the rain on the soggy runway while the flight engineer, clad only in trousers, warmed up the engines. We
had met the crew the previous night when they flew in
from Fiji. They were pilot George Washington, co-pilot
Robin McGrath, and flight engineer Charles Ogilvie, all
genial New Zealanders.

Finally everything was in readiness for our take-off—
Charlie had put on a shirt—and we boarded the plane. The
Heron has a top speed of 120 miles an hour—slower than
some sports cars. It seats twelve passengers in a seating
arrangement that guarantees togetherness. I took a seat directly behind pilot Washington, which meant I was almost
riding piggy-back. My knees were planted firmly in his
back so that if I'd crossed my legs we'd have done a nose
dive. The rest of the accommodations were similarly informal. The powder room was a bucket in the rear of the plane.

As Washington revved the motors, Charlie took his place
in the forward part of the plane to demonstrate the life-
saving equipment as required in overwater flights. "Wel-

come to Fiji Airlines," he said. "Your pilot is George; Robin
here is your co-pilot and I'm Charlie, your stewardess."
Taking a moth-eaten-looking life jacket he grinned broadly
and announced, "Now comes the terrifyin' part." He pulled
the life jacket over his head to demonstrate how to put it on
in case we had to ditch at sea. "After putting on your life
jacket you pull this string to inflate it," he instructed. With
that he pulled the string and it came off in his hand. "Well,
that happens," he said, "but don't worry. A light goes on
if you're in the water for several hours. It doesn't work on
this one." He then showed us a whistle dangling from the
life jacket. "Ships will be coming for you and you'll want to
attract their attention," he added. With that he blew a fee-
ble blast on the whistle.

While this reassuring demonstration was in progress, we
had taxied to one end of the runway for take-off. Then
Washington gunned the motors and the Heron began rolling down the runway, throwing out sheets of water on either
side. On and on we labored, without gaining sufficient mo-
mentum to be airborne. Finally we began picking up speed
but the end of the field was rushing swiftly at us! I felt
Washington and McGrath tense in their seats. Suddenly
George reversed the propellers and braked the aircraft to a
skidding stop in a spray of mud and water. "There will be a
twenty-four-hour delay," he announced, with what proved
to be undue optimism.

All that day and all night tropical rains continued to lash
Guadalcanal. We sat moodily in the Hotel Mendana bar
listening to the unremitting downpour and speculating
gloomily on our prospects of getting away the next day. We
commiserated with the pilots who had some additional bad

news. "Mud got thrown into two of the engines on our take-off attempt," McGrath said. "We're trying to repair the engines."

The next morning it was still raining. Henderson Field looked like a swamp when we drove out to check on the prospects of our flight getting off. It was a dismal sight that greeted us as we pulled up at the field. Parts of the two engines were scattered around on the wet grass while the crew, clad only in swimming trunks, worked in the warm rain to repair them. "We need some new parts," Washington said, "but there's no way to get them while this rain continues. The field is too flooded for a plane from Fiji to land here." Every day we made our pilgrimage to the field to watch the crew struggling to get the engines fixed. And every night we sat around with the pilots cursing the Guadalcanal rainy season—all twelve months of it.

After several days the rains stopped at last. Henderson Field still looked wet and muddy but a relief plane flew in from Fiji with the necessary spare parts and the crew finally got the Heron's damaged motors put together again. The following morning we were up again at 5 A.M. for another take-off attempt. Due to the delay there were enough passengers to fill not only the originally scheduled flight but the relief plane as well. Feeling that the first plane was jinxed we tried to sneak aboard the relief plane scheduled to leave a few minutes later. However, we were herded aboard our original plane along with a motley group of passengers including George Grey, the U.S. Consul in Fiji, and a couple of native women with babies. The runway was still soggy but this time our Heron managed to get up just enough speed to be airborne, barely clearing the palm trees at the end of the field.

1. *Miriam, Randy and unidentified cameraman in Moscow's Red Square.*

2. *Give the people what they want and they'll turn out. Waiting in line at Lenin's tomb.* LOOK Magazine photo

3. *Recording the St. Joseph's school choir on Guadalcanal. The school was formerly a U.S. Army hospital where I was confined during World War II.*

4. *Vouza, a famous native hero in World War II. I bought him a pair of store teeth from a bartender. (Honiara—Guadalcanal)*

5. *Caught in a tropical rain storm with Sadie Thompson nowhere in sight. (Guadalcanal)*

6. *Blackett Strait where Lt. John F. Kennedy's PT boat 109 was sunk. Kolombangara island in the background.*

7. At reunion for PT-109 survivors in New York. Left to right: What's-his-name, Lt. George Ross, Kevu and Evans.

NBC photo

As we headed out over Ironbottom Sound—hardly a comforting locale for a group of nervous passengers—the two damaged engines began acting erratically again. The pilots feathered one propeller and the other engine continued going but with the spasmodic rhythm of a 1923 washing machine. "The trouble is we put metal shields over the air intakes to keep them from getting clogged with mud again," George explained. "Now the carburetors aren't getting enough air."

As we limped toward Espiritu Santo, Charlie decided to relieve any anxiety among the passengers by announcing he would serve a box lunch. Judging by the way things had been going, I fully expected these to be CARE packages. A few moments later he was back with a correction. "There's been a little error," he announced cheerfully. "The box lunches were put on the relief plane by mistake. However, we have some soft drinks for you." He went to the rear of the plane again and we heard the rattle of bottles. Then he was back for still *another* correction. "I guess we won't have the soft drinks after all, folks," he chuckled. "Someone forgot the bottle opener."

So for hours we droned over empty seas while the only passengers who enjoyed any liquid refreshments were the native babies who were being nursed by their mothers. The rest of us looked at the feathered propeller on one engine, listened to the *cha cha* rhythm of the other balky engine and recited the 23rd Psalm.

There was a wholesale sigh of relief when we landed safely at Espiritu Santo about midday. While the crew climbed resignedly out of the plane to resume their uphill battle with the two problem engines, an airline station wagon took us into the little town of Luganville for lunch. Luganville is the most curious town in the Pacific; it is one street wide and six miles long. "There is a French restaurant there," George Grey told us, "so they might have very good food." On the way into town, we amused ourselves by totaling up the mishaps of the jinxed flight: the delayed take-off, the motors acting up, forgetting the lunches and bottle opener. "Has it occurred to anyone," I suddenly remembered, "that today is Friday the thirteenth?" Hardly had I mentioned that when—so help me—a black cat darted out of the jungle and raced across the road in front of us!

At a little restaurant called the Corsican we ordered lunch and decided to celebrate our safe arrival with a bottle of good French wine. Cochran, a wine connoisseur, had a long conversation in French with the proprietor, earnestly discussing brands and vintages. The proprietor produced a dusty bottle that he proclaimed was his very finest vintage. Tommy sniffed the bouquet knowingly, then sipped the wine with the skeptical expression of the true connoisseur. "An engaging little wine," he pronounced it. "Full-bodied but not too pretentious."

The wine did lend a festive air to our lunch which we ate with the gusto of condemned men eating their last meal— which is what we felt like. "You have the last," I said, pouring the end of the wine into Cochran's glass. "Oh dear God," he exclaimed, looking at his glass. Along with the last of the wine, three very dead and soggy flies had plopped into his glass. Vintage flies, no doubt.

Back at the old drawing board, we found our crew putting the finishing touches on another repair job of the temperamental De Havilland engines. Climbing aboard with all the enthusiasm of Kamikaze pilots, we took off on the last leg of our trip—six more hours overwater to Nandi, Fiji. The last lap of the flight was perfectly normal—the two engines began acting up again! George again feathered the propeller of one while the other resumed its bongo drum rhythm. I looked at Cochran and thought I saw his lips moving in prayer. "If you're saying a prayer," I suggested, "be sure to include me in."

"It's not you I'm worrying about," Tommy said. "I'm praying for the pilot."

Hour after hour passed with nothing below us but endless stretches of ocean. It began growing dark and I remembered the reports we had heard that our plane was not equipped for night landings. I sat peering into the darkness and silently composing slogans for Fiji Airlines (Pray Now, Fly Later). As darkness fell George began to take star shots to calculate our position. It did nothing for our morale to see him take a shot with his sextant and then sit down to plot our position, furrowing his brow and shaking his head in apparent bafflement. We knew we were scheduled to land in daylight and our apprehension increased as we droned through the darkness with nothing beneath us but the dark sea. George continued to stand up and take sightings with his sextant, until I began to wonder whether he was taking star shots or imploring Divine intercession. It may have been my imagination, but it seemed to me that George's brow had been furrowed so long over his calculations that it was more wrinkled than Spencer Tracy's. I'm ordinarily not the nervous type about flying, but a feeling kept growing that an airline that could put the lunches on the wrong plane, and even forget the bottle opener, *might* be capable of missing a tiny group of islands in the midst of thousands of miles of empty ocean in pitch blackness. I wondered if the obituaries would remember that Paar is spelled with two "a's." Finally George stood up and smiled. On the far horizon was a faint flare of light. It was the airport lights at Nandi, and to us they looked more beautiful than the Northern Lights. A few minutes more and our poor, weary Heron limped in for a landing like an exhausted gooney bird. Terra firma never felt better.

An airline bus whisked us to a smart, modern hotel with the improbable name of the Mocambo. After the deluge on Guadalcanal, and the terrors of the flight, we were suddenly transported to the lap of luxury: air conditioning, a native orchestra playing, a swimming pool shimmering under a tropic moon. It was almost too good to be true. All the earmarks of civilization including American tourists complete with sports shirts and cameras. "Hey, Jack," one of them yelled. "You keep me awake every night."

I knew we were getting near home.

After the constant rains of Guadalcanal, the dry heat of Fiji was a joy and we spent a couple of days just unwinding in the pleasant weather. Although the very name of Fiji conjures up tales of headhunters and cannibals, because of its location at the crossroads of the South Pacific, Nandi has one of the busiest and most modern airports in that part of the world, with flights arriving and departing frequently from Australia, New Zealand, Samoa, Tahiti, and Honolulu.

We flew to Suva, the capital of the islands, a colorful town of 43,000 Fijians, Indians, Chinese, and Islanders. There we explored the busy wharf and market, visited the museum to see the rudder and other relics salvaged from the *Bounty* at Pitcairn Island, where she was burned by the mutineers, and were entertained by George Grey, the American consul, at his home high on a hill with a stunning view of the harbor. We even sampled yanggona—a Fijian drink originally used as a chaser after a feast of long pig (barbecued missionary). We stayed at the Grand Pacific Hotel, a picturesque colonial structure right out of the pages of Somerset Maugham. Over a gin and tonic we got acquainted with the hotel's piano player, a spry but seedy Englishman who told us that Noël Coward had recently been a guest at the hotel. "Is that so?" I said. "I know Noël. He was a guest on a TV show I do back in the States."

"Oh, you're in show business," he said, with an expression as if he had smelled something unpleasant. "I used to be in show business back in London, but I got out of that rat race." Looking around I had to admit that he'd gotten out all right; about as far out as you could get.

After a couple of days in Suva it was time to get back to Nandi to catch our plane for Honolulu and the United States. We were waiting at the Suva airport for our flight when a Fiji Airways Heron landed and a bedraggled group of passengers climbed out looking like a band of walking wounded. I suddenly recognized some of the passengers as fellow refugees from Guadalcanal and realized that this was the relief plane that had left there just behind us several days before.

"Where have you been?" I asked in astonishment.

"We're just arriving from Guadalcanal," one of the passengers said.

"But you left when we did," I said. "That was days ago."

"I know," the passenger said, resignedly. "We had to lay over at Espiritu Santo. The pilot got dysentery."

On the trip back to the South Pacific I learned of the
Cargo Cult . . . the strange belief of primitive Melanesian
people that all the material things of the white man are
produced by magic and that someday the natives will pos-
sess them too. I first heard of the Cargo Cult in the Russell
Islands. Later I learned more about it on Guadalcanal and
Fiji. Members of the strange cult believe that white men do
not work . . . that they merely write secret symbols on
sheets of paper (checks) for which they receive "cargo" in
the form of automobiles, airplanes, radios, and canned food.
The cult varies in form, from island to island, and even in
name. On the big island of Malaita in the Solomons it is
called the Marching Order, but on most islands, including
New Guinea and New Britain, it is known as the Cargo Cult.

The origin of the fantastic cult is hazy, but it is believed
to have sprung up after World War II. Many of those remote islands were inhabited almost entirely by natives
whose lives were only barely removed from the Stone Age.
Then World War II engulfed them. In the eyes of the primitive natives, what happened then did seem like nothing less
than magic of the white man's god. Suddenly great ships of
every description appeared. White men poured off their
ships and swarmed ashore, bringing with them amazing machines. With their monstrous machines they battered down
palm trees to make airfields and crushed coral to build
smooth roads. They brought in terrible weapons of all kinds:
tanks that spit bullets, submarines that rose from beneath
the sea, planes that dropped bombs, and with them they
drove the Japanese invaders from the islands. They had
trucks and vehicles of every sort. They had mountains of
canned food, little boxes that talked and played music,
strange machines that projected moving pictures on a

screen. All these things and many more, like flashlights, cigarette lighters, and ice cream, came in an unending stream
from the ships of the white men. I can remember myself
from the war the astonishment of the natives on Guadalcanal and other islands when we introduced them to things
like ice cream, flashlights, and chewing gum. Small wonder
all this bounty seemed like gifts of the gods.

Then one day it all ended as swiftly and mysteriously as
it had begun. The white men said that peace had come.
They got back on their ships taking their wondrous machines and cargoes with them. Soon the jungle reclaimed
the flying fields and Quonset huts and the coral roads. The
tropic stillness returned to the islands that had echoed to
the thunder of the white men's guns, the roar of his planes
and the clatter of his machines and vehicles.

Then, apparently, the Cargo Cult had its beginnings. The
superstitious natives saw the coming and departure of the
white man, with all his amazing possessions, as the work of
the white god. Belief sprang up that the white man would
return one day, bringing all his great cargo with him. (To
the natives all trade goods is cargo.) Variations of the belief
grew. One New Guinea tribe worships a white god called
John Frum . . . probably an aviator in the war. They believe
that John Frum will return someday in a great four-motored
plane with lavish possessions for them. In anticipation of
the day they have erected a shrine with a white-faced ef-
figy of John Frum and a model of an airplane, with an airstrip ready to receive the cargo. Tribesmen on the island of
New Ireland are saving their money to "buy" Lyndon Johnson to rule them. They drove off Australian tax collectors
with spears, clubs and stones and fled into the swamps to
await the arrival of President Johnson to liberate them. An-

other tribe has built docks two thousand feet up a mountain-side. They believe a giant wave will roll up to the wharves bringing ships with great carloads of cars and radios and re-frigerators. Strangest of all, one group of natives has been found sitting on hens' eggs hoping to hatch American sail-ors!

There is something pitiful in the thought of these simple people waiting patiently by their rude mountainside docks or makeshift airfields for a plane or ship that will bring the magic cargoes that disappeared with the white men twenty years ago. It is obviously fantastic, pitiful, and bizarre to think that someday an American aviator would return with a ship full of cargo for the natives. Yet . . .

On a steamy June day in 1963 a freighter named the *Piri* appeared off the village of Ewasse on the lonely north coast of New Britain. Word of its coming had preceded it by bush telegraph and a crowd of natives lined the beach as the ship dropped anchor offshore. The natives broke into a ragged song of welcome as a boat from the *Piri* rowed in and a white man jumped ashore. The man was Fred Harge-sheimer, an American flier shot down on the island during the war, and he had come back with a cargo for the natives . . . a cargo and a mission. The story of Fred Hargesheimer is to me one of the great stories of the Pacific war. I first heard of it on my trip to the South Pacific in 1962 when our plane flew over Lake Hargie on New Britain . . . a lake named for the American. The rest of the story I learned later from Hargesheimer himself.

In June 1943, Hargesheimer, a handsome Air Force pilot from Minnesota, was shot down on a photo-reconnaissance mission over New Britain, a boomerang-shaped island about the size of Vermont. The island, off New Guinea, was Japanese-held and its harbor of Rabaul was one of the great enemy bastions of the Pacific. For a month he wandered alone in the jungles, existing on plants and snails. Finally, more dead than alive, he was found by a band of natives. The natives took him to a little village called Nantambu on the coast. There they cared for him and hid him when Japanese patrols came by. Lauo, the chief, took the American into his own hut. A native named Gabu looked after him. He learned to talk to them in pidgin English and found they had saved three other downed American fliers. They never betrayed his presence, even when threatened by the Japanese who had seen his plane crash in the jungle and were looking for him. When he became sick and nearly died they nursed him tenderly. He was too ill to retain food so a native woman named Ida gave her mother's milk to save him. After many months they spirited him through the jungle to three Australian coastwatchers hiding out on a mountain peak. The coastwatcher radioed an American base in New Guinea and a submarine made a secret rendezvous and picked up Hargesheimer and two Australian fliers who had also been shot down. In the darkness, the American whispered a farewell to the natives who had saved and sheltered him for almost a year. He never expected to see them again.

After the war, Hargesheimer married and raised a family. He had a good job and a pleasant life in White Bear Lake, Minnesota, yet he found his thoughts often turning back to the natives who had saved him and sheltered him at the risk of their own lives. Sitting before a crackling fire he would tell his wife and children about them. What had be-

come of them now, he wondered? Finally the urge to go
back and see them again became irresistible. His wife understood his longing to return, and their children shared
vicariously in the adventure.

In the summer of 1960 Hargesheimer took off on his long-
dreamed-of sentimental journey. He flew to New Guinea
where he was joined by Matt Foley, one of the coastwatchers who had helped rescue him. At Rabaul they found an
old trawler, which agreed to take them to Nantambu. It
was night when the trawler neared the little coastal village.
Hargesheimer stood on the bow peering through the darkness as they nosed toward shore.

A strange excitement gripped him. Did the natives know
he was coming? he wondered. Would they even remember
the American flier they had rescued seventeen years earlier?
Excitedly he shouted and waved. Suddenly a big outrigger
canoe glided alongside and he recognized Lauo, the old
chief. Lauo boosted him into the canoe and it headed toward shore.

As they reached shore they saw the natives dressed in
their Sunday best: the men in white calico shirts called lap
laps, barefooted but wearing loyalty medals, the women
in white blouses and lap laps. As Hargesheimer stepped
from the canoe they burst into a full-throated "God Save the
King." The American wept unashamedly.

When they finished singing, grizzled old Lauo spoke. "Me
lukim him," he said in pidgin. "Now me lukim you. He Mastah Number One true." What he said was that the flier they
had saved in the war, and the man standing before them,
was the same. As Hargesheimer looked around him at the
grave, dark faces, he knew why he had had to come back.

The following morning he and Foley went ashore for a

full-fledged celebration. Once more Lauo gave a speech in pidgin assuring them that Hargesheimer was indeed "Mastah Freddy" whom they had sheltered in the war. Then it was his turn. In rusty pidgin he told them he had come back out of gratitude for their saving him. Then he presented them with some simple gifts. Lauo gave him the conch shell they had used to warn him of approaching Japanese patrols.

After a feast and some native songs it was time for the trawler to leave. As Hargesheimer waved goodbye, the natives on shore again burst into "God Save the King."

There was one last emotional experience in store for him. As the trawler tied up at the wharf at Rabaul he was met by a Methodist missionary. He told Hargesheimer that Ida, whose mother's milk had saved him, had come with her family over twenty-five miles of open sea in a tiny sixteen-foot canoe to see him. They went to the missionary's home, overlooking the harbor, where Ida and her six children were waiting. They talked shyly for a time. In clear, sweet voices, Ida and her family sang, "Onward, Christian Soldiers." Then they went down to the beach and climbed into the canoe that was to take them home. Hargesheimer stood waving and looking after the frail craft until it disappeared in the sea haze.

All this seemed unreal only hours later when he was aboard a plane winging back to the U.S. His pleasure at having seen the natives again was tinged with sadness over their lot. Although he had been deeply touched at seeing them again, he found their lives still as harsh as when he first met them. They still eked out a miserable existence with what scant crops they cultivated or fish they caught. They still were prey to malnutrition and disease. He found some of them were members of the "Cargo Cult." Their pressing need, Hargesheimer realized, was education. In a jet roaring back across the Pacific he decided to try to raise funds for a school. At first it seemed like a preposterous undertaking, for a man with a salaried job and a growing family. Yet he decided to try.

Hargesheimer found that, with volunteer labor, a simple but practical school could be built for $15,000. People responded generously when he spoke informally of the project. Soon he was being invited to speak before club and church groups. He spoke to all kinds of groups: to a gathering of four hundred people at the Hilton Hotel in St. Louis, and to a handful of people at a country store in Arkansas. It took two and a half years but finally he had his $15,000.

Then came the problem of actually building the school—ten thousand miles away on a tropical island and with no equipment or materials within a hundred miles. Matt Foley, who had helped rescue him, rounded up materials in Rabaul. A Rabaul contractor agreed to supervise the construction.

In June 1963, Hargesheimer and his seventeen-year-old son Dick, set out for New Britain nearly half-way around the world. At Rabaul they loaded four hundred sacks of cement and other materials on the motor vessel, *Piri,* and set out for Nantambu more than a hundred miles away through treacherous, reef-filled waters.

Word of their coming had preceded them and a crowd of hundreds of natives were on hand as the *Piri* anchored offshore. Three choirs, one from each of the nearby villages, sang in their native tongue as the Hargesheimers paddled in to shore. Once more Hargesheimer was greeted by his old friends, although Lauo, the old chief, had died, willing him his bones.

The site chosen for the school was at a nearby village called Ewasse, about a mile from the beach. There the natives installed the Hargesheimers in a bush house raised on stilts and decorated with flowers. Early the next morning the whole group set to work. About a hundred natives toiled with the Americans to clear the three-acre site chosen for the school. While the men worked clearing the land, the native women brought sand and gravel for cement from the beach.

The second week another ship arrived with the Rabaul contractor and five thousand feet of lumber. It had to anchor about a half-mile offshore, but that didn't daunt the natives. The crew simply dumped the lumber in the ocean and the men and boys swam it in, a board at a time.

The day after the contractor's arrival they began pouring cement. Slowly the buildings began rising. Some of the natives were so primitive that they thought that building with steel and cement was some kind of magic. "I had shown them a postcard with a picture of the skyline of St. Paul," Hargesheimer says, "and when we dug holes to build the school foundation some of the natives thought we were 'planting' buildings and a city like St. Paul would grow from the earth."

When Hargesheimer had to leave, after six weeks, the work was well along. The school, consisting of three bright airy buildings, surrounded by lawns and shrubs, opened in February 1964. It was named the Airmen's Memorial School and the natives called it "something bilong friendship." The three buildings, connected by covered walks, contain four classrooms and an assembly hall which also serves as a community meeting place. The school is staffed by one Australian and two native teachers. One hundred and thirty children come by foot and dugout canoe from several surrounding villages and the bush. When school started the children were inoculated against tropical diseases. Some of them thought that this was how you acquired education—that it was injected by a needle.

The formal dedication took place in July of 1964, and Hargesheimer flew to New Britain once again for the occasion. More than a thousand natives were gathered in the clearing around the school for the ceremonies. Some carried spears and knives, and wore discs made of sea shells in their noses and ears. They listened intently as Hargesheimer spoke to them in pidgin English. He said the school was a gesture of gratitude to the natives for the American fliers saved in the war, and a memorial to those who died. Midway in his speech the tropical peace was shattered by the shriek of a jet plane as a U.S. Navy Sky Warrior roared over the school at six hundred miles an hour. The fly past was the American armed services salute to the new school, and to the natives. As the thunder of the jet diminished in the distance, Hargesheimer finished his speech. The natives described the school best in their own words, he told them. Those words were "Something bilong friendship."

*EAST AFRICA*

August 1962

In 1871 Henry Morton Stanley, a reporter for the New York *Herald,* achieved world-wide renown by going to Africa and finding the Scottish missionary and explorer David Livingstone. The fact that Dr. Livingstone wasn't lost, and refused to be rescued, didn't seem to detract at all from the attention accorded Stanley.

Since that African search for Livingstone did so much for Stanley, I decided in the summer of 1962 to go to Africa and find someone myself. But who? Judge Crater had been missing a long time but he wasn't even turning up at séances. There was always the FBI's "Ten Most Wanted Men" but there were already enough people looking for them. I wanted to find someone all by myself. Then it struck me— William Holden! William Holden had recently gone to Africa with a party of several press agents to make a movie. Since nothing had been heard from him since, I deduced either he was missing or he didn't have very good press agents. I would find William Holden!

Before you could say "Dr. Livingstone, I presume?" Memsahib Miriam, Randy, and I were aboard an Alitalia jet bound for the Dark Continent. Leading our hardy band of adventurers was Joe LeTourneau, who once explored Beverly Hills. Joe regaled us with stories of high adventure on safari while the stewardess plied us with caviar, smoked salmon, and champagne. I was still humming "Arrivaderci Roma" when the stewardess announced, "Please fasten your seat belts. We are now landing in Nairobi."

We stumbled off the plane, fighting down heartburn, into the clutches of a welcoming committee. Among our greeters were Mr. Jamidar, the Minister of Tourism, Denis Mathews of the East Africa Tourist Bureau, and a crowd of askiris who began wrestling among themselves for our luggage, threatening to tear it apart in their enthusiasm.

"I've come to look for William Holden," I announced.

Mathews, a dapper-looking Englishman, seemed not to know who Holden was. I explained he was the well-known American movie star.

"Ah, yes, the mummer chap," he said. "Is he missing?"

"He must be," I declared. "I haven't read a line about him in Louella Parson's column for a week."

The purpose of our expedition established, Mathews led us through Nairobi's modern new terminal to a waiting limousine. There he produced a document as thick as the Manhattan telephone book. "This is your itinerary," he announced cheerfully. "You'll find we've laid on quite a few things for you."

This proved to be a gem of British understatement. Mathews began to read the lengthy itinerary as we sped into Nairobi and the series of receptions and cocktail parties he had "laid on," as he put it, made our adventure in darkest Africa sound like a vacation with Elsa Maxwell.

"I was hoping to see some wild life," I said weakly.

"You will," he said. "Some of these cocktail parties get pretty wild."

While Mathews droned on with his itinerary we reached Nairobi. Nairobi is a clean, modern, bustling city of a quarter million inhabitants, with tall buildings, broad avenues, fine hotels, supermarkets, and smart shops. "I thought it would look more like a Tarzan movie," Randy said plaintively.

By the time he had us settled at the New Stanley Hotel, Mathews finished the recital of our itinerary. "Of course, if there are other things you'd like to do we can probably arrange them," he said. "Perhaps you'd like to interview Oginga Odinga." (I didn't make that name up. Oginga Odinga is a leading politician in Kenya.)

"No politics for me," I said. "I interviewed Fidel Castro once and he immediately turned anti-American. Of course, it may have been coincidental."

Despite my being gun-shy of foreign political figures, I did have a meeting with Charles Rubia, the first African mayor of Nairobi. Rubia is an intelligent, ebony-hued gentleman with a charming British accent. After we had chatted for a while, he greeted a delegation from Wichita, Kansas, who presented him with the keys to that city. In response, Rubia made a gracious speech, thanking the people of Wichita for the honor. He then glanced at me, with a twinkle in his eye, and said: "I say, I wonder if this key will work for one of your bunny clubs?"

The second day of our stay in Kenya we saw our first wild animal. It was a giraffe at a drive-in movie. The giraffe wasn't exactly *in* the audience at the drive-in on the outskirts of Nairobi, but it was closer to the screen than I've been in some of the last rows at New York's Radio City Music Hall.

We were taken on a tour of the Nairobi Royal National Park by Colonel Mervyn Cowie, director of the Kenya National Parks. The forty-four square-mile park, the finest lion preserve in Africa, is only five miles out of Nairobi. "It doesn't require a safari to find big game here," Cowie laughed. "You can go by bus. Or you can take a taxi from downtown Nairobi and ten minutes later be staring a lion in the face."

As he drove us around the rolling, grassy preserve, zebra, giraffe, and wildebeest scattered as the jet aircraft swept low overhead coming in to land at the busy airport. The telephone poles along the road were extra tall to keep the giraffes from breaking the wires with their long necks. Ostrich, hartebeeste, and Grant's gazelle seemed so tame they scarcely looked up as our Land-Rover passed, trailing a plume of dust. Colonel Cowie pointed out that the legs of the male ostrich were a bright red—a sign that it was the mating season. He also debunked the old myth that ostriches stick their heads in the sand. I never believed it anyway, I told him, and certainly it would seem to be inadvisable during the mating season. Some baboons climbed over the Land-Rover, when we stopped to look at them, and peered in the windows scowling like a cop about to give a traffic ticket.

Coming over a gentle, grassy rise, we saw a group of cars gathering in a circle, in the manner of an old-fashioned wagon train. "That means there's lion there," Colonel Cowie said, heading our Land-Rover in that direction. Squeezing into the circle of cars we saw the cause of the attention: a male lion and two tawny lionesses. They were stretched out fast asleep on the open plain—oblivious to the minor traffic jam they were causing. We drove to within a few feet of them and I popped my head out the hatch and began filming. They snoozed on blissfully. Suddenly I realized that shots of sleeping lions wouldn't make very exciting film fare.

"Do you think they'll wake up soon?" I asked.

"They might sleep for hours," Colonel Cowie said resignedly.

People in other cars were filming. Children were pointing and talking. Cars arrived and left. The lions just snored away. While we waited for the lions to wake up, Colonel Cowie told us some interesting facts about lions and other big game in East Africa. Despite the fact that Nairobi is so near that the lions are practically suburbanites, he said, there are more lions in the park now than when it was established in 1946. He also said there is one man in London who makes a living selling surplus lions from overpopulated British zoos to African countries. Although the lion is called "king of the jungle" it is almost never found in the jungle, he said, but prefers the open plains. Incidentally, in Africa people rarely use the word jungle, but refer to it as the forest. When the sleeping lions gave no sign of waking up even to be filmed for television, I asked if we could make a noise to awaken them.

"No, sir," Colonel Cowie said. "There's a fine for annoying the lions. That's what our rangers are for. Not to protect the people from the lions; to protect the lions from the people."

There are fines for getting out of your car, or for honking your horn. Signs posted around the park warn No HOOTING and ANIMALS HAVE THE RIGHT OF WAY, and it is well to ob-

serve them. One car collided with a rhino. The rhino was
killed but the car was a total loss. Another time a giraffe
stepped on a car. A lady in a small European car rounded a
turn in the road and a giraffe stepped on her car and then
toppled on top of it. "There seemed to be legs *everywhere*,"
the dazed lady reported.

I mentioned to Colonel Cowie that he and his rangers
seemed to recognize the park lions individually. He said
they did and told me a story that confirmed it. Although
there are thousands of lions in Africa, when 20th Century-
Fox decided to film a picture called *The Lion* they imported
a lion from Hollywood to play the title role. A Nairobi man
named Monte Rubin, who had the Hollywood lion in tow,
decided to play a little practical joke on the park people. He
bundled the Hollywood lion, a 550-pound black-maned
beast named Zamba, into a station wagon and drove to the
park entrance.

"You should keep a better eye on your lions," he told the
askari at the park entrance. "I found this one wandering
around Nairobi so I brought him back."

The askari peered in at Zamba sitting placidly in the rear
seat.

"Not one of ours," he said, dismissing Rubin with a wave.

A few of the idlers around the Thorn Tree sidewalk cafe
of the New Stanley Hotel snickered as we came out to ven-
ture forth on safari. We were dressed—if not armed—to the
teeth. Miriam, Randy, and I were all resplendent in broad-
brimmed safari hats with leopard bands, bush jackets, khaki
shorts, and Sahara boots. "You look the very picture of the
true white hunter," our tailor assured me.

The only trouble was that when our white hunter pulled

up in his safari truck, *he* didn't look the part. The hunter, Peter Whitehead of the renowned safari firm of Ker and Downey, wore faded levis, an old khaki shirt, brown jacket and no hat at all. Other than sartorially, however, he looked every inch the part. He was a lean, handsome Australian and it was easy to imagine Ava Gardner falling in love with him in a Hemingway movie.

Our safari destination was the Amboselli-Masai National Reserve in the shadow of Mount Kilimanjaro. The 150-mile drive from Nairobi was hot, bumpy, and dusty but enlivened by frequent glimpses of giraffe, wildebeest, ostrich, and zebra. The reserve is some twelve hundred square miles of uninviting, dry bush country, dotted with giant ant hills and teeming with game. In this harsh setting the game, the nomadic Masai tribesmen and their cattle all co-exist, although not always peacefully.

The Ker and Downey camp, which we reached after a teeth-rattling ride of several hours, consisted of a cluster of tents in a little oasis of grass and trees on the dusty plain. An elephant browsed nearby and in the distance we could see zebras and baboons. Despite the proximity of wild game, the camp was highly civilized. There were askaris in white prayer caps and ankle-length green *kanzus* to wait on us, a choice of shower or tub and excellent food and vintage wines. All this with majestic Mount Kilimanjaro looming above and an elephant just a champagne-bottle's throw away.

With Peter Whitehead at the wheel we spent three days filming the game. There are few roads at Amboselli and whenever we spotted game Whitehead simply took off across country after it, crashing through bush and wadies and careening around ant hills or dead trees. We saw sleek, frisky zebras, Thomson's gazelle, beautiful, high-leaping impala, lumbering, foolish-looking wildebeest, the gnu of the crossword puzzle, and massive rhinos with white tick birds riding on their backs.

Whitehead told us that the rhinos are nearing extinction. They are being killed by poachers, he said, and sold to the Chinese and Indians who believe that ground rhino horn is a powerful aphrodisiac guaranteed to make Chiang Kai-shek feel as frisky as Tommy Manville.

Prince Philip of Britain has taken the lead in the fight against the use of ground rhino horn—which, incidentally, is not horn but sort of hairy gristle—as an aphrodisiac. "One look at the population figures of China and India would show how unnecessary aphrodisiacs are in those countries," he said. Moreover, the Prince contends, that ground rhino horn is no more effective in stimulating passion than ground-up chair legs. His campaign should either save the dwindling number of rhinos or else threaten the supply of chairs in England.

While Whitehead told us of the rhino problem we came upon a pride of seven lions near a pool with the carcass of a wildebeest they had just killed. "The females make the kill," Whitehead said, "but then the old boy gets first crack at dinner." The old boy in this case was sleeping off a hearty repast while the other lions slept or gnawed away at the remains of the carcass. Some vultures and jackals awaited their turn nearby. He drove to within about twenty feet of the lions but they only blinked sleepily at us. I observed that the lions we had seen seemed to spend most of their time sleeping and asked Whitehead, tongue-in-cheek, if hunters had to wake them up to shoot them. Lions were no laughing matter to him. "If one comes for you, you never forget it," he said. "When they rush you they seem to be all claws and teeth."

Later we came upon a herd of about a hundred elephants moving purposefully through some trees, the youngsters walking directly underneath the adults but somehow never getting stepped on. We drove near the edge of the trees and stopped to film the big herd. I poked my head out of the hatch and was filming when a big cow elephant suddenly charged us! Whitehead gunned the motor and roared away while my spinal column rattled like castanets as I ricocheted around the open hatch. However, in the best tradition of Hemingway and Ruark, I never lost my poise, and coolly continued filming as the elephant bore down on us. Now if only I hadn't had my thumb over the lens.

After hours in the open country filming, it was pleasant to come back to camp in the late afternoon for a bath, sundowner (as they call the cocktail hour), and dinner by lantern light in the dining tent. After dinner we would sit around a fire, which helped to dispel the chill breeze off Kilimanjaro, and talk about Africa with Whitehead and camp manager Peter Bramwell, a goateed veteran professional hunter. The first night we asked them what precaution we could take to keep prowling animals out of our tent. "Nothing," Bramwell said cheerfully. "Of course you could zip up your tent flap," Whitehead said. "However, if some animal, a leopard say, did happen to get in, the two of you would find it terribly confining with the flap zipped." I asked if animals had ever attacked anyone at the camp. "No," Bramwell said, "but I wouldn't leave my shoes out. One chap did that and a hyena ate them. Nothing left but the laces."

I slept like a baby, thanks to my foresight in bringing Seconal, but Joe LeTourneau got a start early one morning making his way to the lavatory tent. Joe is nearsighted and neglected to put on his glasses for the short walk to the lavatory. At the tent he met a visiting professional hunter bound on a similar mission. "Well, what do you think of *that?*" the hunter asked. "*That's* something you don't see every day!" Joe peered in the direction the hunter was pointing but saw nothing. In fact, without his glasses Joe couldn't even see 19,563-foot Mount Kilimanjaro which was right in front of him. "That's really something, all right," he told the hunter. Then he groped his way back to his tent to get his glasses and see what it was they were talking about. Putting on his glasses, Joe looked in the direction the hunter had pointed. There, about fifty feet from where he had been standing, was a big elephant noisily ripping down tree branches for breakfast.

On our last day at Amboselli, Whitehead announced he had arranged for us to visit a Masai village. The Masai are one of the proudest and strangest tribes of Africa. Tall, lean people, with aqualine features, they live by keeping great herds of scrawny cattle. The cattle are not used for beef but are kept as status symbols and to barter for brides. The Masai also bleed the cattle for blood which they mix with milk to produce a sort of Masai Bloody Mary with real blood. They extract the blood by shooting an arrow into the cow's jugular vein. They then drain a quantity of blood into a gourd and then plug the wound with cow dung. All this may sound a little unsanitary but the gourds are always washed first—with urine. They never brush their teeth yet most Masai have no cavities. They don't need to see the dentist once a year—they see the witch doctor every day.

The Masai are rather individualistic in other ways, too. The women shave their heads while the men plait their hair in elaborate coiffeurs and dye it with a mixture of ocher and the original "greasy kid stuff": cow dung. Both sexes distend their earlobes with wooden plugs and a Masai belle with ears like President Johnson's beagles is worth a lot of cattle in marriage. The women do the work while the men are trained as warriors and are adept with spear and club.

Peter Whitehead imparted this lore to us as we bumped across country to the Masai village to film. It was forbidding country: endless miles of rolling brushland, with an occasional sight of zebras or Grant's gazelle. Finally, seemingly in the middle of nowhere, we came to a village. The houses, made of woven saplings and dried cow dung (I don't know what they'd do without *that*), were surrounded by a thornbush stockade to discourage unannounced visits from lions or editors from *House Beautiful*.

As we pulled up at the village a group of *moran*, as the warriors are called, were assembled ready to make their debut for our TV cameras. They were dressed in loose-fitting brown robes and were carrying spears, clubs, and shields. As we climbed out of our safari truck we were descended upon by clouds of flies. The Masai were covered by flies, too, so thickly we thought at first they were beads, but they paid no attention to them whatever. Their faces were absolutely expressionless and they made no effort to disturb the flies that crawled over their faces and even their eyes. We didn't have the same self-control. The flies buzzed around so thickly and maddeningly that I found it impossible to hold the cameras steady for filming. After a few minutes of filming, twitching, and swatting I told Whitehead we had enough.

"But they expect to dance for you," he said. "I paid them for it."

"We don't need the dance," I said. "These flies are driving me crazy."

"These people don't like to be crossed," Peter said, "and they're pretty handy with those spears."

We had no choice but to stand grimly by while they went into their dance. It was a frenzied dance, with much acrobatic leaping and brandishing of spears, but no more strenuous than our frenzy of fly swatting as we watched. Finally, in perfect unison, they began to dance in a circle with their backs to us.

"This is our chance," I said, leading the dash to our trucks. As we roared away in a cloud of dust the Masai stopped dancing. I noticed, though, they were still brandishing their spears. "Smile," I yelled back at them. "I'm Allen Funt and you're on *Candid Camera.*"

Cutting down Denis Mathews' hit-and-run schedule was really simple. I just canceled all the places I couldn't pronounce. So now I'll probably go through life without having laid eyes on Mweya, the Kazinga Channel, or Ngorongoro Crater. We still saw plenty, though. We managed to hit—and that's the right word—Arusha, Moshi, Tanga, Zanzibar, and Dar es Salaam—*all in two days!* We came out of it suffering from baggage fatigue but it was worth it. I can hardly wait for the next cocktail party when someone starts place-dropping with *me*.

We flew from Nairobi to Zanzibar in an East African Airlines DC-3 that was up and down oftener than a Yo-yo. It's a comparatively short flight, but we stopped en route at Arusha, Moshi, and Tanga, all in Tanganyika. At Moshi we took aboard a load of elephant tusks bound for Zanzibar.

From Tanga it's only a brief hop over the Indian Ocean to fabled Zanzibar, since renamed Tanzania after its union with Tanganyika. Zanzibar, with its white beaches, palm trees, and bright sunlight is truly a picture-postcard island, and the main industry seems to be selling picture postcards to tourists who can't resist mailing them with that romantic postmark. The town of Zanzibar looks as though it might have been designed by Walt Disney when he was suffering from a hangover. It has a white gingerbread Sultan's Palace (the Sultan is since deposed), a harem and similar exotic touches. Arab dhows and outrigger sailing canoes with wild-looking crews ply the waters of the harbor. The maze of crooked streets was crowded with Africans, Indians, Persians, and a half-dozen other nationalities including a few Americans from the U.S. space tracking station.

Somehow our driver, navigating by mental telepathy, negotiated this labyrinth of streets to deposit us at the Zanzibar Hotel. This hotel had to be designed by an architect of the leaning tower of Pisa school. It consists of two old Arab houses, *both* leaning. Fortunately they are leaning against each other, apparently from exhaustion, which holds them up. It also has an annex about a block away—as the crow flies. By foot, through the twisting streets, it seemed like three miles. The hotel also has a combination bar and telephone booth and a garden restaurant with barefooted, white-robed waiters all of whom seemed to be deaf.

After registering, we got a guide and set out on the hike to our rooms in the annex. They proved to be not only about a block away but three flights up. The hotel's magic carpet wasn't working and climbing the three flights to our rooms seemed nearly as exhausting as scaling Kilimanjaro. When I thanked our porter for leading us in the climb to our rooms, he said, "I had to do it because they were there."

Our rooms were furnished with big four-poster beds swathed in mosquito netting, large closets, and an air conditioner that dated from the reign of Seyyid Sir Khalifa bin Harub. I opened one of the closets and so many mosquitoes flew out I was nearly fanned to death. I wasn't unduly concerned, though, since our beds were covered with mosquito netting. However, when we went to bed I discovered that a couple of mosquitoes were *inside* the netting. I struggled up and opened the netting to shoo them out. I got them out all right, but a half dozen others got in during the maneuver. "Why not get them *all* inside," Miriam suggested, "and then we can move *outside?*"

The next day we spent exploring the picturesque town and island with U.S. Vice Consul Dale Provenmire and his wife. We filmed the Sultan's Palace, the home of explorer David Livingstone, and a church built on the site of the old slave market. We also visited the colorful waterfront where a big cruise ship was coming in and several smaller boats were rushing out to greet it. "How picturesque," I said. "Are those natives going out to dive for coins?"

"No," Mrs. Provenmire laughed. "That's the local American and European women rushing out to get their hair done. There's no beauty parlor here so when a big ship comes in there's a mad rush to get permanents."

Only a few of the narrow, winding streets are wide enough for automobiles, and those that are offer a challenge to the pedestrian. When a car comes through you flatten

yourself against a building and hope for the best. Despite
the hazards of walking, the streets were crowded with Indian women in colorful saris, swarthy Arab coffee vendors,
Moslem Indian women in white pantaloons. Rickshaws and
bicyclists wove through the pedestrians with a fine disregard
for life, limb or traffic laws. Miriam was winged by a passing
cyclist while my foot was run over by a hit-run rickshaw
puller out to better the trotting record set by Dan Patch. As
he sped off I yelled after him, "Haraka haraka haina baraka,"
which is an old Swahili proverb meaning "Much haste has
no blessing." He just kept on running and yelled back, "Same
to you, fella."

The streets are lined with dark little shops selling gold
bracelets, Persian rugs, ivory and ebony carvings, silks and
rubies. Hindu and Arab music wails from the dark recesses
of shops and over all hangs the smell of curry, cinnamon
and cloves. It might be a scene from the *Arabian Nights*
except for the Diners' Club signs in the shops. Formerly the
best buys were the massive teakwood Zanzibar doors
studded with brass nails which were the perfect gift for the
man who has everything or the warden at Sing Sing. Now
there is a law against exporting the doors—to save Zanzibar
from suffering an epidemic of cross-ventilation—and the
next best buy are ornate wooden chests which are equally
cumbersome and useless. I didn't want anything that osten-
tatious so I compromised and bought a love potion for
Charley Weaver.

Although there was an air of tropical languor about the
city—except for the drivers and cyclists—some of the ancient
walls were emblazoned with political slogans; telltale hints
of the violence that was to break out later when the British

gave the island its independence and the African majority overthrew the Arab Sultan in a bloody purge.

Vickers Haviland, the owner of the Zanzibar Hotel, invited us for cocktails and a swim at his home. VH, as he is known locally, told us he was a retired British Army officer who turned to hotelkeeping as the result of reading an article in the *Reader's Digest*. I immediately made a mental note to cancel my subscription. His home is a beautiful big house on a bluff overlooking the Indian Ocean. It formerly was the home of Sir John Kirk, the British Consul General and an associate of Dr. Livingstone. Kirk was also a famous botanist and the grounds were covered with jacarandas, flamboyants, and frangipani. We swam in the ocean and had to wade in slowly it was so hot. It was warmer than a heated pool—probably 90 degrees. The beach also sloped very gradually and we had to wade halfway to Tanganyika before the water was up to our waists.

After a pleasant interval with Vickers Haviland, it was time to leave. Reluctantly we said goodbye to Zanzibar, as the last rays of the tropic sun caressed the languid sea, and the American ladies were elbowing each other as they climbed aboard a visiting cruise ship to get bouffant hair teases.

"This is where the road ends," our driver said. "From here on we go on foot. And keep a sharp eye out for elephants."

We were headed for the Treetops Hotel in the Aberdare Mountains of Kenya, and our host was Major Eric Sherbrooke Walker, the owner of that unique game-watching roost. Walker, a tall, white-haired, ramrod-straight Britisher, led the way, warily cradling a rifle in the crook of his arm. It is a quarter-mile from where the dirt road ends to the hotel in the trees, but the grassy trail seemed considerably longer with the suspense inspired by the jungle surroundings. Every few feet there were rustic ladders nailed to the trees to escape if we were attacked by a wild animal.

"If an elephant or rhino attacks just nip up a ladder," Walker whispered. "Remember, eighteen feet up if it's an elephant."

No rogue elephant or angry rhino materialized, much to Randy's chagrin, and we arrived without incident at the hotel in the trees. The three-story eyrie is nestled high amid the massive branches of three chestnut trees in a jungle clearing near a pool where the animals come to drink. We climbed up a ladder to the first level and the ladder was then pulled up behind us. "A precaution against leopards," Major Walker explained. "We found one once in the ladies' room."

Treetops, which accommodates twenty guests, is surely the most ingenious tree house since the Swiss Family Robinson's. Although branches and trunks jut through most of the rooms, Treetops has almost everything most good American hotels have except Gideon bibles and pictures of Conrad Hilton. It has hot and cold running water, flush toilets, and even a telephone. There is a comfortable living room, a snug bar and small, reed-walled rooms where you can hear the people in the next room even better than in a new New York apartment. The bar, framed by arched elephant tusks, is probably the only one in existence where you can drink too much and see *gray* elephants—and they're real.

After barking my shins and bumping my forehead on branches, I got us installed and we repaired to the roof for tea. Teatime at Treetops is more fun than a barrel of monkeys, which it practically is. From our box seat amid the chestnut blossoms we could see long-haired Colobus monkeys swinging through the surrounding trees, while a troupe of baboons scampered around the water's edge. The baboons, noting the arrival of visitors, scrambled quickly up through the branches to join us for tea. They cavorted sportively along the railing around the roof, snatching scones and slices of pineapple from the guests and then disappearing in a flash of pink behinds. Major Walker said a lady guest once asked him why the baboons' bottoms were red.

"For the same reason, madame," he said, "that yours is white."

"Why," she gasped, "how did *you* know?"

While Miriam and Randy fed the baboons, Major Walker told me the history of Treetops. He pointed out the charred stump of a huge fig tree near the pool which is all that remains of the original Treetops. "It was burned down by the Mau Mau in 1954," he said. "These Aberdare Mountains were the last refuge of the Mau Mau." The destruction of the original Treetops was not unexpected. Walker got intimations that the natives were getting restless when signs began appearing nearby reading: KILL YOU BWANA AND YOU CAN HAVE HIS FARM FOR 50 POUNDS. The original Treetops gained world-wide attention in 1952 when Queen Elizabeth II went up one evening a Princess and came down in the morning a Queen when her father died during the night. "When the Mau Mau terror ended I decided to rebuild in these chestnut trees," Major Walker said. Thirty-four cedar poles, as well as the trunks of the three trees, support the tree house. The staff consists of one professional hunter, a hostess and four Africans in green jackets and trousers and red fezzes. There are two powerful lights to illuminate the clearing, and it is sown with salt each day to attract the animals.

As we talked, the animals were beginning to gather in the lengthening afternoon shadows. Waterbuck and baboons rooted around the muddy pool. A number of wart hogs appeared, fly swatter tails erect. They sniffed around the pool for a bit and then trotted off. Then from the forest emerged several African buffalo, big, agile creatures with massive, lethal-looking horns. "They're the only animal that will hunt man just for sport," Major Walker said. The buffalos drank from the pool as two crested cranes swooped in to land on the water.

By now the sun was setting. Snow-capped Mount Kenya glowed in the last light and the forest green took on a special sheen. As darkness fell the flood lights went on and we took our places in the row of airplane seats on a balcony overlooking the clearing. The main event was about to begin.

We didn't have long to wait. Several rhinos came bulldozing out of the forest, low-slung beasts, formidable as tanks. They huffed and grunted along the pool's edge, rooting for salt and eying the buffalo balefully. It was an exciting show, still there was an air of expectancy. Would the elephants appear? Time passed and the rhino and buffalo had the clearing to themselves. Then suddenly, silent and ghostlike, the elephants emerged from the forest, their trunks swinging. First in single file, then in groups, they came heading with rolling gait to the pool. The rhino and buffalo gave them plenty of room as they started sucking up the water in their trunks, drinking and bathing noisily. We tried to count them but they came in such numbers we soon lost track.

Soon there were at least a hundred elephants milling around in the clearing below us. Some were so close we could almost reach down and touch them. Occasionally one of them lurched against the supports of our perch and the whole building shuddered. Several times young elephants rushed at rhinos, or rhinos charged elephants, but there was no actual combat. They are both great bluffers, Major Walker said, and the dim-witted rhinos usually forget in mid-charge why they're charging. "Once in a great while we see a real fight," Walker said. "The night Queen Elizabeth was here two male waterbucks fought and one killed the other."

After hours of watching the animals it was time for dinner by lantern light at the long refectory table. Although the plates rattled occasionally, when an elephant or rhino bumped one of the supports, it was an excellent dinner with vintage wines topped off by peaches flambé. Over coffee and cognac Major Walker talked about the cost of providing such items as champagne and peaches flambé in a tree. The rate at Treetops is now $25 per night, but Major Walker said it formerly was higher. His charming wife, Lady Bettie, said that when she visited England some years ago a London paper carried a story on her and the unique hotel, stressing how expensive it was. Accompanying the article about the rates was a picture of Lady Bettie with the caption: *TEN POUNDS A NIGHT.* "A man clipped the story and mailed it to me," Lady Bettie laughed. "On it he wrote: 'Judging by the picture it's not worth it.'"

After dinner we returned to the balcony overlooking the clearing. The show was in full swing, with elephant, rhino, buffalo, and bushbuck mingling in the flood-lit clearing, grunting and snuffing around the water. Major Walker recalled that he had once experimented with the effect of music on the animals. He got a phonograph and played waltzes, like "The Blue Danube," which the animals, particularly the rhinos, seemed to enjoy. "They raised their heads and seemed to be listening with pleasure," he said. "However, when I played jazz they snorted and ran away." After hours of watching the show, and pondering what effect the music of Lawrence Welk would have on an elephant, I decided to retire for the night. Going to my little reed-walled room, I decided to read myself to sleep with a volume of Hemingway with the sounds of the animals outside providing a real life background to his African stories.

I was midway through *The Snows of Kilimanjaro* when there was a tap on my door.

"Pardon me," said the pretty Irish hostess, "but would you care for some hot Ovaltine before you go to sleep?"

I declined with thanks.

"All right," she smiled. "Then here is your hot-water bottle."

Somehow Africa wasn't the same in Hemingway.

Driving from Treetops to the Mount Kenya Safari Club at Nanuki we crossed the equator. On shipboard, crossing the equator is the occasion for a lot of folderol about King Neptune and his court, and I wondered whether it called for any such ceremonial on dry land. Since we were in the heart of former Mau Mau country, I thought our native driver might have some sort of oathing ceremonial in mind and we might have to stop and whisper a few incantations over chicken entrails. However, he breezed along oblivious to everything (including the road) so we observed the crossing with an old American tribal rite—picture taking.

By now I felt we were closing in on Bill Holden. We had searched for him without success in the Nairobi Game Park. He was nowhere to be found in the bush at Amboselli. When I asked about him at Treetops a man said, "Bill *who?*" But now I thought we must be getting close. Holden and a wealthy California oil man, Ray Ryan, own the Mount Kenya Club so perhaps that was where he had disappeared. At Nanuki, we turned off the highway and drove up a winding, tree-lined road to the club.

We were greeted by a slim Englishman who turned out to be Jack Mills, the club manager.

"I've come to find Bill Holden," I said.

"Oh, too bad," Mills said. "He's in Switzerland. He heard you were coming, though, and said to take good care of you. We've got his private banda for you."

So that's how my efforts to remake the Stanley and Livingstone story for television ended. Maybe it was too ambitious. Next time I may try the story of Alexander Graham Bell, but with a new ending. When Bell invents the telephone and rings up Watson, his assistant, Watson's line is busy.

The Mount Kenya Safari Club is a plush pleasure dome set in a glamorous chunk of real estate which shows, as S. N. Behrman once said, "what God could do if He had money." The main building was formerly a charming small hotel. Then Holden and his partners bought it and sunk millions into making it one of the most luxurious clubs in the world.

Beautiful new bandas (cottages) arch in a graceful crescent around the main building. Peacocks and other exotic birds stroll through the acres of luxuriant gardens and manicured lawns that slope down to a big swimming pool, with snow-capped Mount Kenya in the background. Holden's private banda, which we occupied, had cedar-paneled walls, white telephones and walk-in black tile bathtubs that looked like a setting for a Roman orgy. There was also a big fireplace and every time we turned around the native servants would rush in and make a fire—whether we needed it or not. Since it was August—and the club is almost on the equator—most of the time we didn't, but since my Swahili was limited to "*jambo*," which means hello, I didn't have much success dissuading them. They seemed to be so intent on fire-making I began to suspect they were actually a secret band of arsonists left over from the Mau Mau terror.

On the subject of fires, Jack Mills told us an interesting story. A few years ago, he said, the club employees threatened a strike. Owner Holden went to a strike meeting and made a speech. "We've put five million dollars into this property," he announced. Then he lit a match. "See these matches?" he said. "If you go through with a strike I'll burn the whole place down."

There was no strike and the natives now get along well with the owners. There are more than two hundred servants —about three to a guest. Women do the outdoor work, such as gardening, while the men do the inside chores like cooking and bedmaking. They have their own modern village with hot showers in the thatched huts and a private school for their children. Whenever Holden or Ray Ryan pay a visit, the one hundred and fifty children rise and sing "God Bless America." Once Ryan took the then British Governor of Kenya to see the school. The students broke into "God Bless America." "Well, it's fine for *you*," the Governor said, "but it isn't doing very much for *us*."

One day during our stay at the Mount Kenya Club we drove into the nearby town of Nanuki to have a drink at the Silverbeck Hotel which is bisected by the equator. Over a beer we were regaled with stories of the old days in East Africa by the hotel's proprietor, Commander Logan Hook, who told us he arrived in Kenya in 1922. He showed us his bar on which was a large brass arrow proclaiming "Latitude Zero."

"How do you know precisely where the equator is?" I asked. "Are the calculations magnetic or astronomic?"

"When one owns a bar," Hook said, "one knows exactly where the equator is."

The Mount Kenya Club is probably the only club in the world with its own movie studio. When 20th Century-Fox made *The Lion,* Holden, who starred in the picture, got them to build a modern studio on the grounds of the club. Mills showed us around the studio and pointed out a large steel cage used in the film.

"Was that where they kept the lion?" Randy asked.

"No, the lion was *outside,*" Mills explained. "The cameraman was *inside* the cage. They were afraid the cameras would excite the lion."

Filming with wild animals can be a highly dangerous business, Mills said. He told us that a woman animal trainer named Diane Hartley was killed by a lion during the making of *Hatari,* a John Wayne picture filmed nearby. Peter Whitehead, the professional hunter who accompanied us on safari, shot and killed the lion.

Mills also told us of the special problems created by making pictures at the club. "One of the Hollywood people involved in shooting *The Lion* was an animal trainer," he said. "He kept a lion cub in his bedroom and three big pythons in his bathroom. One day when he was out one of the pythons wrapped itself around the hot water tap of the tub and turned it on. Since no one was in a hurry to unwrap the angry eighteen-foot python, the bathroom was flooded and the three snakes nearly parboiled before we got them out."

Although Nairobi is surprisingly modern (Chubby Checker dancing the twist was a big attraction when we were there) it still is not to be confused with Grand Rapids, Michigan, or Spokane, Washington. The attractive capital of Kenya is a city with the modern cheek by jowl with the primitive. The New Stanley Hotel is as good as a fine New York hotel, yet porters wax the floors by skating around them with mops on their feet and beggars, many of them pitifully deformed, roam the sidewalks outside. The broad boulevards, with brightly flowered traffic circles, are crowded with cars and motor scooters, yet occasionally a lion wanders into town.

The Kenyans have some crack soccer teams but games are disrupted by medicine men who roam the sidelines muttering incantations. Hovering white-gloved European waiters serve osso bucco Milanese and Scotch salmon in the Grill Room of the New Stanley, but those who like to dine dangerously can find places that serve such exotic fare as hippo, crocodile or puff-adder steak, plump roast porcupine, or a crackling dish of fried termites. There are good golf courses but they have some unusual hazards such as hippo wallows, and one has a sign that says: "Members need not play a ball lying closer than 10 yards from a lion."

Nairobi had just built its first television station when we were there but it was not yet in operation. However, TV sets were displayed in many store windows and natives would gather outside and stand for hours just watching the test pattern on the screen. Joe LeTourneau told us a joke about two African head-hunters watching television. "It's a box that shrinks the whole body," one explained to the other.

There are a goodly number of educated Africans in the Kenya government, yet the day we arrived government agents trying to take a census were routed by a hail of poisoned arrows from a hostile tribe. Even the most sophisticated of the new Kenyan leaders still practice some of the old tribal customs. When Tom Mboya, one of the political leaders in Kenya, married Pamela Odede, a recent graduate of an American college, he promised to pay the "bride price" of sixteen cows. However, there was one modern touch to the ancient custom. The cows will be paid on the installment plan.

Kenya was about to receive its independence from Britain at the time of our visit there, and there were heated differences of opinion among white Kenyans and British over the future of the country. Some, particularly white Kenyans, insisted bitterly that after its imminent independence the country would explode into chaos as the Congo had. They were particularly bitter on the subject of Jomo Kenyatta, who had been imprisoned by the British as the suspected leader of the bloody Mau Mau uprising and who was destined to be the leader of independent Kenya. Some of these disillusioned Kenyans and Europeans predicted a blood bath and told us they were getting out before independence. Some were selling their farms or businesses for whatever they could get, they said, while others, who had worked in the government, were departing reluctantly after what they called the "golden handshake" . . . a farewell accompanied by severance payment. Others, like Jack Block, a white Kenyan who owns the New Stanley and Norfolk hotels, and Ray Ryan, the American oil man, felt sure that Kenya would remain politically stable and that there would still be a place for whites in business and even the government there.

We saw occasional small signs of the underlying tension, but nothing serious. Once, on a plane, I heard a white colonial bark at a native steward, "Boy, bring me a gin and tonic." The black steward eyed the white man coldly and said, "Me no boy. Me airline stewardess." The gin and tonic were a long time coming.

Because of the strongly opposed views on the subject we heard in Nairobi, it is interesting to observe what has happened since Kenya has become independent. Kenyatta, who was pictured by most British and white Kenyans as a bloody butcher has proved to be a moderate and genial chief of state. In fact, on December 12, 1963, when Kenya officially became independent, he had the ceremony of transition held at night. "I want the lights lowered," he ordered, "so the people won't see the British flag come down." After independence, when his army staged an abortive mutiny over low wages, Kenyatta asked for and got British army assistance in putting it down.

Although the new republic has a variety of problems, including serious unemployment and a growing Communist Chinese influence, whites are still active in business there, the safari business is booming, and, ironically, the chief worry of the Europeans and white Kenyans now seems to be who will succeed the once feared and hated Kenyatta who is now seventy-four years old.

There is one personal and tragic epilogue to our trip to East Africa. One of the people there with whom we discussed the future of Africa was George Clay, NBC's Nairobi news chief, who assisted us in filming there. Clay seemed optimistic about the future of Kenya as an independent country and felt it would not disintegrate politically after independence as did the Congo. Ironically, Clay, a bearded South African, was shot and killed while accompanying Congolese government troops advancing on rebel-held Stanleyville at the time of the massacre of the white refugees during the joint American-Belgian parachute rescue in November 1964. Clay was buried in a small, neglected cemetery in the jungle near Stanleyville. He was laid to rest in a sheet with his name written on it with a ballpoint pen. Shortly before his death he told a friend: "I've come to the end now. For a long time I could keep on going because of the marvelous television it was producing. But a little while ago, on a lovely calm night by Lake Kivu, it was so peaceful, and I suddenly felt sick at heart at the whole thing, at the blood and stupidity, and at me, making a living by putting it down on tape and film to divert the wife of a Kansas City milkman for a few minutes."

*TAHITI*

July 1963

A beautiful vahine rushed up, threw a flowered lei around my neck and kissed me. Another tawny-skinned lovely in a printed wrap-around paraeu clutched me and did likewise. So did a third. I sighed contentedly. Tahiti *was* just as it said in the travel folders. Then a tiny, beautiful Japanese girl came flying out of the crowd, hurled herself on me like a panther, and cried, "Welcome to Tahiti!" She looked like Reiko, the cute singer wife of my writer friend Jack Douglas, but it *couldn't* be! In New York a month before I had seen Reiko and Jack off for Tokyo. How could she be in Tahiti? Then I spotted Douglas, a pleased smile on his face, filming the whole wild scene at Tahiti's Faaa airport.

"I thought you were in Tokyo!" I yelled.

"We surprise you," Reiko squealed.

That they did. It seemed they thought it would be funny, while en route to Tokyo, to detour a few thousand miles to Tahiti and surprise me. The pretty Tahitian girls, who had been kissing me, were all part of the plot.

For years I had been wanting to visit Tahiti. It's strange

about the lure of Tahiti. The beautiful island has had a troubled history, and it's the troubles that have been the big attraction. The troubles started with the English circumnavigator, Captain Samuel Wallis, who discovered the island in 1767. He found that his sailors were trading nails from his ship for the favors of the local vahines at such a brisk rate that his ship was threatening to fall apart. This shocking situation resulted in a boom in enlistments in the British Navy. The first missionaries complained bitterly that the Tahitians were allergic to wearing clothes. It isn't that the Tahitians are immodest. It's just that the men and women believe in airing their differences. This brought an influx of visitors bent on investigating the interesting charges. These visitors raised so much hell Tahiti was called "the filthy Sodom of the Pacific." That proved to be such an attractive slogan it brought a fresh influx of tourists.

These days people are arriving in ever-increasing numbers in hopes of getting into some of the kind of trouble Tahiti is famous for. In July of 1963 I decided to visit Tahiti before the trouble was settled. My wife Miriam couldn't come with me as she was tied up—to the bedpost. Armed with credit cards and cameras, my friend John Reddy and I boarded a TAI jet in Los Angeles for the eight-hour flight.

For some reason known only to the French, the jet for Tahiti leaves at 2 A.M. which allows time for a leisurely cocktail hour—nine hours. Then, as you are lifted gently aboard, the plane starts *its* cocktail hour. Aboard the plane with us were Anna Kafshi, the former Mrs. Marlon Brando, their young son Christian, and Mrs. Brando's lawyer in the divorce suit and *his* family. Miss Kafshi, fetching in stretch pants, enlivened things by chasing their son up and down the aisles while we started on our second cocktail hour. The progressive cocktail hour seemed to blend, or perhaps blur is a better word, into breakfast which began not with orange juice but white wine.

Arrival by jet in Tahiti is unforgettable. For nearly eight hours we had been roaring through pitch darkness with nothing beneath us but the vast Pacific. Then day broke with dramatic swiftness, illuminating vast stretches of empty ocean. Suddenly Tahiti was below us, beautiful in the tropic dawn.

Peering down we could see the figure eight outline of Big Tahiti and Little Tahiti, joined by their narrow isthmus. Our greeting at the airport was as noisy as a Fourth of July celebration which was appropriate since it *was* the Fourth of July. We blended perfectly into the patriotic atmosphere with our red, white, and blue eyes. An orchestra was playing and flash bulbs popped. People yelled greetings in French, Tahitian, and English. Then the Douglases sprang their surprise with its orgy of kissing. A man even kissed me on both cheeks. I was beginning to wonder about *him*, until I found out he was a French official and the kiss on both cheeks was the formal civic welcome.

We were then herded into a car for the drive to the Hotel Tahiti. The Douglases were staying there, too, with their cute, rambunctious two-year-old son Bobby, and Jack was writing a very funny book about their trip called *The Adventures of Huckleberry Hashimoto*. Our driver, who turned out to be someone we had been kissing, introduced herself as Irene Teamo. "I'm your guide from the French Tourist Office," she announced. "This is Miss July who will preside over Bastile Day." Miss July, a pretty vahine, smiled winningly. I wished I had remembered to bring nails. "She doesn't speak English," Irene explained.

Irene (pronounced Ear-wren) is a bouncy, voluble, intelligent, and moody girl who knows Tahiti like the back of her hand, which she sometimes gives you. She speaks Tahitian, French, and English—and is frank in all of them. "Jack, don't be so goddam nervous," she commanded as we sped toward the hotel. "You're here to relax. Now relax!"

Irene got us installed in cottages at the hotel which is between the airport and Papeete. The Hotel Tahiti is situated on the lagoon looking out over the reefs to the island of Moorea about a dozen miles away. It consists of a spacious main building and a cluster of cottages, all of bamboo and pandanus thatch roofs, with showers, electric lights, and hot and cold running lizards. Guarding the doors of our cottages were wooden tikis, Polynesian totem poles with a wealth of anatomic detail which reveals that Tahiti's wood carvers are as uninhibited as its hula dancers. The hotel and cottages are set amid lush lawns and gardens extending out to a sea wall. There is a swimming pool and a dock extending out over the coral ledge and you can dive off the end into sixty feet of water.

The hotel is owned by Spencer Weaver, an American who also owns hotels and restaurants in Honolulu. Although Weaver is a tycoon, the democratic Tahitians, including his employees, all call him "Spence." Our first night at the hotel Weaver and his beautiful Tahitian wife sat with us and watched the sun go down with dramatic suddenness behind the jagged peaks of Moorea. We were joined by Irene and Coco, her slim, handsome Tahitian husband, who is also a guide. I mentioned that the former Mrs. Brando had been on the plane with us which touched off a lively discussion.

The Tahitians seem fascinated by Brando, whom they refer to as "Marlon," and all speak highly of him, perhaps because of his affection for Tahiti and Tahitians. Irene knew him from having worked behind the scenes on *Mutiny on the Bounty*. Coco had worked on the *Bounty* picture, too, and had also appeared in a picture called *Tiare Tahiti* with James Mason. We asked about Brando and Tarita, the beautiful Polynesian girl who appeared in the picture with him, and Irene said Tarita was back in Tahiti and we could meet her.

Some musicians were playing softly in the jasmine-scented night and Irene got up to dance the hula for us. The Tahitian hula bears no resemblance to its languid counterpart, the Hawaiian hula. It is a thing of fire and fervor, in which pelvic gyrations sometimes called bumps and grinds are performed with an abandon and at an rpm never dreamed of on a burlesque runway. The way Irene danced it would make a belly dance look as dignified as a performance of Swan Lake. She threw back her head, her black hair trailing down her back, and her hips quivered and quaked in a manner which would have brought out the worst in a stone tiki. "Watch the hands," a little old lady sitting near us told her husband. "She's telling a story with her hands." I meant to ask Irene what the story was. For some reason I missed her hands.

"This is the only cafe I know," Jack Douglas muttered, "with bicycle traffic between the tables." We were sitting drinking the local Hinano beer at a table outside Bar Vaima on the Papeete waterfront. Bicycles and motor scooters were whizzing by so close it seemed at times as if they *were* weaving in and out between the tables.

Probably nowhere else on earth is there a scene any more colorful than that from Bar Vaima. A juke box blares rock n' roll music from famous Quinn's next door. Bronzed Tahitian girls in bright pareaus, French sailors in white shorts and red pom pom hats, Chinese merchants, bearded American beachcombers, all amble by. And the traffic! Buses from the districts, crowded with laughing Tahitians, careen past. A fat Tahitian lady bicycles by, eating a watermelon and nonchalantly spitting out the seeds. A man whizzes by on a motor scooter carrying a guitar. Two pretty girls—bicycling in opposite directions—stop, kiss on both cheeks, then peddle on.

The quai, just across the busy street, is equally active. Beautiful yachts from Paris and Los Angeles are tied up alongside dingy ferrys from the atolls, crammed with pigs, poultry, and seasick passengers. There are always lots of yachts tied up at Papeete due to one of the occupational hazards of sailing to the island. It seems that sailors landing in Tahiti after a long spell at sea are given to taking to the hills with a local vahine, leaving the yacht owners with no one to run their boats. It happened to Captain Bligh and it's still going on. The only change is the sailors don't take the nails from the ships any more for trading purposes, the price of vahines having gone up like everything else. Or so Irene told us.

We spent one day filming the colorful scene along the waterfront, and it was pretty frustrating. I tried to film Jack Douglas staggering out of Quinn's—he was just acting—and there were more people in the background than the mob scenes in *Cleopatra*. They were staggering, too, and they *weren't* acting.

After finishing our filming we sat around Bar Vaima with

Irene and drank Hinano and listened to the juke box music
from Quinn's for a while. Irene seemed to know almost everyone and lots of people stopped to greet her warmly. An
attractive young American boy, who had been working as a
guide, stopped to say goodbye. They greeted each other
with great enthusiasm, hugging and kissing warmly.

"I guess you've heard," the boy said. "I have to leave tomorrow."

"It's a dirty shame," Irene said. "I heard the French won't
renew your visa."

"That's right," the American said dejectedly. "It's a lousy
deal."

Then he and Irene embraced some more and he went
sadly on his way. I said it was too bad he had to leave Tahiti when he wanted to stay so badly.

"Too bad, nothing," declared Irene. "I told the French officials about him. Why should we have American guides in
Tahiti? Tahitians need the jobs. Listen, Jack, don't forget
whose island this is."

Tahiti comes joyously alive at night. It is lively enough
during the daytime but at night it fairly jumps for joy. As
darkness falls the lights pop on. Juke boxes begin blaring
and guitars strum. The bicycles and motor scooters and cars
get thicker. The wildest place of all is Quinn's famous waterfront dance hall. Quinn's is a dilapidated-looking establishment of bamboo construction with swinging doors like an
old-fashioned saloon. The orchestra is behind the bar—a
wise precaution. The entertainment on a flimsy wooden balcony overhead is strictly volunteer; usually tipsy vahines
doing the hula for a bottle of Hinano. The co-educational
powder room is something to behold. Despite its uninviting

appearance, Quinn's is usually jammed as it was the night we went there. On the dance floor vahines in pareaus and sailors were jammed together so tightly they could only undulate to the musical din. A vahine got up and sang:

"'Allo Papa, 'ow are you? 'allo Papa, 'ow are you?
I love you. Yes, I do!
Censored, censored, censored, censored,
Whassamatta you!"

Irene said you might run into almost anyone at Quinn's, and she was almost right. *They* run into *you.* The dancers kept bumping into us. Drunken sailors and happy vahines kept stumbling into our table and once we were nearly struck by a carelessly flung jitterbug.

One of the famous island characters who was pointed out to us at Quinn's was Thousand Franc Colette who it seems was available for that sum before inflation set in. In fact, several different ladies were pointed out to us as Thousand Franc Colette. Finally a drunken sailor nudged Jack Douglas, pointed toward another sailor, and said, "Hey, there's Thousand Franc Colette." Douglas had no wish to get into an argument with a hulking sailor.

"She's lovely," said Jack.

"Yeah," growled the sailor, "and *you're* drunk."

One day Irene drove the Douglases, Reddy, and me completely around the island, stopping from time to time to allow us to film and to settle our nerves which were somewhat unstrung from her driving. Irene has a unique way of driving. She loves to describe everything as she goes along, which is helpful, but she insists on looking you in the eye when she talks to you—even if you're in the back seat. Which

I was. She also gestures a lot while driving, which doesn't improve her aim at the wheel. Between the two, I think Irene's driving has done more for prayer in Tahiti than anything since the first missionaries landed.

Our first stop was the tomb of Pomare V, the last King of Tahiti. The tomb, made of native stone, looks like a Dutch windmill and is topped with a funeral urn that resembles a Benedictine bottle. Since the king was quite a tippler, some people contend that the urn was purposely made to resemble a Benedictine bottle. This is said to be a warning against the dangers of drinking Benedictine—possibly sponsored by the Bourbon Institute.

We also filmed at Point Venus, where Captain Cook observed the passage of the planet Venus, and at Matavai Bay where M-G-M built an ersatz native village for the *Bounty* picture. The village is gone now, although Irene did point out several places on our circuit of the island where "Marlon lived." "Marlon Slept Here" houses seem as numerous in Tahiti as "George Washington Slept Here" houses are in New Jersey, although apparently Washington was a sounder sleeper. Matavai Bay, Irene explained, was where the *Bounty* first landed in Tahiti. Later Captain Bligh found the anchorage on the windward side of the island too rough and moved his ship around to the more sheltered anchorage where Papeete now stands.

We had a pleasant lunch at the Faratea Restaurant, near the isthmus that links Big Tahiti and Little Tahiti, and then continued around the west side of the island back to Papeete. One of the sights along the route around the island is the bread boxes, like our rural mail boxes, and we trailed the bread truck awhile to film it. The driver would pull up, slip a loaf or two of long French bread into the box, and then go on. Occasionally "Le Truck," as the island buses are called, would whirl by, crowded with happy Tahitians with bicycles, bananas, and chickens all jumbled together on the roof.

Along the way we stopped at the place where Paul Gauguin had lived during his tormented years in Tahiti. Gauguin left his wife, family, and a comfortable job as a stockbroker in Paris to come to Tahiti in 1891 to paint. Illness and misfortune dogged his steps. His lush paintings of Tahitian scenes brought him only a pittance. Some brought a few francs and others were traded for a bottle of wine or a loaf of bread. Others were thrown away or lost. Finally, sick and discouraged, he moved to the Marquesas where in 1903 he died a pauper. Among his effects was a note saying, "*I am now down and out, defeated by poverty.*" In 1957 it was sold in Paris for $1430. When Somerset Maugham visited Tahiti he found a painting that Gauguin had done on the door of a native hut as a gesture of gratitude for some small kindness. Maugham bought the door for two hundred francs —a few dollars—and sawed off the painting. Today it is one of the most valuable modern paintings in the world. Recently a Gauguin painting *Tahitienne et Garçon* (presumably his mistress and son) sold in London for $236,000! Before leaving Tahiti, Gauguin sold this little plot of land and the hut that stood on it for five thousand francs. Years later his painting of the same hut sold for thousands of dollars. Now only a small wooden sign marks the spot where his hut stood. The land is an open lot with a few coconut shells lying around.

"Did you know," Douglas asked, "that Gauguin offered to give a plot of ground to the French government on the condition they build a school on it and call it the 'Two plus two equals four school'?"

"Where did you learn that?" I asked, impressed.

"Our taxi driver yesterday told me," Douglas said.

One of the landmarks of Papeete is Emile Gauguin, the natural son of the painter. Gauguin, whose mother was a Tahitian, is an enormously fat man whose immense stomach lops over his faded shorts which is about all he ever wears. For years he was a familiar sight on the sidewalks of Papeete, making fish traps out of bamboo, drinking beer, and posing for tourist photographs for a few francs. He was also known to commit a little petty larceny which landed him in the local jail from time to time. Emile's most celebrated bout with the law was told me by H. Allen Smith whose *Two-Thirds of a Coconut Tree* is one of the best books ever written on Tahiti. One night, according to Smith, Emile crept into the house of a nurse bent on burglary. The nurse was taking a shower and Emile thought the house was deserted. While ransacking the bureau he hit the jackpot: a cache of four thousand francs. He stuffed the money in his pockets and was tiptoeing out when the nurse stepped into the room. It was hard to tell who was most surprised: Emile, who thought there was no one home, or the nurse who had nothing on. Emile was pop-eyed at the sight of the unclad nurse. He eyed her ardently and murmured words of admiration. In fact he suggested she make love with him. The nurse was outraged. She told him to get out or she would scream for the gendarmes. Emile continued his amorous pleas. He also pulled out the fat wad of francs he had just stolen. The nurse, never suspecting the francs were hers, began to lend an ear to Emile's pleas. After all, he was a friendly sort and she would have to work hard at the hospital for that much money. Finally she succumbed to his blandishments—and the francs. A little later, broke but happy, he crept away in the dawn. Then the nurse went to the bureau to add Emile's francs to her cache in the drawer. She found the drawer empty! Bitterly she realized she had been had. Two ways. She rushed to the police station and demanded they arrest Emile. The gendarmes collared him and hauled him before a judge. The judge was puzzled. "After all," he told the nurse, "you still have your money." He found Emile not guilty.

Emile's fortunes were on the rise at the time of our visit to Tahiti. H. Allen Smith had launched him as a painter by commissioning him to do several paintings. I believe Smith had tongue in cheek about this enterprise. However, other well-meaning people plunged into the efforts to make a painter out of Gauguin with deadly seriousness. I saw some of Emile's efforts, including a horse with six legs, and they looked like childish finger paintings. They also varied widely in style, which gave rise to rumors that Emile had a small boy or two in the back room who daubed away while he drank beer. Eventually he came into the clutches of a lady journalist named Josette Giraud. She took him to her house outside Papeete and watched him like a hawk while he painted.

I decided to try to film Emile and show some of his paintings for American television. "You won't get anywhere," Irene warned me. "This French lady won't let anyone near him." Nevertheless, we set out one day to try to track him down. We drove to the Punaauai district where Irene thought the French lady lived. En route we stopped at the home of Carlos Garcia Palacios, a good friend of Emile's. Carlos showed me several of Emile's paintings and gave me a couple of them. He said the French lady lived farther along the road. He confirmed that she was holding Emile a virtual prisoner, and said it was unlikely we'd be able to film him.

We drove on, stopping a couple of times to let Irene plunge into the lush growth along the shore in search of Mademoiselle Giraud's house. Finally she emerged from the palms with Emile bouncing along behind her like a happy walrus. He was dressed only in frayed shorts and his huge stomach was jouncing like a tub of jelly.

"Where's the French lady?" I whispered to Irene.

"She's gone into town," she whispered. "Emile says he will pose for you, but hurry up. She'll be back any time."

Douglas, Reddy, and I leaped out of the car and began frantically setting up our cameras. There hadn't been such a flurry of film activity in Tahiti since M-G-M packed up its cameras and stole back to Hollywood. Emile waited patiently, wreathed in smiles. "Me Gauguin, me paint," he said.

After we'd gotten films and stills, I asked Irene if we could buy some of his paintings. She talked to him in Tahitian and French. "He says the lady has them all locked up," Irene said. "Me Gauguin, me artist," Emile said. I gave him a wad of francs for his performance. It was probably the most money he'd seen since he burgled the nurse. Pleased with our coup in getting Emile on film we piled into Irene's car and headed back toward Papeete. Just as we pulled away, a little Dauphine sped up and turned into the driveway we had just left. It was Mademoiselle Giraud!

As we drove back toward town, Douglas sat lost in thought. "Wouldn't it be strange," he said, "if Emile gave up his painting and his wife and children in Tahiti, and left to become a stockbroker in Paris?"

He meant it as a joke, of course, and we all laughed. Yet something nearly as amazing *has* happened with Emile.

Shortly after we left Tahiti, Mademoiselle Giraud did take him to Europe. He had one man shows in Geneva, London, and Paris, and some of his primitive daubings brought substantial prices. Then she brought him to the United States. She takes Emile's art very seriously. "From the beginning," she said, "he started painting with ability as if he had always painted—strange compositions full of beauty. His paintings tend to abstractions. Some of Emile's creations adapt themselves perfectly to commercialization."

So, apparently, does Emile.

There are two subjects about Tahiti that arouse wide disagreement: the girls and tipping. They say that there is no tipping in Tahiti, and the French are trying valiantly to keep it that way. They don't want to spoil the Tahitians. They don't seem to mind if you spoil the French. One of the first things you see on landing at the airport is a sign reminding you not to tip. Just as you're thinking how nice this French concern for your pocketbook is, you discover the government plans to charge you a tax of more than four dollars just to leave the island.

At the hotel I was told that the Tahitians would resent being tipped. "The thing to do if you're pleased with your maid or waitress," I was advised, "is to buy her some material for a paraeu or a little French perfume. Or just ask her to dance." Since I don't dance, and didn't want to spend my visit on shopping expeditions, I just tipped. Anyway, like most Americans, I found it hard to break the habit. And the Tahitians just smiled and took the tips. None of them seemed the least offended and some of them looked downright overjoyed. Once I even tipped the men's room attendant. She smiled prettily and said, *"Merci."*

The beauty of Tahitian girls is a similar subject of debate. Some qualified girl-watchers claim they are the loveliest creatures on earth. Others insist their feet are too big and that most of them could do with a little dentistry and maybe a Maidenform bra. After a careful study of the subject, purely in the interest of anthropology, I find myself a middle-of-the-roader. We did see some beautiful Tahitian girls, but there were others who would be a sensation only on Halloween. Some are fat with jack-o-lantern grins that dispel all illusions of romance. The most beautiful, it seemed to me, were those of mixed Polynesian and Chinese strains, or, as they say, "A little bit sailor, a little bit whaler. Beaucoup Tahitienne."

One of the most beautiful girls we met in Tahiti was Tarita, the lovely part Polynesian, part Chinese girl who had a featured role in *Mutiny on the Bounty*. Tarita is a native of Bora Bora but came to Tahiti where she was discovered by M-G-M and given a role in the picture. I wanted to film her for our TV show. Since this required a bit of doing, I turned to Carlos Garcia Palacios. Carlos is the Chilean Consul in Tahiti which is nice work since there is only one Chilean in Tahiti. He and his vahine Agnes are friends of Tarita and he said he would ask her to allow us to film her for television. One afternoon he brought Tarita and Agnes to the hotel and we filmed her on the grounds, against the beautiful setting of the lagoon with Moorea in the distance. Afterward I took some stills of Tarita and Agnes. To get expression in the stills, I called to the girls, "Say cheese." Photographers have their subjects say "cheese" as pronouncing it forms the mouth into a natural and smiling expression. However, Tarita and Agnes chorused *"Frommage"*—French for cheese—which had just the opposite effect.

René Pailloux has a magnificent view from his thriving
curio shop on the bustling waterfront of Papeete. In the
distance, the stocky, wavy-haired Frenchman can see the
jagged, cloud-capped peaks of Moorea. Nearer at hand, set
like a small emerald in the harbor, is the tiny island of Motu
Uta. Yet to Monsieur Pailloux, Motu Uta is not simply a
beautiful island. For him it is a constant reminder of a
strange, nightmarish ordeal. He told me of that ordeal one
evening sitting sipping Scotch in his beautiful home in the
hills above Papeete.

Pailloux came to Tahiti from France in 1924 as a missionary teacher. He acquired a vahine, a native of the Tuamotus,
and they had three children. He learned to speak Tahitian
fluently and soon was an aide to the French governor in
charge of Tahitian affairs.

In 1939 when World War II broke out in Europe, Pailloux
was caught up in the repercussions in Tahiti. The island's
French divided into opposed Vichy and De Gaulle factions.
Pailloux argued for compromise. However, when the De
Gaullists gained the upper hand he was clapped in jail. Suddenly his whole world collapsed. Although there were no
charges against him, the community turned its back on him.
Even his vahine turned against him. She refused to visit
him or to bring their children to see him.

In 1941 Pailloux was interned with a motley assortment
of prisoners on Motu Uta, about a half-mile off the Papeete
waterfront. "There were thirty-one of us," he recalled,
"fourteen Frenchmen, nine Japanese, seven Germans, and
one Italian." The French guards treated them with Gallic
tolerance. They could swim on the beaches, fish, or grow
vegetables. There were reports that some of them even
swam in and joined in the merriment at Quinn's dance hall,
or that vahines rowed out with cases of beer.

Yet Pailloux hated this seemingly idyllic confinement. He was bitter because the French would not tell him why he was being held. He was angry at his vahine for deserting him. Moreover, he was an energetic man and couldn't stand the enforced idleness. To pass the time he grew tomatoes and planted ironwood trees.

One day Pailloux noticed one of the Germans busily working with his hands. He watched curiously and found the man was fashioning little curios out of mother-of-pearl. He expressed admiration for the German's skill and the man offered to teach him how it was done. Pailloux became an avid pupil. Day after day he watched and learned. He persuaded the French guards to bring him some shells which contained mother-of-pearl and some tools with which he could shape and polish the gleaming, iridescent substance. Soon he, too, could fashion artistic little curios.

Then came a day when his life took another sudden and disastrous turn. Without warning or explanation, he was shipped to his estranged vahine's native island of Kaukura. There the islanders were told he was their prisoner. His vahine's family became his jailers. He was made to do menial work around the native village. When he protested about his cruel treatment, his vahine's father, a burly islander, beat him in front of the villagers.

It had now been three years since he was interned. The mistreatment, coming on top of the years of confinement, had reduced him to a physical wreck. His once stocky figure was gaunt and his expressive face lined and haggard. Finally a passing schooner took him to the hospital in Papeete. For six months he lay in a hospital bed. It gave him time to think how to rebuild his shattered life. He had no money. His health was broken. His vahine was gone and his children scattered. His once-respected reputation in the community was tarnished. He could not go back to the government which had interned him. Then he recalled how he had learned to make curios from mother-of-pearl on Motu Uta. Perhaps he could do that.

When he got out of the hospital he began fashioning little curios and selling them to the few tourists. When the war ended more tourists began coming and his little business began to pick up. He became more original in his work. He taught some Tahitians his technique and opened a little shop. Ironically, the shop was facing the quai and looked directly across the harbor to Motu Uta.

He also resumed his old campaign of writing to government officials, demanding to know why he had been interned. The answer was a Gallic shrug. The French were anxious to forget old animosities. However, Pailloux would not let them forget. He nagged them like a guilty conscience, demanding vindication. At last the French government summoned him to Paris in 1950. There for six solid hours he poured out his pent-up grievances. "The French said only that they would study the case," Pailloux recalled, "and I came back to Tahiti."

In Papeete his business continued to grow. Soon he had a group of artisans turning out hundreds of different kinds of curios. He became one of Papeete's leading businessmen.

Finally he heard from the government in Paris. He was vindicated! The government ruled his internment was unjust and granted him a pension for life. A French *fonctionnaire* pinned a medal on him and gave him the traditional kiss on both cheeks.

Pailloux likes to stand in front of his busy shop, looking out across the harbor. He sees Motu Uta, with the ironwood trees he planted now grown tall and green. "It's strange the turns life takes," he says.

8. *President Kennedy with Kevu at the White House. Ben pronounced him "Number One."*

Wide World photos

9. *Near Treetops Hotel in Kenya, East Africa. The elephant seems to be trying to remember something.*

10. *On safari at Amboselli, Kenya. This camp had hot and cold running hyenas.*

*11. Enroute with Tom Cochran and John Reddy to visit Dr. Albert Schweitzer at Lambaréné, West Africa, on the Ogove River.*

Louis Hepp photo

*12. Dr. Schweitzer showed us around his jungle hospital by jeep.*

Louis Hepp photo

*13. Although nearly 90 when we visited him, Dr. Schweitzer made the rounds of his patients every day.*

Louis Hepp photo

14. *Emile Gauguin, son of famed painter Paul Gauguin, in Tahiti.*
*Emile gave me a self-portrait titled "Les calories ne comptent pas."*
*(Translation: "Calories don't count.")*     Jack Douglas photo

15. *When Pauline dances the Ta-*
*hitian hula it makes a belly dance*
*look as dignified as Swan Lake.*
Jack Douglas photo

16. *"Whatta ya mean you can't*
*understand my Japanese?" Reiko*
*and Bobby Douglas in Tahiti.*
Jack Douglas photo

17. *Eating with these chopsticks was like knitting a meal.*

18. *So THIS is what you do with a geisha girl.*

# A VISIT WITH DR. SCHWEITZER
November 1963

Getting there is half the fun," I kept telling myself, as our Trans-Gabon DC-3 hit another air pocket. The cabin, into which I was crammed with some Africans and a jumble of cargo, was stifling hot and there was not a breath of air. Everyone was *holding* his breath, waiting for the next bump. Even if there had been any air in the cabin I don't think any of the passengers would have inhaled. The air was too turbulent even to *breathe.*

The Africans, however, seemed not in the least perturbed by the rough flying conditions. Several of the Gabonese women around me were calmly nursing their babies and I had a terrible vision of what might happen if they were still nursing them when we landed and the plane came down with a jolt! In fact, everywhere we flew in Africa some of the passengers were nursing mothers. I always half expected the stewardess to announce, "We are now about to land. Please fasten your brassieres and observe the no nursing sign." The African lady next to me on this flight sat with her seat belt tightly fastened throughout the flight. This I assumed was because of the bumpy air. However, when it

became especially turbulent, and the FASTEN YOUR SEAT
BELTS sign flashed on, she promptly *unfastened* hers. Either
her English wasn't very good or she was an extreme non-
conformist.

I was on Trans-Gabon's popular white-knuckle flight
bound for the jungle hospital of Dr. Albert Schweitzer . . .
a journey that had begun by jet plane in New York a few
days earlier and seemed to move swiftly backward in time
to an earlier century. It was also a $10,000 and 15,000 mile
gamble. I had long admired Dr. Schweitzer and had wanted
to film him at his work which I felt would be of great interest to American television viewers. However, efforts to arrange to see him had been frustrating. Schweitzer, then
eighty-eight, had been seriously ill, and associates of his in
New York and London had discouraged the idea of visiting
him. Finally, in October 1963, I decided to just take the
gamble and fly to Lambarene in Equatorial West Africa on
the chance of being able to interview him.

With Tom Cochran and John Reddy I had flown by jet
from New York across the South Atlantic to Dakar, Senegal,
on the westernmost tip of Africa. From there we hopped
down the steamy west coast of Africa, with stops at Monro-
via, Liberia, Accra, Ghana and Lagos, Nigeria, finally landing at Leopoldville in the Congo after seventeen hours of
flying. At Leopoldville we were met by Louis Hepp, NBC's
Nairobi bureau chief, who had flown from Kenya across
Africa to join us. Things were still chaotic in the Congo and
Hepp, a handsome Greek who had nearly been killed earlier
covering the fighting there, proved to be a handy man to
have around when the natives got restless.

Among the minor confusions in the Congo are the names
of the countries. When both the former Belgian Congo and

the former French Congo became independent they both re-
tained the name Congo. The former Belgian Congo became
Congo-Leopoldville, and the former French Congo is Congo-
Brazzaville and that's how it remains—subject, of course, to
change without notice.

Leopoldville is a city with modern buildings and broad
boulevards and once had been a miniature Brussels with
palm trees, Hepp told us, but the prolonged troubles had
turned it into a shambles. The city was half deserted and
any kind of service strictly catch-as-catch-can. Electricity
and water sometimes just petered out, and attempting a
phone call was an invitation to madness. We heard some
wry stories of the chaotic conditions. One concerned a
woman who called the gendarmes to report a prowler.
"We'll come right away," the police replied, "if you can
send someone to come and get us."

The Hotel Regina, where we stayed, was the best hotel,
Hepp said, but it was operating on the do-it-yourself plan.
The only food obtainable was eggs and bread and it had to
be flown in because of the upset conditions. Incidentally,
Leopoldville was the only place in the world I ever found
where they would not cash travelers checks. I tried to pay
our hotel bill with them but the Belgian lady behind the
desk acted as though I had said a dirty word—Patrice Lu-
mumba. She insisted on our paying cash. While I was dredg-
ing up fistfuls of tattered franc notes, Cochran checked the
bill and pointed out that the lady had *under*charged us.
"I don't care," she said, "just so long as you pay cash."

After our bout with the erratic finances of the Congo-Leo-
poldville, we set out to sample the confusion of the Congo-
Brazzaville from where we were to fly to Gabon where the
Schweitzer hospital is situated. In a wheezy ferry boat we

crossed the mile-wide Congo River, dotted with clumps of floating water hyacinth, to Brazzaville, a smaller tropical town with a Catholic Cathedral where the worshipers are called to mass by the beating of a tom-tom. Although the French Congo did not explode, like the former Belgian Congo, there was political unrest there and the chief of state, Abbe Youlou, had only lately been deposed. We got a vivid sample of the unrest when some native gendarmes roughly manhandled a Congolese at the slip as we got off the ferry.

From Brazzaville we caught an Air Afrique DC-8 jet for Libreville, the capital of Gabon. Libreville is a sleepy tropical town strung out along the coast of the Gulf of Guinea. From Libreville we caught the Trans-Gabon DC-3 for Lambarene, the village nearest the hospital. Crowded in among the natives and the bulky cargo, I mentioned to Louis Hepp we hadn't exactly caught the Champagne flight. "This is nothing," he grinned. "You should take a flight in Cameroon, the country next door. There they slaughter cattle at the airport and hang the sides of beef in the cabin with the passengers. You have to keep ducking to avoid the swinging sides of beef as you fly along."

Apart from the discomfort and turbulence our flight from Libreville to Lambarene was uneventful: the plane landed smoothly and none of the nursing mothers got anything nipped off. However, the wait at the airport took nearly as long as the flight. The Africans have picked up the white man's burden—red tape—and the Gabonese lassoed us in yards of it. We spent an interminable time in the sweltering little terminal filling out lengthy forms . . . for what I'll never know. I haven't signed my name so often since the time a group of little old ladies with autograph books trapped me in an elevator at NBC—under the impression I was Van Johnson.

Finally we climbed into a jeep station wagon for a wild ride into Lambarene. The driver was a jaunty Gabonese in a beatnik outfit featuring a heavy wool sweater (in the above 90-degree heat!) and a beret that was pure Greenwich Village. He careened over the winding dirt road to Lambarene with the reckless abandon of Sterling Moss at Le Mans, while kids, dogs, and chickens scuttled out of the way. Whirling around a corner, he winged a dog and set off a chorus of outcries. The dog yelped in pain, the Gabonese passengers howled with glee and we yelled in protest. "Do you get the feeling," Louis Hepp asked, "that Dr. Schweitzer's reverence for life hasn't caught on everywhere here yet?"

After crossing the Ogoue River in an asthmatic barge, our demon driver dropped us at our hotel in the village of Lambarene which is situated on an island in the middle of the broad river. The Hotel de L'Ogoue is a small but reasonably comfortable hotel on a hill with a sweeping view of the surrounding countryside. The heat and humidity were oppressive, but the country was much more beautiful than I had expected. The river, cutting through the thick jungle, was like twin streams of silver as it divided to flow around the island, and the whole scene was soft and beautiful.

The Schweitzer hospital is about three miles downstream from Lambarene, on the far side of the river. It can be reached by pirogue (native dugout canoe) or by a primitive ferry. We crossed on the ferry in a hired Land-Rover and bumped over a rough jungle road toward the hospital. On the road we were met by Schweitzer's daughter, Mrs.

Rhena Eckert, and Erika Anderson, an American woman film producer, who is a close friend of the doctor. They greeted us graciously but Mrs. Eckert said her father had been ill and she did not know whether he could see us. The best she could do, she said, was to get a note to us at the hotel in the morning telling us whether he would see us and let us film the hospital.

We returned to the hotel to sit and brood—something I do rather frequently. In fact I could feel the first symptoms of Kakorrhaphiophobi.* "Do you suppose," I wondered, "that we've come fifteen thousand miles for nothing?" I knew that Dr. Schweitzer had been ill, and his daughter had been very noncommittal in talking with us. A note delivered to the hotel in the morning would be a graceful way of refusing us. Between my foreboding and the intense humidity it was a restless night.

In the morning there was nothing to do but wait for the note from the hospital. Tom Cochran, a devout Catholic, announced he was going to church in the village and I decided to go along and lend moral support. Cochran is one of five handsome Erie, Pennsylvania, brothers, another of whom is World War II flying hero Colonel Phil Cochran who was portrayed in the comic strips as Flip Corkin. Tommy has been with me through thick and thin—mostly thick—and is one of the finest men I know. He is so devout that he sometimes goes to several Masses on Sunday. If he can't find a Mass he'll go to a *clean* Italian movie. Although he has no vices that I know of, he goes to confession regularly. I suspect he's trying to get a reputation. It was characteristic that we no sooner arrived in Lambarene than

---

* Exaggerated fear of failure. I wanted to get that in *somewhere*.

Tommy wanted to go to Mass. Since it looked as though our hopes of seeing Dr. Schweitzer could stand a little prayer, I went along. To get to the church, we had to take a pirogue down the Ogoue. A pirogue is a very frail craft, and the Ogoue is full of hippos and crocodiles, and I suddenly found myself wondering what I was doing in a tippy canoe with a Catholic. A Baptist would make sense, since they believe in total immersion. Tommy doesn't smoke, drink, or swim. I comforted myself with the thought that I was in good company and if we drowned I could probably gain admittance to Heaven as a friend of Tom Cochran's.

The church was a little bamboo hut with open windows near the river's edge. The congregation was entirely Gabonese except for Cochran and a couple of French people. Since I am not a Catholic, I waited outside during the Mass which I could hear through the open windows. The Mass was in Latin, of course, but the priest preached the sermon in French. There were several little Gabonese boys playing near me outside the church, and their chatter and laughter began to intrude on the sermon. Even with my fragmentary knowledge of French, and the chatter of the boys, I could gather that the sermon dealt with brotherly love. Finally the talk and laughter began to distract the priest. *"Et Jesus dit* (and Jesus said) . . ." he said. A burst of laughter came through the window. *"Et Jesus dit . . ."* he repeated. More squeals from outside the window. The priest walked suddenly to the open window, made a fist, and rapped the offending youngsters smartly on their heads. They scattered in a final burst of glee. The priest adjusted his vestments, walked back to the front of the church, and resumed, *"Et Jesus dit . . ."*

Cochran's prayers must have worked. When we arrived back at the hotel there was a note from Dr. Schweitzer's daughter. The doctor would be happy to see us, it said, and would like to have us as his guests for lunch.

Within minutes we had piled our camera equipment in pirogues and were being paddled downriver to the hospital. The jungle on either side was lushly green and the humid air like steam rising out of a green mist. The native paddlers increased the tempo of their rhythmic strokes as we neared our destination. Then the hospital came into view: a sprawling cluster of tin-roofed wooden buildings straggling down a green slope to the water's edge. Small cooking fires winked through the haze. Our pirogues slid up on a sandy beach and I jumped ashore. Looking up I saw the familiar figure of Dr. Schweitzer coming down the winding path to greet us. He wore a white pith helmet, thin white shirt and black bow tie, and baggy white pants. A smile lighted his craggy features as he greeted us in French and invited us to join him in a cup of tea.

I had arrived at a troubled time in the life of Dr. Schweitzer. He was in his eighty-ninth year and his fiftieth year at his jungle hospital. For years he had been hailed as one of the great men of our times. He had given up notable careers in philosophy, music, and theology to go to Africa to minister to the natives. His philosophy of reverence for life was known around the world. He had been awarded the Nobel Peace Prize. Yet now he had suddenly become a controversial figure, caught in the winds of change sweeping across an emerging Africa. There were cries of "Colonialist" and "Jungle doctor go home," hurled by newly independent Africans. There were charges that his hospital was dirty and antiquated and that time had passed him by.

Despite his recent illness, and the controversy raging around him, he looked well. His piercing eyes, drooping mustache, and strong, aqualine nose gave him the appearance of a pioneer of the old West. His hands, which had so beautifully interpreted the music of Bach and Wagner, looked strong but worn from wielding shovel and saw. Over a cup of tea he told us of his work at the hospital he had literally built with his own hands. He had given up operating at seventy-five, he said, but still supervised the hospital and the new construction. With obvious pride he said he had worked eight hours the previous day pouring cement for a new building. He told us something of the special problems of his jungle hospital. "We get many cases of hernia, malaria, and sleeping sickness," he said, "but cancer and appendicitis are almost unknown here." Natives are occasionally brought in injured by gorillas, and one man had been treated for being "hit by an elephant." "This is how to act if you come face to face with a gorilla in the jungle," he said. Smiling, he walked slowly backward.

After finishing our tea we set out on a tour of the hospital. "Do you mind if we film you as we go?" I asked. A smile creased his grizzled face. "I'll do anything with you but box," he said.

Dr. Schweitzer's jungle hospital is not a hospital in the sense that we envision one; it is more an African village. There are some fifty ramshackle buildings, mostly little more than shacks and huts. There is no electricity and the only water comes from one hand-pumped well. The only sanitary facility is an old-fashioned privy for the staff. Only the little operating room, the gift of Prince Rainier of Monaco, has electric light. The place is a bedlam of sound: goats bleating, dogs barking, children squalling. Occasionally there is a sharp crack like a pistol shot as a mango or breadfruit falls on a tin roof. Chickens, pigs, and turkeys are everywhere underfoot. All of the noise and clutter disturb Dr. Schweitzer not at all. "Circumstances require that the hospital be primitive in keeping with the primitive state of the people," he said. "We save money by not having electricity and it is more poetic without it."

The doctor led us down a winding path to the buildings near the river's edge. Despite his eighty-eight years he moved along spryly. He is not comfortable speaking English so his daughter and Erika Anderson translated as we walked along. He stopped first at the long pharmacy building, which he called his "tape worm building," where he usually sits at a battered old desk issuing drugs or prescribing treatment.

I remarked about the oppressive heat that soaked us all in perspiration. "We have no thermometers here," he said, "because if we knew how hot it was we couldn't stand it." The patients greeted him gravely as we passed. Sometimes he stopped to say a few words to one or to pat a youngster on the head. The patients wore paper tags around their necks with their name, village, and tribe. Some wore bandages. One man had no nose. Many of the women puffed on pipes. Some patients lay on rude wooden bunks while their families crouched outside around smoky fires cooking for the sick relatives. "When a patient comes to the hospital the whole family comes along to care for him," Dr. Schweitzer said. "Sometimes when they recover they don't want to go back to their village because they are old or handicapped or lonely. We let them stay on and work around the place." He showed us some of them working. Women were sewing or ironing, and laundry flapped everywhere from trees and bushes. Men passed carrying bunches of bananas. Naked children splashed in the river. Several pirogues were beached at the water's edge. "It was on the river here," he said, "that I conceived my philosophy of reverence for life."

As we walked the doctor spoke of some of the cases. An appealing little boy of about ten was helping Louis Hepp to carry our film equipment. "He is deaf," the doctor said. "We hope to send him to Paris to study lip reading." Climbing back up the slope we came to a pygmy woman whom Dr. Schweitzer called "Maman Sans Nom" (Mama without a name). "The natives found her in the jungle and brought her to us," he said. "She apparently was the last of her tribe. She speaks a language no one understands." The little pygmy was a pathetic sight. She dislikes wearing clothes, we were told, but was persuaded to wear a loincloth. She tries to communicate by doing a sort of undulating dance, and making clicking sounds with her tongue and teeth.

Chickens, ducks, and dogs scurried out of our way as we passed. "We have over two hundred sheep and goats and about a hundred hens and ducks," the doctor said. Under his principle of reverence for life they are never molested. They seemed to get along peacefully, although Dr. Schweitzer once saw a dog chasing a chicken. "Please," he yelled, "remember that we got the Nobel Peace Prize."

He showed us some of his pets including several antelopes, a pelican and two chimpanzees. One of the chimpanzees had only one arm. "We had to amputate the other," the doctor said. "The poor creature was caught in a trap." While we stood watching them, the one-armed chimpanzee lunged at Louis Hepp. "*Attendez!*" the doctor shouted.

He showed us fruit trees of which he had planted more

than a thousand. "The African jungle contains almost no indigenous fruit trees," he said. "These mangoes, papaya, and breadfruit all had to be imported, but they flourish here."

At midday we joined the doctor and his staff at lunch in the dining hall. There were about forty doctors, nurses, and visitors at one long table. Dr. Schweitzer sat in the center and I was directly across from him. "We feed over a thousand people a day," his daughter told me. "No one is ever turned away." Lunch consisted of fresh papaya, lamb chops, rice, and stewed mangoes, and was cooked and served by natives. Dr. Schweitzer did not eat the lamb chops. I mentioned that the fact they were serving meat seemed inconsistent with his reverence for life. "The people in the kitchen," he smiled, "are not of the same opinion as Dr. Schweitzer." There were ants on the table and I reached over and brushed one off the doctor's shoulder. "He was mine," he said. "Let him go in peace."

The doctor, who had once called television "the beginning of stupidity," asked about my program. I told him that I had done an hour and three-quarter show each week night for five years. "How did you do it?" he asked. I reached in my pocket and fished out a Dexamyl. "Ah, that is not good," he scolded. "Science does not know the long-range effects of such drugs."

After lunch the doctor retired for a brief siesta while we filmed and talked with some of the other doctors and nurses. The staff is drawn from a dozen nations. Dr. Rolf Muller, a young surgeon, is Swiss. Dr. Takahashi, who handles the lepers, is Japanese. Dr. Richard Friedmann, a psychiatrist, is Israeli. Ali Silver, a nurse with a deeply spiritual face, is Dutch. Marie Louise Cullum and Virginia Schneider, nurses' aides, are Americans. Some are paid a small sum while others work as volunteers. Some, like Mathilde Kottmann, the doctor's first nurse, have been with him for decades; others for only a few months. All are dedicated people, working under primitive conditions in brutal tropical heat with scant comforts.

From them we learned more of the sometimes bizarre problems of operating a hospital for primitive people in the midst of the jungle. The patients are mostly from the Fang and Galoa tribes and have to be housed separately or they will quarrel. They are given food to prepare themselves because of their belief that food prepared by someone else might poison them. Also, we were told, witch doctors still have a strong hold on native minds. Sometimes late at night, when the hospital staff is asleep, witch doctors creep in and treat the patients in the old jungle ways. However, even superstition is being modernized. "The natives now hold tribal dances around a Coleman lantern," a nurse told us.

We saw touching examples of the feeling of the staff for their black patients. One English nurse was making her rounds with a tiny African baby strapped to her back like an Indian papoose. "That's Joan Clent, an English girl," Mrs. Schneider told us. "She came here all the way from England by bicycle. It took her two years. The baby's mother, a mental patient, hanged herself. Joan has adopted the baby."

Marie Louise Cullum, an attractive New Yorker, was also caring for an African baby. The boy was prematurely born and his mother died in childbirth. In accordance with tribal custom they were going to bury the infant with the dead mother. However, the father got it away from the fetish ceremony and brought it to the hospital. The baby was nearly starved and covered with tropical ulcers. Marie Louise took the baby and cared for it as if it were her own. Eventually, with love and care, it recovered.

The staff all spoke with great affection of Dr. Schweitzer, even in telling of his human foibles and his deep concern for any living thing, even insects.

Someone told of the time a tsetse fly lighted on a patient while Dr. Schweitzer was treating him. The patient's wife moved to swat the insect. The doctor caught her arm and shooed the fly out the window. "The fly thanks you," he said.

Adlai Stevenson visited Schweitzer at the time when there was trouble in Lebanon and the U.S. Sixth Fleet was standing by. While talking to the doctor a mosquito landed on Stevenson and he swatted it. "You didn't have to use the whole Sixth Fleet," the doctor said reproachfully. Another time, we were told, a goat wandered into the operating room while an operation was in progress. Someone had dropped a rubber surgical glove on the floor. The goat proceeded to eat the glove and died as a result. "Dr. Schweitzer was furious," an aide said. "Not because the goat was in the operating room; because someone was careless enough to drop the glove so the goat could swallow it." The doctor sometimes employs macabre humor to impress on his guests his concern for all living things. "Be careful here," he will say on a jungle path, "because the serpents nest along here." As his visitor recoils in horror, the doctor adds, "I wouldn't want you to step on the snakes and harm them."

Dr. Schweitzer has a saying that "help comes to us from Heaven" and this is sometimes literally true, his daughter told us. Once they had to perform two major operations on a six-months-old child. The surgeon was concerned about

the operations because they did not have a skilled anesthetist or modern anesthesia equipment. Just before the
operation an English anesthetist arrived by plane with his
equipment. He had been at a medical meeting in neighboring Nigeria and came to Lambarene to meet Dr. Schweitzer.
He administered the anesthetic and the operation on the
baby was a success. In a similar instance, a man's back was
broken by a falling tree and he was paralyzed. He could
be helped only by a skilled neurosurgeon. A crack neurosurgeon happened to arrive by plane from the Philippines
and performed the difficult operation. The man now walks
on crutches and will eventually be able to walk unaided.

Jet travel has made remote Lambarene more accessible
and now there is a steady stream of visitors: doctors and
Peace Corps members, celebrities and the merely curious.
Some stay on to work for weeks or months. Hugh O'Brian,
TV's Wyatt Earp, appeared in full Western regalia and
worked for a week. "The natives thought he was a white
witch doctor," a nurse told us.

A wealthy American woman appears periodically to stay
at the hospital, passing out dresses, shirts, baseball caps, and
even $20 hand-painted silk neckties to the native patients.
The influx of such visitors is not an unmixed blessing, I
gathered, although Dr. Schweitzer treats them all hospitably. We heard of one American woman who pestered the
busy doctor with her attentions and silly questions. While
talking with him she dropped her comb. The doctor picked
it up and started to hand it back. Then he smiled and said,
"My dear, may I keep this as a memento of you?" Sometimes, though, there is an end to his patience. One young
man persisted in discussing reverence for life with Dr.

Schweitzer at lunch while their food got cold. "Couldn't you practice reverence for life on me?" the doctor finally asked. "I am also a life, and I would like to eat my soup while it is hot."

After awaking from his nap, the doctor invited us to his little room to talk. It is a spare, plain room with a bed, a couple of chairs, a wooden table and a wash basin. The table, where he writes, was littered with books and papers. Both ends of the room are open, with lattice-like construction which Dr. Schweitzer said keeps the room cool even in the hottest weather. Outside the window is buried Mrs. Schweitzer, who died in 1957, at the age of seventy-five. Tools are propped on the porch railing outside his door as a precaution against their being stolen. "The chickens roost on the railing," the doctor said. "They make a good burglar alarm." He instigated his unique burglar alarm system after he discovered the natives were stealing the hospital's chamber pots and using them as cooking pots in the villages.

In this small, cell-like room, Dr. Schweitzer lives a spartan existence. He shaves with a straight razor, without soap or water. He cuts his own hair. Recently a member of his staff appeared with a fresh haircut. The doctor asked him who cut it. "A brother at the Catholic mission cut it for five hundred francs," the man said. "I'd have done it for less," declared the doctor.

He always dresses the same: white pith helmet, white shirt and pants, and a black tie. He has had one hat for forty years and a tie for more than twenty years. He was told that some people had dozens of neckties. "For *one* neck?" he said.

This spartan living is part of Dr. Schweitzer's philosophy. "True comfort is simplicity of one's means," he says. Sitting in his little room, where he writes late into the night after a hard day's work, he spoke of his work and his philosophy. He talked gratefully of the assistance he had received from the United States which he visited only once. He recalled the visit was in 1939 to speak at the Goethe Festival in Aspen, Colorado. He was surprised then at the warmth of his welcome by Americans. When asked how he should be introduced, he said, "Just say that this fellow who looks like a collie is Albert Schweitzer."

"Few people realize," he said, "that this mission at Lambarene was started by an American, a Dr. Nassau. When he retired and returned to America I read of the need of a doctor here and decided to study medicine and come here. When I got here in 1913 the slave trade was just ending. The slaves didn't want to be free because it meant they would have to buy their own wives. An African could buy a wife then for sixty empty bottles."

Dr. Schweitzer recalled that his first hospital was an abandoned chicken house. His only assistants were his wife and a native named Joseph Azowani. In those days, witch doctors tried to beat the "evil spirits" out of the sick, and the mentally deranged were drowned in the river. Patients sometimes ate the ointment given them to put on infections. I spoke of how much he had achieved in the half-century since. "The other doctors can't make the natives work the way I do," he said. "You need great authority to get them to work on time or to work at all. I have this authority because I am an old man. Authority over the natives comes with age."

Schweitzer places great store by hard work and toils like a coolie at his construction. "I'm the only peasant here," he sometimes says. He was much impressed with the way cameraman Louis Hepp moved swiftly about to film him as he walked. "A good man," he said. "I could use him here."

He was impatient with charges that he was living in the
past and that he had never trained any Africans to be doctors. "We don't have the facilities to train them here," he
said. "Africa is so vast that if one feels he can do good in
this continent why not go and do it? Why climb on this old
back?"

After we had talked a long time Dr. Schweitzer suggested
we visit the leper village. We rode by jeep along the winding dirt road past the little cemetery through a grove of mangoes to the village. There are about 120 lepers and their
families in the village, many of them pitifully disfigured.
Like the other patients, they live with their families in bar-
rack-like buildings of wood and palm weave with tin roofs.
Beautiful tulip trees all around contrasted with the sad condition of the lepers. In one building costumed leper children
sat solemnly waiting to rehearse a nativity scene they would
perform at Christmas. Dr. Schweitzer reached up and
tapped one of the tin roofs. "These were paid for by the
money from the Nobel Prize," he said. Dr. Takahashi showed
us through the building where he treats his patients. We
talked with one girl whose arm was so badly burned it was
webbed from forearm to shoulder. "Dr. Muller will operate
on her tomorrow," said Dr. Schweitzer.

On the way back to the hospital we met Joseph Azowani,
the doctor's first native assistant when he arrived in 1913.
He was a very old man, his head almost like a black
skull. "Joseph is old but in good health," a doctor told us.
"Sometimes, though, he pesters Dr. Schweitzer for pills to
restore his virility."

Talking with Dr. Schweitzer, as we walked through the

sprawling hospital compound, I could not help but be struck by paradoxes in his character. He obviously loved the Africans, and had given most of his life to caring for them, yet he seemed to have little faith in their ability to govern themselves. "You can't change their character," he said. He believes deeply in brotherhood yet his hospital is strictly segregated and in a half century he has never trained an African to be anything more than an orderly. When I asked him about the Berlin Wall he said, "I know nothing of politics." Yet when United Nations forces intervened in the Congo he called them "bandits" and "assassins" and he told me he corresponded with intellectuals around the world in an effort to ban atomic warfare. He showed me a letter he had written to President Kennedy praising him for his efforts in achieving the test ban treaty.

There was something magnificent yet sad at the sight of the crusty, stubborn old man going his way as he had for half a century while the world around him changed even in the African jungle.

When he first came to Africa in 1913 it took him three days by paddle-wheel boat to travel from Port Gentil on the Atlantic to Lambarene 175 miles up the Ogoue River. Yet we had flown it in an old DC-3 in little more than an hour! The natives still traveled in pirogues, but now many of them had outboard motors. The hospital, with its ramshackle buildings and natives crouching around smoky fires, might be a scene out of Conrad's *The Heart of Darkness*. But just three miles downstream in the town of Lambarene is a modern, antiseptic government hospital and a good hotel with air conditioning, telephones, gourmet food, and vintage wines. For years Dr. Schweitzer had been universally acclaimed for his humanity in serving the natives in this inhos-

pitable place. Now the educated Africans were grumbling
that he was a remnant of colonialism. "If it were up to me
I would burn the place down," an official of the newly independent Gabonese government had said.

Dr. Schweitzer clings fiercely to his ideas despite criticism
or change. "I know what is best for Africans," he said. "The
natives still come here because they know they will be
cured."

Although Dr. Schweitzer admits he is opposed to change,
the inexorable passage of time has brought changes in his
own life at Lambarene. Once a friend told him, "You cannot burn a candle at both ends." "Oh yes you can," the doctor said, "if the candle is long enough." Now his candle was
burning low and he worried about who would carry on construction when he is gone. "I am a king in friendship and a
beggar in time," he said.

He no longer preached at the Sunday services, with a native standing on either side of him to translate the simple
sermons into the language of the Fangs and the Galoas.
Other members of the staff now do this. The zinc-lined piano, on which he played Bach and Mendelssohn in the stillness of the jungle night, is now gone. It was shipped back to
his old home village of Gunsbach in Alsace because it was
falling apart in the tropical humidity. Otherwise his days
are as they have always been: caring for the sick, building
obsessively, writing at night after the long day's work. He
has no plans to leave his hospital except "to go to heaven."

After three days it was time for us to leave. The doctor
walked with us down the crooked path to the river's bank
to say goodbye. It was late afternoon and the palm trees cast
long shadows. Cooking fires burned redly in the gathering
dusk. Children trailed behind us and dogs and chickens

scrambled out of the way. The doctor asked us to come again and I said I'd be honored. "Never use that word with me," he said. "One need not honor another man."

Two pirogues were pushed out in the river to take us back to Lambarene from which we would begin our long flight home. We climbed into the teetering craft and the native paddlers steered them out into the current. All alone, the old doctor walked out on a little jetty. It was a sight I will never forget. We waved at him and shouted farewells. He removed his worn pith helmet and his long, white hair blew in the breeze. He bowed low, like a great actor acknowledging a tremendous ovation. That was our final sight of him . . . still standing and bowing gravely . . . a frail, fierce figure, seeming to defy time.

*BRAZIL*

August 1964

Miriam seemed a little startled when I suggested a trip up the Amazon.

"What is there to see *there?*" she asked with wifely skepticism.

"I'm glad you asked," I told her, looking up from my travel folders. "There are swamps as big as Texas. There are schools of piranha fish that can strip a man down to a skeleton in two minutes. There are Indians with blow guns, and bargains in shrunken heads. There are snakes called anacondas that can swallow a deer whole. There are anteaters as big as bears and spiders so large they catch birds. What else would you like to know?"

"I can hardly wait to go," she said with what seemed a certain lack of enthusiasm.

Even the name of the Amazon trip sounded irresistible: Green Hell Tours. After years in the gray flannel jungles of New York I could hardly wait to take a Green Hell tour.

We were scheduled to fly to Brazil anyway, to film Mary Martin and her husband Richard Halliday on their ranch near Brasília, so why not go up the fabled Amazon at the same time? It would be like killing two *toucons* (a Brazilian bird) with one blow gun. After all, there was nothing to stop us except those piranha fish, anacondas, hostile Indians, and various other perils.

The next thing I knew I was sitting drinking *gim-tonicas* in the bar of the Grande Hotel in Belém poised to plunge into the green hell of the Amazon jungle. From Belém, where the Amazon enters the Atlantic, we were scheduled to take the RMS *Hubert* a thousand miles up the river to Manaus, the old rubber capital of the Amazon. Belém doesn't have a great many tourist attractions. After you've seen the big water tower, squarely in the middle of town, you've seen it all. It's one of those towns where *both* sides of the track are wrong. To complicate things, either the RMS *Hubert* was running late or our Green Hell Tour schedule was running early. Or maybe it just *seemed* like the *Hubert* was as long overdue as the *Titanic*. In between sipping *gim-tonicas*, and drumming my fingers impatiently on our table at the Grande, we wandered around town taking in the water markets, the Goeldi Museum, the opera house, a railroad station built in 1896 (which looks it), and the zoo. You can get very tired of looking at anacondas, we found, even if they can swallow a deer. We also sat around listening to the Brazilians speak Portuguese which doesn't sound as you expect it to. Instead of having the liquid sound of Spanish, as I thought, it sounds almost guttural like German or, as author Richard Bissell says, "like a Frenchman speaking Polish." Written Portuguese looks like Spanish, slightly misspelled. Whenever we didn't have anything else to do we looked at the Amazon, and you can look at it a long, long time without seeing it all. In fact, at Belém the river is so wide you can't even see across it. In between exploring the mouth of the river in a boat we listened to legends about it.

Belém's principal exports are rubber, fish, and legends, and I hope the rubber and fish are more reliable than the legends. Almost everyone we met had some bizarre tale to tell, and most of the stories turned out on checking to be pure fancy (or *im*pure fancy) or else highly exaggerated. The only stories we heard that weren't exaggerated were about the Amazon, and it's impossible to exaggerate about the Amazon. At Belém, the huge, muddy stream is forty miles wide. It is so deep that oceangoing vessels can go up it as far as Peru—a distance of 2400 miles. The islands are similarly huge. Marajo Island, in the mouth of the river, is larger than Switzerland. Another, Gurupa, is fifty times larger than Manhattan Island. The state of Amazonas is twice as large as Texas.

So powerful is the swift-flowing Amazon that it tears away great chunks of its banks which form floating islands which drift down the river and into the ocean. Brazilians along the river often climb on these floating islands and ride them downstream, much as hoboes in America catch freight trains. One man we heard of had part of his farm, on which he had cattle grazing, torn away and borne off down the river. He pursued it in a boat, stopping along the way to ask, "Has anyone seen my farm go by?"

Typically, the Amazon got its name through a false legend. Francisco de Orellana, the Spanish explorer who first traveled the length of the great river in 1541, told of being attacked by fierce women warriors like the legendary Amazons of mythology. Another Spanish chronicler spoke of women warriors who amputated their right breasts to facilitate their use of weapons. Modern historians tend to debunk the whole idea of the single-breasted women warriors.

They say what Orellana saw was undoubtedly Indian men with Beatle haircuts, but nevertheless the river wound up being called the Amazon.

After a few days of listening to Amazonian legends, and cruising the river around Belém, we concluded that the tardy RMS *Hubert* must be lost. We had seen enough of the river by then to know that getting lost would be no trick at all on the Amazon. Consequently we decided not to wait any longer but to fly to Manaus. Varig Airlines came through nobly. They not only booked us on a flight to Manaus but sent along two very efficient public relations people to hold our hands and make sure we didn't get lost in the jungle or devoured by piranha fish.

As our Varig Caravelle circled over Belém we could look down and see the Amazon flooding into the Atlantic with such force that it turns the ocean muddy for a hundred miles. Then we were over the island of Marajo, in the river's mouth, and could see cattle and water buffalo grazing on the palm-studded plains. Our Varig guides, Charlotte Franklin and Fernando Markan, briefed us on the country as our plane followed the river deep into the interior. The Amazon, they told us, is 3900 miles long; only the Nile is longer. Below us we could see hundreds of islands, including one of the famous floating islands. "No one knows how many there are," Charlotte Franklin said. "They appear and disappear." We could see boats on the chocolate-brown waters, including an ancient paddle-wheel steamer. "Some of them are veterans of the Mississippi," Fernando Markan told us. The thick jungle crowded to the water's edge. It is so dense that when a tree is cut it cannot fall because its branches are interlocked with the trees around it and interwoven with vines. There are no bridges the length of the Amazon because there is nowhere to go. For the same reason there are almost no roads or railroads. Virtually all travel is by boat or plane.

High above the jungle and river, we could observe the changing course of the mighty stream. Sometimes it was a maze of channels. At other places it widened into lakes and swamps, broad as inland seas. When it floods, our Varig friends told us, it creates swamps as big as Texas. Then another large river—the Tapajoz—joins the Amazon. Near the confluence of the two rivers we sighted the red-tiled roofs, church spires, and docks of a good-sized town.

"Santarém," says Charlotte Franklin. "It has a fascinating history." It is a history laced with irony. Santarém was established by Americans, Charlotte told us, and their descendants still live there. After the Civil War, Southerners, embittered at losing their slaves, moved to this remote spot in Brazil where slavery was still practiced. Then Brazil, too, outlawed slavery. Today there are residents of Santarém with American names like Vaughn, Jennings, and Riker. They speak only Portuguese and know nothing of the land their forebears left in bitterness a century ago.

Next into sight came the Rio Negro . . . a dark stream as mighty as the Mississippi. Veering away from the Amazon we followed the Rio Negro a few miles and then swept in low over the jungles to land at the colorful city of Manaus. Today Manaus is a shabby city of 180,000, dozing in the jungle, but it still retains a few spectacular reminders of its fleeting years of glory. It had a skyrocket growth at the turn of the century when the rubber trees of the surrounding jungles began providing tires for the new horseless carriages.

The boom was like the California gold rush in a jungle setting. Overnight rubber barons, cruelly exploiting the Indians, made millions in rubber. Garish Victorian mansions
sprang up along the Rio Negro. The wealthy people sent
their children and even their laundry to Europe. The city
built a forty-million-dollar dock system. Soon Manaus was
the richest city per capita in the world. An opera house,
with crystal chandeliers and Italian marble, was prefabricated in England and then transported across the ocean
and up the Amazon. Entertainers, including Pavlova, the
great dancer, were imported to perform there. Some died
of yellow fever, while others married oil barons.

Then, as suddenly as it had skyrocketed, Manaus plum-
meted. An Englishman smuggled some of the rubber seeds
out. They were planted in the Far East where they grew
even better than in Brazil. Soon Brazil could no longer com-
pete in the world market. In 1912 the crash came. The big
fortunes melted away and Manaus became almost a ghost
town. Bats flitted through the beautiful opera house.

Today Manaus produces jute, oil, and Brazil nuts. Only a
trickle of rubber comes out of the surrounding jungles now.
It has a modern hotel, a few big office buildings and a busy
dock where freighters from Liverpool, New York, and Ham-
burg tie-up. Yet there are no street lights, no covers on
the manholes and the city garbage collection system is the
vultures who are thick and nonchalant as pigeons in an
American city. There is one traffic light, run on a car bat-
tery, but it's mostly a status symbol. Manaus doesn't have
enough traffic to really need a traffic light, but it apparently
makes the citizens feel better. There are no roads out of
Manaus. Same old problem. No place to go. There is a floating market, where you use a canoe instead of a push cart,

and there are attractive specials in such items as ocelot skins, macaws, and snakes. The Rio Negro—three miles wide at Manaus—rises as much as forty-five feet during the rainy season, so the city has floating docks that bob up and down with the seasons.

The famed opera house is something to see. We had heard stories that it was falling apart, and I had visions of the jungle creeping in to reclaim it, but this, like so many Amazon stories, proved to be spectacularly incorrect. In fact, it had recently been refurbished and was gleaming in fresh gilt and red velvet. It was empty; no customers but no bats, either. Although the architecture is early Charles Addams, the opera house is overpoweringly sumptuous. It is set in a huge square of serpentine mosaic and inside is decorated with lavish murals and frescoes featuring armies of plump cherubs. In fact, if all the cherubs were laid end to end they would probably reach to Iquitos, Peru, 1300 miles farther up the Amazon. The scenery is still hanging in the flies as though awaiting the ballerinas who died of yellow fever while dancing there. I asked if they ever have performances there now. "Only a local string quartet a few weeks ago," I was told.

For all its plush and new paint, there is a sadness about the old opera house standing in the tropic sun literally a thousand miles from nowhere. For the dense jungles of interior Brazil around Manaus are among the least populated areas in the world. Only Antarctica is a larger area with less population. If you had a string a thousand miles long, and drew a circle with Manaus as the center, it would encompass nothing but jungles and a few hidden Indian villages; no cities, no roads, no bridges.

One day the Governor of Amazonas kindly provided his boat for us to explore the rivers around Manaus. We went through the floating towns of flimsy houses on log rafts, with their own floating markets, cafes and gas stations, and past the ghostly decaying mansions of the rubber barons. Near the banks we peered into the thick jungles, so dense we could see only a few feet into the green tangle of trees and ferns. Occasionally a baleful pair of red eyes would glow in the shadows. These were caymans, the Amazonian counterpart of the crocodile. One Manaus plant tans twenty thousand cayman skins a month, we were told. Parrots and macaws screeched in the trees. Occasionally there was a plop as a fish jumped near us. I asked about the piranha fish, supposed to be able to devour a man in two minutes. Our guide told us they had found skeletons fully clothed of men who had been devoured by a school of piranhas. The vicious foot-long fish stripped the man to the bone without touching his clothes. Even more menacing, our guide said, were giant catfish, weighing as much as two hundred pounds, who sometimes pull a swimmer under never to be seen again.

A few miles below Manaus, the Rio Negro enters the Amazon. It is an awesome sight. There is a sharp line where the dark Rio Negro surges into the yellowish Amazon and our boat rolled precariously in the waves. Side by side the two rivers rush along for a few miles until the dark waters of the Rio Negro are absorbed in the muddy Amazon.

In the evenings, after exploring the river, we would walk through Manaus, carrying flashlights because of the absence of street lights, or sit in the terrace cafe of the Hotel Amazonas and watch the characters go by. Manaus seems to have a corner on characters and I half-expected to have

Humphrey Bogart slip in and try to sell me some hot diamonds. We saw botanists stalking exotic butterflies, bearded ancients that seemed left over from the rubber boom and American lady tourists who apparently took the Green Hell Tour in the belief it went to Disneyland. Manaus is awash with dreamers and every time I turned around someone had me by the lapels telling me about a place where diamonds were lying around loose or where we could find gold nuggets as big as bagels. All they needed, they said, was a grubstake. The only trouble was, from the figures they mentioned, they wanted the grubstake to be catered by the Colony or Pavillon.

After a few days in Manaus it was time to unhitch the hot-eyed dreamers from my lapels and move on to film Mary Martin and Richard Halliday at their ranch near Brasília. Varig does not fly directly from Manaus to Brasília, so it was necessary to fly a thousand miles to Belém and then another fifteen hundred miles on to Brasília on the country's vast, rolling central plateau six hundred miles from the sea.

After the musty, rococo opera house and ghostly deserted mansions of Manaus, Brasília came as a vivid contrast. The new capital of Brazil is the newest and most modern city in the world and we got a magnificent view of its striking architecture and design as our plane circled the city before landing. For hours we had been flying over dense jungle and then deserted uplands, with scarcely a sign of human habitation. Suddenly a beautiful city seemed to spring from the vast, empty red plains below us.

Brasília is laid out in the form of a plane, and its soaring towers, spaciousness and broad avenues were a magnificent sight when first seen from the air. For more than a century,

Brazilians had talked of building a new capital city in the sparsely settled interior plateau to draw industry and population westward from the coast to which the people seem to cling for dear life. Finally, when President Juscelino Kubitschek took office in 1956, he decided to build the new capital come hell, highwater, or inflation. He almost bankrupted the country but he got the new city built, or almost built. Striking buildings, designed by brilliant architect Oscar Niemeyer, were thrown up in a frenzy of activity by an army of construction workers. Kubitschek would often pop up in the middle of the night to urge on the workers toiling under floodlights. In April of 1960 Kubitschek cut the ribbon marking the formal opening of the new city.

When we arrived in August of 1964, more than four years and $600,000,000 later, we found Brasília, sadly, still not finished. At first we were dazzled by the imaginative design of the city and buildings. The low concrete and glass presidential palace mirrored in its reflecting pool, the tall twin towers that house congressional offices, the Hotel Nacional and apartment complexes, are all beautiful. Yet the shantytown that housed the workers is still there, although work has been suspended, and there is a serious unemployment problem. The graceful concrete crown 108 feet high, that will form the framework of Brasília's Catholic cathedral, is still only a skeleton covering a forlorn-looking excavation. Some of the gleaming new buildings are already showing signs of disrepair and we saw venetian blinds shredded like spaghetti. Despite the bold planning and high hopes, Brasília's very spaciousness gives you a strange feeling like being in a deserted city.

The first days of our visit the Hotel Nacional was crowded with an international convention of engineers gathered to view the wonders of the new city. Then the engineers departed and the hotel was almost deserted.

Although governmental crises and galloping inflation have brought construction to a halt, the argument over Brasília goes on as heatedly as ever. The idea of moving the capital to the thinly populated center of the country may be a good one, and Brasília already has a population of 200,000, but the fun-loving Brazilians are loath to give up a city as gay and charming as Rio and flee back at every opportunity. In fact Varig has a shuttle service with planes leaving the capital every hour on the hour for Rio.

"Brasília is a beautiful city and we will finish it one day," one Brazilian told me. "But who would leave Rio unless he had to?"

In Brasília, as everywhere in Brazil, we found the people's hospitality overwhelming. They were so anxious to do things for us that we soon found ourselves hard put to keep up with the hospitality. What's more the Brazilians won't take no for an answer. If I tried to get out of an engagement, by pleading a headache, they would shower me with remedies and postpone the affair until I recovered.

On our last day in Brasília we were informed that Governor Mauro Borges of Goiás state had made plans for us. Borges, who was ousted shortly afterwards on charges of plotting against the government, was sending his plane to fly us to an island called Ilha do Bananal in the Araguaia River, we were told, where we could see and film Indians in their primitive state. The Brazilian Indians are some of the most primitive people on earth. They do not even know of the wheel although they did invent the hammock and you can't knock that. I had hoped to see some of them but they had proved hard to find.

Centuries of oppression have made them wary of white men and they have withdrawn farther and farther into the interior jungles. Now the Brazilian government is doing its utmost to protect and aid the some 800,000 remaining Indians, but they remain suspicious and often hostile and occasionally kill a government official or farmer. Much as I welcomed a chance to see the Indians, we were due to drive the next morning to the ranch of Mary Martin and her producer husband Richard Halliday. "Would you thank the governor," I told his representative, "and explain that we are expected at the Hallidays tomorrow." The governor's man responded with unshakable Brazilian hospitality. "No problem," he said. "After you have seen the Indians the governor's plane will fly you to the Hallidays. Be at the airport at nine o'clock sharp."

Promptly at nine we were at the airport, laden down with cigarettes and 22-caliber shells for the Indians, all set for the two and a half hour flight to the Ilha do Bananal. The shells and cigarettes would come in handy, we were told, in case we saw anything appealing in shrunken heads or wanted to stir up a fertility dance. Nine-thirty came and no plane appeared. Ten o'clock and still no plane. Eleven. No sign of a plane. Apparently the pilot had succumbed to the *mañana* spirit. It was after noon when our plane finally did appear. However, the pilot wasn't at all perturbed by his tardiness. He was a short, dark chap, reminiscent of TV's José Jiminez, and the soul of nonchalance. He told us to put our equipment on the plane, while he had a *cafe-zinho,* the hot, sweet little cups of coffee the Brazilians love, and he would whisk us off to see the Indians.

After he had several *cafezinhos* he suddenly remembered he had to have the plane refueled. I was just finishing stowing our cameras and luggage aboard the little three-place plane when I began doing some mental arithmetic on our timetable for the day. It was then about one o'clock. The flight to Ilha do Bananal, I knew would take two and a half hours. To visit the Indians, and film a rain dance or blow gun exhibition, would take another few hours. Then there would be a two and a half hour flight back to Brasília. After that we would still have to get to the Hallidays, a considerable distance away. I realized that with our late start there simply wasn't time to make the trip.

"Tell the governor thank you very much," I told the pilot, "but there just isn't time to make the trip. We'll just have to forget it."

I started back toward the terminal, staggering under all our luggage, with the pilot trailing after me explaining he would get into trouble with the governor. "At least let me take you for a little ride," he said.

"Okay," I said. "How about flying us directly to the Hallidays?"

With that I had to drag all our luggage back to the plane, load it again, and we took off. It was a half-hour flight to the little town of Anápolis, which is the nearest airport to the Halliday ranch. As we climbed out of the plane the pilot flashed us a big grin, shook hands, and took off in a cloud of red dust. We sat down on the luggage waiting for someone from the little terminal to come get us. Strangely no one came. Then we all grabbed luggage and cameras and trudged over to the terminal building. Nothing. It was absolutely deserted. I poked around the empty building. No taxis, no telephone, no people. The only sign of life was a

couple of chickens scratching around in the thick red dust.
I finally plodded off down a dirt road and eventually flagged
down a farm truck. After some sign language the Brazilian
driver drove us into the town of Anápolis. There we found
a driver with a dilapidated Chevrolet who agreed to drive us
the twenty-five miles to the Hallidays.

When we finally arrived at *Nossa Fazenda* (Our Ranch)
we must have been the most bedraggled-looking group since
Pizarro got lost in Brazil in 1541. We were hot, weary, and
covered with red dust, but Mary and Richard welcomed us,
revived us with their warm greetings and cold daiquiris
and got us installed in the comfortable guest house adjoin-
ing their main house. The houses and other ranch buildings
are set in 1200 acres of rich, rolling red land reminiscent of
Arizona or New Mexico. Mary calls their house Brazilian-
Chinese. Originally it was a small house; no bigger, she told
us, "than the house in *Peter Pan.*" They rebuilt and enlarged
it and today it is a handsome, white-pillared residence with
brightly painted iron trim. There is no electricity, light is
provided by candles or kerosene lamps. Water comes from
an old-fashioned well. Both the main house and guest house
are brightened by rugs made of gaucho blankets, the vivid
colors of Mary's paintings and sprays of yellow orchids from
their own trees. In the kitchen are two bright tiled wood-
burning stoves on which Mary cooks. "I'd never cooked a
meal in my life until we came here," Mary laughed. "All
those fancy gadgets on our big stove in New York scared me.
But here I learned to cook on this old wood stove using a
Portuguese cook book and a dictionary." Now she whips
up Southern fried chicken, wonderful fudge, and her own
strawberry jam.

We quickly fell into the comfortable routine. When we woke up in the morning Randy would give a blast on a horn, hung in our bedroom, to notify the Hallidays that we were awake. From the main house would come the answering sound of Mary tooting a bugle to let us know they had heard our signal and breakfast was on its way. Moments later the Hallidays' American butler, Ernest, would be rapping on our door with breakfast, and what a breakfast! Juicy melons, just off the vine, flavored with freshly picked limes. Scrambled eggs, gathered that morning. Strong Brazilian coffee, freshly roasted, smoking in the cups. With a breakfast like that, who needs civilization!

Mary and Richard love their *fazenda* and their warm pride in it was plainly evident as they showed us around. They have six thousand chickens in a series of long chicken houses with nine hundred cages in each (one for each hen). They also raise Brahma cattle, pigs, and turkeys, and have twenty thousand coffee trees, avocados, limes, lemons, and corn, rice and other vegetables.

Audiences who saw Mary as Nellie Forbush in *South Pacific* or *Peter Pan* on television would scarcely recognize Donna Maria, as the Brazilians call her, in blue jeans, herding her Brahma cattle, feeding the chickens, whizzing over dusty roads in her jeep or supervising the damming of a spring to create a little pool. I have always considered Mary Martin one of America's natural wonders, since first hearing her sing *My Heart Belongs to Daddy*, but this was a new and startlingly different Mary than I knew from *Annie Get Your Gun* or *Sound of Music*, or from visiting her in her luxurious New York penthouse overlooking the East River. Yet she's as much a revelation in one world as she is a star in the other. She's a marvel.

Mary can sing opera, dance ballet, blow a bugle. She can bake bread, needlepoint a rug, help build a dam. She can treat a sick chicken, paint a house, a picture or a welcome sign. She's equally at home with Noël Coward or a Brazilian gaucho. She can grow a Texas watermelon in Brazil, cut her husband's hair, make water run *up* hill (and we all know she can fly!).

Mary and Richard are busy from dawn to dusk at their *fazenda*, and we got tired just watching them. They gathered eggs, picked avocados, and weeded the tapioca. Mary worked with Ivan, their four-foot Indian carpenter, fashioning a fine piece of furniture. She showed Geronimo, the Brazilian bricklayer, how she wanted some tiles set. She fed the pigs and roasted coffee. She scrubbed floors and washed windows. "When she plunges in with mops and pails," Richard said, "it reminds me of those old pictures of a lady prohibitionist descending on a saloon to wreck the place."

The Hallidays are very much a part of the surrounding community which has taken them to its bosom. When they arrived the chief of police gave them a notice to put on their windshield that the Hallidays were not to be arrested under any circumstances. The Brazilians love Donna Maria not because she is a star but because she is so much one of them. She sang *Ave Maria* in Latin at a wedding at the little local church. When one of the women on the *fazenda* had a baby there was no doctor available so Mary rushed to the rescue. When she got to the woman's house the baby had already been born. "I couldn't think of what else to do," Mary recalled, "so I gave her two aspirin and a cup of tea. It seemed to work wonders. Now whenever a woman on the *fazenda* has a baby they insist I bring my aspirin and tea."

On Sunday the local children come up the hill to present Donna Maria with a bouquet of flowers. She is like a Texas tomboy on the *fazenda,* with her close-cropped hair and blue jeans, and her favorite expression is "dag burned." Yet she is always beautifully dressed and groomed and every inch the lady when she goes into Anápolis to shop or entertain Brazilians at home.

The Hallidays gave a party while we were there and the guests came from miles around. In fact, the country around *Nossa Fazenda* is so sparsely populated that some of the guests drove as much as half a day to get there. The guests were a cosmopolitan group: Brazilians, Lebanese, Orientals, English, and they chatted away in a variety of languages. One couple was an English doctor and his American wife. He was educated at Cambridge, the doctor told me, while his wife was from Mississippi. They spoke Portuguese most of the time, he said, but at home they spoke English. However, from exposure to his Mississippi-born wife, the Englishman now speaks English with a southern drawl!

Mary laughingly told of her own problems with the language. "When I first got here I went around saying '*si*' to everything," she said. "That can get you in trouble when you're a girl." Now Mary speaks fairly good Portuguese, although she still has problems occasionally.

One day she came a cropper in asking her workmen to kill some bats that had taken up residence in the roof of her house. The Portuguese word for bats is *morcegos* but in asking the workmen to kill the bats Mary said *manteigas* which means butter. "There are many, many, *manteigas* in the roof," Mary said. "I want you to kill the *manteigas*." The workmen looked puzzled, shrugged, and began to take off the tiles.

"They told me they didn't find any butter," Mary said. "All they found was some bats."

In this colorful, relaxed atmosphere, four thousand miles from garish Broadway where Mary won fame, the Hallidays seem to have found peace and contentment that rubs off even on the visitor. The days are full of active, outdoor work and the nights are quiet with a peacefulness unlike anything we had ever experienced before. Darkness falls swiftly in those remote uplands of Brazil. We would sit around in the darkness on the broad white-tile terrace, sipping magnificent daiquiris made with the *fazenda's* own freshly picked limes. Sometimes we would listen to the *Voice of America* news at seven o'clock . . . our only contact with the outside world of strife and crisis. Every time the newscaster mentioned a new problem I had another daiquiri and the problem dissolved in a roseate glow. "The first six weeks we were here we didn't have a radio," Richard said, "and we didn't see a newspaper or magazine. We didn't miss them."

In these quiet conversations in the darkness we got a wonderful insight into the warm, relaxed, bantering relationship of the Hallidays. Mary spoke nostalgically of her childhood in a small Texas town. "I had my first love affair at five," she said. "I fell in love with an audience at the Fireman's Ball."

Richard talked of Broadway, where Mary had her first success, and of Hollywood where they met when she was a budding star and he was a studio story editor who voted against her screen test. "Fortunately I was outvoted," he laughed. They both spoke affectionately of their daughter Heller who had just made them grandparents. When Heller was a youngster, Richard told us, Mary undertook to help her with her homework, with disastrous results. One day Heller was kept after school and Mary asked her why.

"I misspelled boat," the child said.

"Well, how did you spell it?" asked Mary.

"B-o-t-e," confessed Heller.

"Well," said Mary, "what's wrong with *that?*"

Above all I loved to hear Mary reminisce about the great roles she had played in Broadway musicals. She spoke tenderly of the late Oscar Hammerstein who with Richard Rodgers wrote the songs she had sung so beautifully in shows like *South Pacific* and *The Sound of Music.* She recalled how annoyed Hammerstein's wife Dorothy used to get that Oscar often didn't get credit for writing a song because he wrote the words rather than the music. Finally one night at a party Mrs. Hammerstein overheard someone say that Jerome Kern wrote "Ol Man River." "Oscar wrote 'Ol Man River,'" she corrected. Then she hummed the melody. "What Jerome Kern wrote was Ta-Ta, Dum-Dum."

Hammerstein was the first person to audition her in Hollywood she remembered, and then called her years later to tell her that Rodgers and he wanted her to play Nellie Forbush in *South Pacific.* She remembered, too, the last time she had ever seen him. It was during the rehearsal of *The Sound of Music* and she was hurrying toward the stage door of the theater. Oscar was standing just outside looking pale and haggard. "I knew he had been ill," Mary said, "but I was shocked to see how gaunt he looked. He started away, then turned back and slipped a piece of paper into my hand. 'I don't know whether we'll ever use it in the show,' he said, 'but I want you to have it.' Then he hurried

away. Inside I met Dick Rodgers who told me that Oscar
was to undergo a serious operation the next day. Hesitantly
I unfolded the crumpled piece of paper he had given me.
On it were four lines of one of the loveliest lyrics he ever
wrote." Mary's voice broke as she spoke the words in the
darkness . . .

"A bell is no bell till you ring it,
A song is no song till you sing it,
And love in your heart wasn't put there to stay,
Love isn't love till you give it away."*

"That was Oscar's farewell," Mary said softly. "I never
saw him again."

Sitting there at night, sipping Mary's icy daiquiris, listening to her reminisce, or sing, or watching her dance or
clown in the moonlight . . . *well,* all I could say was *"Oba!"*
(Portuguese for Wow!).

Yet my single most vivid memory of our visit was not even
of those wonderful nights, so full of good talk and compan-
ionship and music. It was of a day when we were out riding.
Mary was racing toward us full tilt on her stallion, the sky
at her back, laughing, her tousled hair flying in the wind,
glowing with the sheer joy of living. "People sometimes ask
me, 'Why do you like Brazil?'" Richard said to me. "They
say, 'What do you and Mary do all the time?' At times like
this I think: Oh, if they could just see Mary now!"

The change from the leisurely informality of the Hallidays' *fazenda* to gay, crowded, busy Rio de Janeiro was so

* Copyright © 1959 by Richard Rodgers and Oscar Hammerstein
II. Used by permission of Williamson Music, Inc., New York,
N.Y., owner of publication and allied rights.

startling we almost got the bends. Coming in by plane, after flying six hundred miles over open uplands and thick jungles, Rio is a stunning sight from the air. As our plane descended for a landing, we could see the spectacular bulk of Sugar Loaf rock, the curving white beaches of Guanabara Bay, lined with its gleaming steel and concrete apartments and hotels, and, looming over all, the giant figure of Christ atop the peak called Corcovado, the hunchback.

The Cariocas, as the residents of Rio call themselves, are as unique as their spectacular city. They are so gay and effervescent that just walking around the streets of Rio gives you the feeling of being part of one big conga line. Although Brazil is beset by problems, including poverty, inflation, and government instability, the problems don't seem to daunt the carefree Cariocas. They are warm, funny, and wildly emotional. They drive like demons. Their *futebol* (pronounced footyball) players hug and kiss when they win and weep bitterly when they lose. The *abraco* (embrace) is the Brazilian form of greeting, which is like substituting Sumo wrestling for the handshake. After our first day in Rio we had been clasped, squeezed, and hugged so often and so hard in a variety of *abracos* we all felt as done in as Y. A. Tittle of the New York pro football Giants after a hard afternoon on the gridiron.

The Cariocas, particularly are fiercely individualistic. A story we were told illustrating this concerns Rio's ancient *bondes* or open trolley cars. A crowded *bonde* was rolling along with passengers clinging to it like flies. A tall Carioca tried to get off the rolling trolley, tripped and fell flat. His fellow passengers roared with laughter. The man got up, dusted himself off with dignity, and yelled after the laughing passengers, "Everyone descends from the *bonde* in the way he wants to."

The Brazilians are as informal as they are individualistic, and we saw many evidences of this during our stay. They call almost all their political and public figures by their first names or nicknames. Even Brazil's national hero, an eighteenth-century dentist executed for plotting independence from Portugal, is known by his nickname of *Tiradentes,* "the tooth puller."

They are similarly informal about dress. You can go to the best restaurants and hotels in Rio in slacks, sandals, and without a tie. George Guinle, a well-known figure in international society, took us out at night wearing only a sweater and slacks. Women, however, are seldom seen in slacks and I never saw a pair of Bermuda shorts on men despite the tropical climate.

Brazilians are also a sentimental people, sympathetic to any misfortune, and a word we heard frequently was *coitado* . . . "poor thing." When President Kennedy was assassinated, we were told, lighted candles appeared suddenly everywhere in windows throughout the city. They are also a happy people, slow to anger. We were told of a Brazilian walking down the street with a friend when he was insulted by a stranger. The man ignored the insult. "Aren't you going to do anything?" his friend asked. "Are you a man or aren't you?"

"Oh, I'm a man, all right," the insulted man shrugged. "But not *fanatically.*"

Racial discrimination is virtually unknown in Brazil, we found. The country has a large Negro population and Brazilians pride themselves that they are treated like anyone else. Randy interviewed a group of Rio children on what they considered the difference between our two countries, and almost all singled out their greater racial harmony. Brazilians are a mixture of many racial strains—we were surprised to see so many blond, blue-eyed Cariocas—but they are all emphatically Brazilians. "Are you German or Scandinavian?" I asked several such Nordic-looking Brazilians, meaning of German or Scandinavian origin.

"No," was the inevitable reply. "I'm Brazilian."

Although there is no racial conflict in Brazil, the Brazilians are immensely proud of their home cities and inclined to scoff at the unfortunates who live elsewhere. We found this particularly true of the Cariocas. They love their beautiful city with a passion and feel only sympathy for the poor souls who live in bustling, industrial São Paulo—Brazil's largest city—or modern but dull Brasília. And several of them almost fell down laughing at word that we had been up the Amazon. "The Amazon!" they cried, in disbelief. "But *why?*"

"There is little cruelty in the Brazilian character," a Carioca told me. "We gained independence without war. We abolished slavery peacefully in 1888 and never had a lynching. Unlike other Latin American countries, Brazil has never even had bullfighting. It is too cruel for us. Even our revolutions are usually bloodless."

We arrived not long after an Army group had forced the ouster of President Joao Goulart and the installation of General Humberto Castelo Branco as his successor in a typically Brazilian coup. It lasted less than forty-eight hours and practically nobody got hurt. Perhaps Brigitte Bardot, who was there at the time, best summed up the coup. "What a lovely revolution," said the French sex kitten. "How chic." Cariocas described the coup to us as casually as they would a soccer match, but without as much emotion. They chuckled over their descriptions of typically Brazilian touches to the crisis. One Carioca told us of a column of tanks, weapon carriers, and troops moving menacingly down the street—and then stopping for a traffic light. Someone else told us of another armed group setting up mortars and machine guns to shell a main public building, and then calling off the whole thing when it started to rain. They made the coup sound almost like a lark, although it probably prevented a Communist takeover.

"The kids loved it because they didn't have to go to school," one man said. "The women liked it because they had a big hand in it. More than a million women took part in a march against the Goulart regime. And the men liked it because it was exciting on television."

George Guinle, a wealthy Brazilian businessman who is well known in the United States, told me he watched the coup on television from bed. "It was an interesting revolt," he said, "but the sound was bad."

"What in the world do you mean by that?" I asked.

"Well, the long-range cameras could get good shots of the fighting and military maneuvering," he explained, "but it was impossible to get microphones in close. Consequently, you could see the action very well on TV, but the sound was terrible."

One day during our stay the Brazilian Air Force provided a helicopter for us to film Rio from the air. It had a tiny passenger compartment, with barely enough room for the pilot, Randy, and myself. Then they removed the doors, to enable me to film, leaving us feeling as exposed as a witch on a broomstick. Hanging on for dear life, we soared up over the rooftops of what is probably the most beautiful city in the world. Rio is squeezed picturesquely between jagged mountains and the sea. Below us unfolded the waves breaking on the great crescent curve of beach, the skyscraper business and apartment buildings, and the giant statue of Christ, arms outstretched. Directly below the huge concrete figure, the squalid shantytown *favelas* sprawled down the steep hills, and a cogwheel railroad crawled upward toward the statue. It was a fantastic vista. Mist and clouds swirled around the eleven-story Christ, atop its 2310 foot mountain, and our pilot tried to maneuver in close so I could film it.

I began getting nervous buzzing around the massive 130-foot statue that kept appearing and then disappearing in the mist. It was clearer behind the statue, but when we tried to approach from the front it seemed to disappear in the swirling mist. "If only the statue would turn around," our pilot growled.

The appointment of General Castelo Branco as President has resulted in greater governmental honesty but the easy-going Brazilians still talked of political corruption as a sort of game. They look on official misdeeds with amused tolerance if not downright admiration and passed along reports of governmental chicanery with obvious relish. One lady told me gleefully of a big Rio politician who sent his ne'er-do-well son to the hinterlands with a letter of introduction for a government job. "I'll appoint you the official piano player for the state," the local political bigwig told him. "But, sir, I don't play the piano," the young man protested. "That's quite all right," the politician grinned. "We haven't got a piano anyway." For all their tolerance of governmental vagaries, the independent Brazilians don't like to be pushed around by officials. One lady got a tax form which said in one place: *"Do not write in this space. For official use only."* She wrote in the space: *"I am a Brazilian, I am vaccinated and I write where I please."*

The Cariocas love to joke and laugh although some of their jokes seemed to lose something in translation. In fact, a few of them lost everything. One thing I noticed is that any mention of the figure 24 seemed to send them into hysterics.

I tried to determine what was so funny about 24, and it took a bit of sleuthing. It seems the slang term for a homosexual in Portuguese is *veado* which means deer. In the national lottery there is the head of an animal and a number on each ticket. It happens that a deer head is on the tickets numbered 24. As a result, if you are in room 24 at your hotel, or 24 years old or taking flight 24 on an airline the Brazilians laugh fit to kill because to them it means homosexual. I've heard of comedians so funny they could make audiences laugh by reciting a laundry list, but Rio was the only place I ever got howls by just asking for the key to room 24. With this bit of knowledge, I was tempted to import some Brazilians for my studio audience. They could be the biggest thing since canned laughter.

Although Brazilians love jokes and laughter, and refuse to get excited over anything as serious as inflation or armed coups, they get wildly excited over their *futebol* (which we call soccer). When Santos, Brazil, won the World Club championship before 150,000 delirious fans in Rio, Brazilian broadcasters clobbered the Italians with microphones and photographers bopped them with umbrellas. Small wonder they are the world's best soccer players as everywhere we went we saw Brazilians playing on street corners or along the beaches.

"Goulart would have been overthrown sooner," one Brazilian told me, "but the people were too interested in *futebol* to get excited over the Communist threat." We also heard that during the coup, soldiers marching on the Copacabana Fort asked some boys playing *futebol* along the beach to move along as there might be shooting. "Just wait until we take this penalty," the boys asked.

Their greatest player, and the greatest in the world, is a slight, jug-eared Negro with the resounding name of Edson Arantes do Nascimento, but known to Brazilians by his nickname of "Pele." Pele is the highest-paid athlete in the world and is looked on in Brazil as a national asset like coffee or the samba. When he led Brazil to victory in World Cup play, a million cheering Brazilians turned out to welcome the team back. A Spanish team once offered more than a million dollars for Pele, but Brazil's then President Quadros acted quickly in the national emergency. He had Pele declared a national asset not to be exported at any price. However, Pele's team had no thought of parting with him. "If we sold him," a team official said, "the people would lynch us." So impulsive are Brazilian soccer fans that in Rio's huge stadium —which is twice the size of Yankee Stadium—the playing field is surrounded by barbed wire and a watery nine-foot moat.

The only thing besides *futebol* that brings out the wild side of the normally cheerful, friendly Brazilians is getting behind the wheel of an automobile. For some reason, even the mildest Brazilian in an automobile becomes as reckless as the Kamikaze taxi drivers of Tokyo or the Freeway Freedom Fighters of Los Angeles. The cars on Rio's streets are in various stages of decrepitude, but the Brazilian drivers tear around in them in pursuit of pedestrians seemingly oblivious to danger, direction or traffic laws. "We should send the Peace Corps down here," Randy suggested, "to teach them to drive." The bus drivers are paid by commission so they whip their ancient buses around furiously, boosting their pay and, incidentally, the traffic toll. However, while we were in Brazil the authorities were taking measures to make drivers obey the traffic laws. The Director of Traffic in Rio, Americo Fontenelle, has devised some unique methods for combating disregard for traffic laws. Parking fines now are the same as years ago when twenty cruizeros equaled about a dollar. However, because of Brazil's galloping inflation, the cruizero was 1600 to the dollar, so that a parking fine is less than a penny. As a result, motorists simply parked where and when they wanted, and gladly paid the insignificant fine. Before Fontenelle, that is.

Fontenelle instructed police when they find a car parked illegally to simply let the air out of the tires. They are so strict that they even let the air out of police cars if they are parked illegally. This impartiality is impressive, except when police want to pursue a traffic violator and find their own tires flat. However, Fontenelle's drastic methods have made their imprint on Rio's driver. They are now paying much more attention to parking regulations, and the bus drivers are not as quick to pursue pedestrians up onto the sidewalk. A street urchin who saw me eying a car with flat tires told me that the sun said to the full moon, "Watch out for Fontenelle." Authorities in São Paulo have a variation on the Fontenelle method. When police find several cars parked illegally, they simply chain them together, lock the chain, pocket the key and saunter off, leaving the frustrated illegal parkers to figure out their dilemma.

So, as the tires of the illegally parked cars sank slowly to the street, it was time for us to leave beautiful Rio. We were exhausted but happy after three weeks of Brazilian hospitality.

"Don't you hate to leave?" I asked Miriam.

"I do," she admitted, "but think of it this way. One more *abraco* and our ribs would probably give out." And besides I was afraid it was making her flat-chested.

# ODDITIES AND ENDITIES

They say that travel is broadening and it's true. After five years of traveling by jet, ocean liner, camelback, helicopter, pirogue, Land-Rover, and rickshaw I now wear size 36 shorts. That's two inches broader than when I started traveling. However, I have a lot to show for our trips. I have about two million feet of home movies, so many inoculations that my arms look like the dart boards in an English pub and some colorful memories. Everywhere we went we were royally treated—sometimes literally. I flew over Jordan in a helicopter and the people below threw kisses and prostrated themselves on the ground. I thought this was a very handsome way for the Jordanian people to greet me until I realized I was in the royal helicopter and they thought I was King Hussein. Incidentally, we flew at midday and the smoke from thousands of kitchens all cooking lamb was as thick as fog over London. I've flown through gales, lightning, and snowstorms, but that was the only time I'd flown blind through shish-kebab fumes.

We visited dozens of countries in our travels and naturally we have our favorite places and people. I found the British the most interesting, the Italians the most amusing, the Tahitians and the Brazilians the friendliest, and the French the least friendly. The French smile so seldom that if Ed Sullivan were French he could probably beat De Gaulle in the next election. One of the few smiles I saw in France was on the Mona Lisa and you had to pay to see it. Fred Allen once observed that the national pastimes of France are eating and shrugging, and there is nothing more eloquent than a French shrug. With a mere lift of the shoulders and the eyebrows the Frenchman can tell you that he doesn't know the answer to your question and also convey the impression that you must be an idiot to have asked.

I always seem to arrive in France in the midst of the annual shrugging festival. The last time I was coming back from Africa and my Air Afrique flight terminated at Paris. I was anxious to get on to London so I went directly to the information desk and asked the girl when the next flight was.

"Not for three hours, monsieur," she told me.

I said with so many airlines operating between the two cities there must be a flight sooner than three hours. "*Non,*" she assured me with a happy smile. (I should explain there is one time when the French *do* smile: when they are imparting bad news. It seems to absolutely delight a waiter to tell you they are just out of frog legs Provencal, or a taxi driver to inform you he can't find the Eiffel Tower.) The French girl was smiling winningly and assuring me there was no flight for three hours when it was announced over the loudspeaker that a plane was then boarding for London.

"What about *that* flight?" I asked triumphantly.

"Ah, monsieur, it is too late to catch that flight," she said. "There would not be time for the formalities."

It wasn't the fact that I couldn't get on the flight that irritated me so much; it was just that it seemed to make the French girl so pleased. So what to do for three hours in Paris? Of course, I could visit the Louvre or Napoleon's Tomb or the Folies Bergère but I was afraid if I asked directions to any of those landmarks I would set off an epidemic of shrugging. Then I noticed a sign saying BAIN. That was it; I'd take a bath! I could spend a couple of hours soaking away the fatigue of the long flight and my frustrations with the French airline girl. I followed the BAIN sign to a lower floor and arrived at twin doors marked DAMES and MONSIEURS. The sign saying BAIN pointed to the door marked DAMES. The idea of taking a bath in the Ladies' Powder Room seemed a little odd to me but by now I was conditioned to the unusual in France. I cautiously opened the door and the lady attendant greeted me as heartily as Texas Guinan.

An inspection of the facilities reassured me. The tubs were in individual rooms so I could close the door and bathe in privacy without a bevy of French women observing me. I had stripped down to my shorts and the water was running in the tub when there was a frantic pounding on the door. What surprise lay in store now? I wondered. I opened the door a crack. It was my friend the French airline girl.

"Monsieur, your plane is about to take off," she blurted.

I don't know what happened to the "formalities." Hurriedly I turned off the water and scrambled back into my clothes, losing one sock in the process. Then I fled through the terminal yelling *"Merci"* as I ran. I got a last glimpse of the airline girl as I ran toward the plane. She was talking to a tourist and shrugging.

The French themselves have lately been taking note of

the adverse effect of rudeness and incivility on the national image. The French newspaper *Le Figaro* admits a certain *lacune d'accueil* . . . a certain "absence of welcome" which has become so noticeable even the French leave France to vacation. To counteract this the government started a campaign to get Frenchmen to smile, but it has not been noticeably effective. "I tried smiling," a French model reported, "and I never felt more foolish or got into more trouble with the opposite sex." Although the smiling campaign seems bogged down, a French woman named Beatrice Ferret founded an organization called Le Club de la Gentillesse aimed at promoting cordiality. Madame Ferret says she has been studying people's vibrations and she can tell if a person is polite or impolite by holding a plumb over his head. (I don't need a plumb; I can tell by their shrug.) A reporter went to Madame Ferret's apartment to interview her on her politeness campaign but was chased away by her concierge who complained the campaign was attracting too many oddballs.

Another group has formed a Doulce ("gentle" in medieval French) France Committee to encourage civility. It decided to award a "Golden Rose" to the most courteous and considerate French taxi driver. It wasn't easy. It took six weeks but they finally turned up a cab driver who was courteous and cheerful in his work. He was also, it turned out, a Bulgarian refugee!

I hope the various campaigns to promote civility and good will take hold, and that smiles are soon as plentiful as artichokes in France, but meantime I prefer to visit other countries, particularly England. I have become almost a commuter to England of late years and, although it has changed

greatly even in that time, with skyscrapers and Beatle haircuts sprouting everywhere, I remain a card-carrying Anglo-
phile. I like so many things about the British: their speech,
their eccentricities, their sports.

When we first visited there in 1960, English friends took
great pride in showing us their old traditional sights such as
the Tower of London, Westminster Abbey, and Windsor
Castle. They seemed crazy about *anything* as long as it was
old and became downright rapturous over anything in
ruins. We did all the usual things like visiting Parliament,
watching the speakers and hecklers in Hyde Park, and taking in the Changing of the Guard at Buckingham Palace.
On our last visit there, in 1964, our London friends wanted
to show us all the *new* things like the American-owned,
eighteen-story Carlton Tower Hotel and the twenty-seven-
story $17,000,000 Hilton Hotel. The new hotels and office
buildings near Buckingham Palace are a source of annoy-
ance to the royal family and Prince Philip has complained
that they interfere with his television reception of the
cricket matches.

The people seem to be changing, too. On earlier visits
English friends took us to see traditional things like the
races at Ascot or the theater in London's West End. The
last time they suggested a Beatle concert or a visit to a
shore resort to watch a rumble between the Mods and Rock-
ers. Because of the influence of the Beatles, many of the
young men have hair as long as girls' and some even feature ponytails. "That's why I favor the topless bathing suits,"
Malcolm Muggeridge grumbled to me. "They're the only
way to tell the girls from the boys any more."

However, some things remain resolutely, unchangeably
British. One is their custom of "booking" or making an ad-

vance reservation for everything but going to the bathroom.
One night I had dinner at the Rib Room of the Carlton
Tower Hotel with Robert Morley, the British actor, and duti-
fully booked our table well in advance. We were ordering
when the waiter wheeled by a magnificent side of beef on
a rolling cart.

"I think I'll have some of the roast beef," I said.

"I'm sorry, sir," the waiter said, "but there is no roast
beef."

"But what is *that?*" I asked, indicating the succulent side
of beef.

"Ah, I'm sorry, sir," he said politely, "but that beef is all
booked."

Another thing that seems to remain immune to change is
the English as only the British speak it. On a recent trip
we were driving to an inn in the country when our driver,
an estimable gentleman named Gorman, suddenly slowed
up.

"What's the trouble?" I inquired.

"There are some loose clippings on the verge of the dual
carriageway," Gorman said. "I think we'd better take the
next way out and cross on the flyover. I just hope we won't
find the road up."

Fortunately we had a translator along. What Gorman had
said was that there were some loose rocks on the shoulder
of the divided highway we were on. He suggested that we
go out the next exit, take the overpass and hope that the
road wasn't under repair.

The charming peculiarities of British expression can be
seen and heard on every hand in London. We saw one sign
which cautioned, WALK WARILY. And in the paper I spotted
a mention of a sign posted in the locker room of a boxing

19. *I wonder if Sessue Hayakawa really started this way?*

20. *Mary Martin in her own Never Never Land on her ranch in Brazil.*

21. *"I Gotta Crow!" Mary has six thousand chickens.*

22. *They say a school of these piranha fish can strip a man down to a skeleton in two minutes. We took their word for it.*

*23. With bowler, brolly and Jonathan Winters in London.*

*24. The things I won't do for my art.*

25. *There's more ways than one to skin an onion.*

26. *Leica and Schnapps. Leica is the eccentric one.*

Raimondo Borea photos

27. *Leica seems to no lika getting vacuumed.*

club. It said: *"All contestants after each bout will remove their gloves so as not to get blood on Lord Fyfe who will be awarding prizes."* At a club swimming pool I spotted a sign warning, *"Members are requested not to vault over the side of the pool as it may cause injury to the marble."* You're never quite sure whether expressions like those are native eccentricity or whether the British sign-painters are subtly pulling the public's leg.

The British also write marvelously quaint notes. Columnist John Crosby reports having received one which read, *"Messrs. Steinway beg to intimate that their tuner will attend on Tuesday 12th instant."* And actor Hugh Griffith, who raises Corgi dogs in the country outside London, told me of a Corgi bitch sent to him to be bred. To the dog's crate was attached a note from the lady who owned her. It said: *"I would be obligated if Queenie could have misconduct twice over the weekend."*

English papers—which are some of the best and worst in the world—are another repository of British quirks and foibles. From the letters to the editors to the ads, the papers bristle with fey items. In a London paper I spotted a notice which read: *"At the last Cheltenham amateur hunt meeting Mr. Michael Vance inadvertently put his front teeth in someone else's coat pocket before going out to ride. Would the finder kindly return them via the course valet as their owner's tight-lipped smile is beginning to wear thin, and his digestion is suffering from impaired masticating facilities."* Another ad asked for the return of *"an African grey parrot called Percy. Speaks English, French and Welsh."*

British understatement is apparent in many newspaper stories, particularly in their coverage of sports. In reporting a cricket match the *Times* deplored the number of dropped catches. "Further incidents of this sort," the paper rumbled ominously, "and we shall name the offenders."

My favorite British sporting event is the six-hundred-year-old "bottle kick" between the neighboring villages of Hallaton and Medbourne. The object of the game is to get two nine-pound casks of beer—called bottles—over the goal line. The players can kick the cask, run with it, throw it or wrestle it. To insure spirited competition the players warm up for two hours in neighboring pubs and several players and spectators are usually laid out cold during the contest. Even this bizarre event is reported with characteristic British calm. "As the goals are several miles apart," one paper noted of a recent contest, "there was understandably very little scoring."

The same sort of droll outlook is employed by British television critics. Once, when we were taping my show in London, one paper described me as a "suavely nuanced front-of-curtain solus," whatever *that* is. On this occasion I had a wild encounter with the Goons, a wacky trio comprised of Peter Sellers, Michael Bentine, and Spike Milligan. They buried me under an avalanche of inside jokes, repeating phrases like "Oy Charleeaay!" and "Pass me the blowlamp mate," endlessly, and finally making off with the desk I was sitting behind. A television columnist reported that I had been "outcountenanced" in the chaotic encounter and that the Goons had "taken the mickey out of the visiting American."

I had a similarly confusing time when I appeared on England's *Tonight Show* which is their counterpart of NBC's *Tonight Show* in this country which I did for five years.

I had scarcely sat down when I was set upon by two interviewers with obviously loaded questions. Although taken off guard, I did my best to parry their questions which were larded with sarcasm about me and American television. Finally they went too far.

"Isn't it true," one of them finally asked, "that you once flounced off your television program?" I didn't mind this reference to the time I walked off the program in a censorship dispute with the network; what annoyed me was the implication of the word "flounced."

"An American never flounces," I shot back. "That's only done in the studios of the BBC or your Admiralty Headquarters. (England had just had a homosexual scandal in the government.) An American walks off like this." With that I stalked out of the studio with John Wayne's bowlegged cowboy walk, leaving my attackers with ten minutes of empty air to fill.

Another problem in traveling, I've discovered, is the matter of trying to sleep in the mornings. Each country seems to have some fiendish method all its own of waking the sleeping traveler. In Japan I once left the radio on and was awakened in the morning by a program of bird twitterings. In Hawaii we were awakened by bird calls, live and in Stereophonic sound. (The myna birds outside the Royal Hawaiian Hotel are louder than the Mormon Tabernacle Choir.) In Italy and other predominantly Catholic countries it's the church bells. At six every morning the church bells start ringing and it sounds as if there's a church on every corner. That's the end of sleep for the day, even for Protestants.

In Arab countries it's the muezzin calling the faithful to

prayer. The first time nobody warned me. In Amman, Jordan, I was awakened at 5:30 A.M. by an unearthly caterwauling that sounded like Tarzan yelling in Arabic. I groped sleepily for the phone, called the hotel desk and told the clerk I thought an ax murder was being committed in the next room. He explained politely that the sound was coming from the neighboring minaret and was the Moslem call to prayer at dawn. Later I discovered the call to prayer was not live but recorded. This meant that not even the muezzin had to get up and the Moslems, who were used to all the noise, could sleep right through it. It was only the Christian tourists who were awakened. Between the Catholic's church bells and the Moslem's morning call to prayer, it's tough for a Presbyterian to get any sleep in a lot of countries. I'm thinking of suggesting we start a call to prayer at 3 A.M.— with a cannon.

*I SHOULDA STOOD IN BED*

There is a New York newscaster named John K. M. Mc-Caffrey who opens his nightly newscasts with, "What kind of a day has it been? A day like any other day."

I've been analyzing those lines and I'm stumped. Either I'm crazy or John K. M. McCaffrey leads a very sheltered life. When he says, "It's been a day like any other day," just what does he mean? Does he mean it's been a day like the day of the San Francisco earthquake? Or the day prohibition ended? It seems to me that every day is *un*like every other day. Someone once said that a day away from Tallulah Bankhead is like a month in the country. The day of the stockmarket crash wasn't exactly the same as National Smile Day. And certainly St. Patrick's Day isn't a day just like Yom Kippur.

I don't know about McCaffrey, but my days are spectacularly different. The day I spent with Billy Graham was quite different from a day I spent with Zsa Zsa Gabor. (In fact *all* days were different from the day with Zsa Zsa.) The day I spent fighting a bull in Spain, and was nearly gored to death, was nothing like the day I spent at a party with Elsa Maxwell, and was nearly bored to death.

There are days when my rating's in orbit and all's right with the world, and other days when I feel, as Joe Jacobs so aptly put it, that "I shoulda stood in bed." I had a day like that not long ago. I called a friend and the line was busy. Then I called back a few minutes later and there was no answer. In disgust I decided to drive to his home in White Plains to see him. On the parkway I got in the exact-change lane at the toll station and discovered I didn't have the right change. I moved over into the right lane but it was jammed up behind a little old lady in an Edsel who was holding everyone up while she carried on a lengthy conversation with the attendant. "What's the trouble?" I finally asked.

"Oh, it's nothing," the attendant said. "I'm just trying to explain to her how to get to Vancouver, B.C., by way of the George Washington Bridge."

When I finally did get to White Plains I spotted a nice parking place but when I pulled in I nearly ran over a Volkswagen that was hiding there. (They've got to do something about those compact cars so small you can't see them in a line of standard cars. Now the Japanese are making one so small they put the license on *your* back.)

When I finally did find a parking place, twenty minutes later, I went to my friend's apartment and took the self-service elevator. I pushed the up button and the elevator went down to the basement. *That* did it. I decided that God just didn't want me to see that man. I gave up, went home and got back into bed. I knew it just wasn't my day.

Days like that, I've concluded, are just the inexorable working of what I call Paar's Law. Paar's Law was discovered in much the same way as the law of gravity: Newton and I both got our inspiration from being struck on the head.

With Newton it was an apple and with me it was a whole tree, but that's what happens when you try to put the star on top of the Christmas tree after five martinis. (But that's another story.) Paar's Law formulates the hypothesis that when Paar comes, can trouble be far behind? For some reason I seem to invite disaster the way Barbara Hutton attracts husbands.

I go to some lengths to lead a secluded home life, but even then I can't avoid trouble. People keep falling in my moat. When I take a simple drive to the supermarket people persist in staring. You'd think they'd never seen a Rolls-Royce before. With stained-glass windows.

Even when I'm right things go wrong. Once a policeman stopped me on New York's 57th Street and said: "You're doing something wrong, I *think*." What I had done was put my 1964 license plates on three weeks *early*. Another time I let Jose Melis drive our new car and he backed into a truck. He thought the "R" on the automatic shift stood for "Rapido." Everything happens to me and I've stopped trying to fight it. It's just Paar's Law.

Even playing the good Samaritan I can get into trouble. One winter morning I was driving to my office, minding my own business and thinking positive thoughts. Rounding a corner I encountered a lady in distress: a pretty young mother in a station wagon with the horn stuck. She was dressed in housecoat and babushka, with three kids in the back seat, and the horn was blaring away fit to wake the whole neighborhood.

I gallantly pulled up in back of her to try to help, and what happens? That's a signal for the three children to start crying. Although she was parked her motor was still running

and so were the kids' noses. "How do you open the hood?"
I asked, since every kind of car's hood is different and to
open some you have to be Willie Sutton and sandpaper
your fingers.

"My husband never showed me," the lady wailed.

By this time the kids were howling, the horn was blasting
and the lady and I were up to our shins in snow while I
wrestled with the hood. It was, as they say in Brooklyn, "the
most noise I ever seen." Her response was to wipe the children's noses. (That's the first law of the jungle: wipe the
kids' noses.) While I struggled with the hood the lady, in
desperation, whipped off her housecoat and threw it over
the steering wheel, figuring *that's* where the noise was
coming from. That left her standing in her babushka, night-
gown, and feathered slippers looking quite helpless and
lovely. Now *she* was crying.

Finally I figured out the combination of the hood and it
sprung open, nearly decapitating me. I reached in and began grabbing wires that looked like they might have any
connection with the blaring horn. In the process I discon-
nected the little water hose that connects with the windshield wiper and it squirted water all over my trousers. At
last, after grabbing wires as indiscriminately as if I were
picking radishes, the horn blowing abruptly ceased. It was a
climactic moment, like the split second of silence at the
opera just after the tenor has reached the high note.

There we stood facing each other: she in her filmy nightie
and me with my wet trousers and greasy hands. It was a
kind of quick-frozen togetherness. It was one of those magi-
cal moments when anything might have happened . . . if
it weren't for those three kids with their runny noses. No
word was spoken but her eyes spoke volumes as I handed

her my handkerchief to blow their noses. It all ended as suddenly as it had begun. She uttered a sharp little cry as she got in the car, which I thought was a word of farewell. Then I realized it was only an exclamation of surprise as her bottom hit the cold seat.

Then she was gone. All I had were my memories, wet pants, greasy hands and her license number. So if you happen to read this, New York 63–947321 I'll never forget you. Also, if you're through with that handkerchief it would be nice to have it back. Miriam is beginning to wonder.

The relentless operation of Paar's Law seems to extend even to such facets of my life as the telephone. Since I seem to have some magnetic attraction for nuts, my number is unlisted and at the office I take refuge behind an array of telephonic devices calculated to confuse even Don Ameche. One of these is an answering service. When no one is in the office, or when I don't want to answer the phone, any call is answered by a recorded announcement. It says: "Your call is being answered by an answering machine. Please leave your name, number and any message at the sound of the tone. This is a recorded announcement."

Sometimes when I answer the phone, and get what I sense is a crank call, I impersonate the recording and reel off the instructions ending with, "This is a recorded announcement." Recently I called the office, forgetting it was a holiday. The service answered with the usual instructions and concluded, "This is a recorded announcement." I was so confused that I blurted, "But this is a recorded announcement *calling.*"

Another of my telephonic devices is a gadget that dials numbers automatically. There is an attachment on the phone with an alphabetical listing of the names of people I call frequently. All I have to do is to flip to the name of whomever I want to call and just push a button. The device then automatically dials the number. It's ideal for the man who has everything—including tired fingers.

One day recently I decided to dial Marano's barber shop, about a block from my office, to make an appointment for a haircut. I flipped to the "M's" on the automatic dialer and pushed the button that I thought was Marano's. Unfortunately, I didn't have my glasses on. A moment later a voice answered cheerily, "Good morning, Channel Eight, Portland."

What I had done was push the number of Bob Maynard, the general manager of WMTW-TV & FM, my station in Portland, Maine.

"I'm sorry," I stuttered. "This is Jack Paar. I dialed this number by mistake."

"Would you like to speak with Mr. Maynard?" the station operator asked.

"No," I said. "Just tell him I was calling to make an appointment for a haircut."

I'm afraid the station is still trying to figure out that call. But it could have been worse. I might have called the barber shop and told them I thought someone should climb Mount Washington and check the antenna.

As part of my defense in depth against crank calls my number at home is unlisted and I guard it as zealously as if it were the hot line to the Kremlin. The operators at NBC have instructions not to give out my private number and on occasions they have carried their protection of me to rather epic lengths. The night we televised the story of President Kennedy's PT boat adventure, I watched the program at home with friends. After the show the phone rang and it was a very flustered NBC operator. "I know you've asked that we not give out your phone number to anyone, Mr. Paar," she said, "but the White House is trying to reach you. Is it all right if I give President Kennedy your number?"

Another night the phone rang about two o'clock in the morning. Since so few people have my private number, I immediately thought it must be some emergency. My first thought was that something had happened to some member of my family.

"Is this Jack Paar?" a voice asked.

"Yes," I said, beginning to do a slow burn. "Who is this? How did you get my number? I thought I had an unlisted bed?"

I could hear two voices on the call. "We're from *Time* magazine," one voice said. "We'd like to ask you a few questions."

Suddenly I heard a telltale beep. I knew then that the conversation was being recorded as there's a law that there must be a beep every ten seconds if a phone call is being recorded. I realized then that the call must be some kind of a joke, and was all the madder at being awakened at two o'clock in the morning.

Then I recognized the voices. It was Johnny Carson and Steve Allen calling from Steve's TV show in Hollywood. Johnny was guesting on the program and they got to talking about the fact that all three of us had done NBC's *Tonight Show*. At two o'clock in the morning it seemed like a hilarious idea to call me.

"Did we awaken your wife?" Johnny asked apologetically.

"Yes, my wife's awake, our dachshund's awake and the German shepherd puppy's awake," I grumbled.

"I hope we didn't wake Randy," Steve said.

"Well, she doesn't sleep with us any more," I said. "There's just my wife, me, and Noël Coward."

Since I was awakened to find myself talking to a national television audience I tried to toss off a few merry quips, and I could hear the studio audience laughing in the background. They seemed to be enjoying it, even if I wasn't. Then Carson and Allen hung up and I spent most of the rest of the night trying to get back to sleep.

A couple of days later I read a review of that Allen show in a TV column. It said that Allen's program was sparkling and that Carson was a delightful guest. Johnny and Steve were great together, the review added. "Jack Paar's phone call," it concluded, "was nothing."

Now the critics are even reviewing my *phone calls*.

Dave Garroway once remarked that New York's taxi cabs are soluble—they always disappear in the rain. It's true. One night, after I had appeared on *Candid Camera*, it was pouring rain when we came out of the CBS studio. Naturally the taxi cabs had dissolved. Miriam and Randy were with me and we planned to have dinner at a midtown restaurant. We huddled in a doorway watching the rain pelting down and speculating gloomily on our chances of getting a cab. Minutes before we had been sitting in a warm studio chuckling at the plight of people trapped in fiendishly contrived circumstances. Now we were caught up in a rather miserable plight ourselves, and it didn't seem funny at all. Finally—wonder of wonders—a cab pulled up at the curb directly in front of us and we splashed out through the downpour to get it. However, the two men in the cab were involved in an argument with the driver and just sat there wrangling while we stood in the rain waiting. They were musicians and one of them was threatening to clobber the cabbie with a clarinet.

"Excuse me," I finally butted in, "but are you guys coming or going?"

"We're getting out," one of them said, "but this clown can't change a five." (New York cab drivers seemingly can *never* change anything larger than a quarter.)

"I've got change," I said, giving the man five singles and taking the five-dollar bill in exchange. The men paid the driver as we climbed into the cab and told him to take us to Trader Vic's. It was only a few blocks and as we pulled up I dredged into my pocket for change to pay the sixty-cent fare. Then I discovered that the five ones I had given the two musicians was my last change! *I* was right back where *they* had been, and I didn't want to go through *that* argument again.

"Keep the change," I said, handing the driver the five-dollar bill and mentally charging it off to Paar's Law. I wonder if stupidity is tax deductible?

The perverse workings of Paar's Law were never better illustrated than the time I took Randy to the opening night of Richard Burton's *Hamlet* on Broadway. Randy's been a fan of *all* Elizabeth Taylor's husbands, and was crazy to see Burton as Hamlet. Finally I agreed that I'd take her to the opening and we'd film it as a feature for my program.

"Papa will hire a limousine," I said, "and we'll get all dressed up and drive up just like all the celebrities, and I'll get an NBC cameraman to film it for my show."

Well, Randy was enchanted but as the occasion drew near I began to have dark forebodings. I'm not one for formal occasions and once horrified Elsa Maxwell by lighting a cigar at a fancy dinner at the Waldorf-Astoria. "That just isn't done," Elsa huffed, although I'd seen Hermione Gingold do it. I'd been to lots of closing nights (usually my own) but never to an opening night. In fact, my dinner jacket had been in dry dock so long five generations of moths had grown up in it. However, Randy was so enthused over our big occasion that I allowed myself to be trussed up in dinner clothes complete with boiled shirt, sapphire studs, and cummerbund. I looked like Lucius Beebe at a very social funeral.

Randy looked beautiful. She had a becoming, grown-up gown and her mother had allowed her to use a touch of lipstick to accent her blonde youthfulness. She chattered away excitedly as our limousine purred toward New York. "What will we do," she asked, "if the people cheer and applaud as we arrive?"

"Just smile and wave," I told her. "Without those nice people Papa would be in the tire business or something."

We were early and our long black limousine was the first to draw up in front of the Lunt-Fontanne Theatre, but there were already thousands of people massed behind the police barricades. However, there were no cheers, as we got out of the car, and no one even waved. The only sign of recognition came from a lady who trotted along beside us thumbing her nose at me. "I'd rather you did that, madame," I said, "than run along beside our car and bark at the wheels."

I tried to maintain my composure and kept looking around for the NBC cameraman as we walked toward the theater. "Keep smiling," I whispered to Randy. "The cameraman will be filming."

Finally I spotted the cameraman. He hadn't even seen us! He was staring into space and scratching himself. He finally saw us, but by then it was too late. We were just disappearing into the lobby to a deafening silence.

That was my introduction to a Broadway first night. We took our places among the chic first nighters; Randy looking radiant and I feeling deflated and uncomfortable in my formal clothes. I enjoyed *Hamlet*, and Burton's performance was magnificent, but it soon became further apparent that it just wasn't to be my night. Burton was uttering one of the bard's poetic lines when I heard an ominous *boinnnggg*. One of my studs had popped out and my starched shirt front sprang open revealing a patch of hairy chest. A few minutes later there was another *boinnnggg*. Another stud had popped out. It was the first time *Hamlet* was performed to a tympani accompaniment. I retrieved a couple of the studs but one fell into my shorts and I drew the line at grappling for that one. "Stop fussing, Papa," Randy whispered. "People are beginning to stare. I looked around and they were. "Where were they when I needed them?" I asked darkly.

By intermission time I was so unnerved I decided to leave. "If any more of these pop out," I told Randy, "I will have pioneered the topless tuxedo. I'll bring you another time but let's go. With this open shirt people will think I'm Harry Belafonte."

So we sneaked out with me clutching my shirt front and scuttling along with what Jack E. Leonard calls the chafed ankle walk, to keep the missing studs from falling out of my shorts. I was just trying to escape as inconspicuously as possible but *now* the cameraman sees us. "My God, Jack Paar," he exclaimed, focusing his camera on our retreating forms.

Then came the problem of our limousine. There were now about fifty limousines lined up around the block, all of them identically long, black, and sleek. How could I ever find ours? I thought of yelling, "Will the *real* Jack Paar chauffeur please stand up," but I didn't want to be conspicuous—at least at that late date. I finally decided to go to dinner and have our limousine service contact our driver and send him to the restaurant. Randy and I caught a cab for the Laurent Restaurant at 56th and Park Avenue. Then I called the limousine service and explained we had left the Lunt-Fontanne Theatre and were at the Laurent Restaurant. They said they would have our driver pick us up there.

Randy and I ate a leisurely dinner while I explored the mysterious recesses of my formal clothes for the missing stud. Incidentally, I never did find the missing stud although I offered a handsome stud fee for its return. Hours passed and still no stud. Also still no limousine. Finally I called the limousine service to ask what had become of ours.

"Our driver says there is no Laurent and Fontanne restaurant," the service said. Paar's Law again.

Poor people have more fun than rich people, they say, and I notice it's the rich people who keep saying it. It's true, though, that having a lot of money can lead to trouble, and I've been able to get into big trouble on even a little money.

Since I have a tendency to buy things I don't really need (I once joined the Yacht of the Month Club) my family have long tried to curb my extravagance. My mother always stressed the importance of thrift although she was as generous as she could afford to be. She always gave me five dollars

on my birthday and she still does. Since I've been married
to Miriam she, too, has tried to get me to be less impulsive
in buying things, and now I have platoons of lawyers, ac-
countants, and financial advisers all engaged in a grim effort
to control my financial vagaries. Even so I seem to be a
compulsive buyer and the only solution may be joining
Spenders Anonymous. (When you feel a craving to buy
something you call a friend. He comes over, gets drunk
with you and rolls you for your wallet.)

My most recent buying binge was on my last birthday. I
drove into New York in my new Jaguar XK-120 to have
lunch with several members of my show staff. We had a
long, pleasant lunch at "21" and the champagne flowed in
toasts to the occasion. Afterward the staff headed back for
the office while I walked toward the garage where I had
parked my car. I was in a state of euphoria. It was a beautiful spring day, I felt a pleasant glow from the champagne
and I had my mother's gift—the usual five-dollar bill—in my
pocket. I'll buy some little foolish thing with it I wouldn't
get ordinarily, I decided.

I looked in the windows of several fashionable shops, as
I walked down Park Avenue, but didn't see anything that
caught my fancy. Then I saw *it!* Glancing in the show room
of the Rolls-Royce agency I spotted a beautiful antelope-
colored Rolls with bright orange upholstery. I was trans-
fixed. With a bravado induced by the champagne, I decided
to have a closer look. I was greeted by a very proper Englishman.

"It's my birthday," I announced, under the mellow glow
of the bubbly I had imbibed.

"Well, happy birthday," the salesman said cheerfully.
"May I show you anything?"

As though I were listening to someone else, I heard myself saying I'd like to look at the antelope-colored Rolls with the orange upholstery. I was in a sort of dream state. Buying a new car, particularly one as expensive as a Rolls-Royce, was ridiculous, I knew. For one thing I already had a beautiful new Jaguar. For another, all the money I had in my pocket was my mother's five-dollar bill and some small change. Yet I was hypnotized by the gleaming Rolls.

"I believe I'll take it," I found myself blurting.

"Splendid," the salesman said. "That will be eighteen thousand dollars."

"Fine," I said. "I wonder if I could give you this five dollars as a down payment?"

The man glanced around nervously as though trying to signal someone to call the men in the white coats.

"I'd also like to trade in a new Jaguar XK-120," I offered.

The salesman looked considerably relieved. He hastily figured out what they would allow me on the Jaguar. After considerable signing of papers, they even let me drive the Rolls home.

Miriam was a little surprised when I drove up in the beautiful new car, but no more than I was. "I wanted to get something extravagant with my mother's five-dollar gift," I explained. From her pained expression I don't think she understood what generous terms I got: five dollars down and twenty-seven years to pay. At least she drew a moral from it. "Never leave Papa alone on his birthday with five dollars, if he's been drinking," she told Randy.

Some public-spirited citizen has just invented a phosphorescent belt for dogs that enables you to see your pet in the dark. What I wish is that someone would invent pajamas that would make me *invisible* to our dog in the dark. The problem is that our dog is an insomniac, among other things, and she likes to share her sleeplessness with people. In fact she believes in sharing *everything*.

We acquired our dog not long ago as a puppy. Schnapps, the dachshund we have had for years, had reached dowager status and Randy wanted a younger, livelier dog. The one we got exceeded all expectations, particularly as to liveliness. She is a beautiful, fawn-colored German shepherd and a wonderful companion if you don't mind a dog running your life.

From the start life with her has not been simple. First Randy decided the puppy should have a German name. The only German words I knew were "Gesundheit" and "Volkswagen" and neither seemed very practical. You might call "Here Volkswagen, Here Volkswagen," and a real Volkswagen would come. Finally Randy named her Leica for the German camera.

Leica sprouted rapidly and she scarcely knows her own strength. When I take her to pick up Miriam or Randy she rides in the front seat with me lashing me with her tail as she wags it. I may be driving a Rolls-Royce but with her tail flogging me I feel like a galley slave.

Another of Leica's idiosyncrasies is that she's an early riser—which means we are too. She may be a dog but she has the sadistic instincts of an Army bugler. She apparently can't stand the thought of anyone sleeping blissfully when they could be up cavorting with her. About six in the morning I'm awakened with a start by a wet tennis ball being shoved firmly in my face. I groan and roll over and tell her to go away but nothing fazes her. I invariably pull the covers over my head but Leica has the burrowing skill of a

badger and invariably succeeds in getting her head under
the blanket and shoving that chewed tennis ball in my face.
Her nose under the blankets is like a Fuller Brush man's
foot in the door: once it's there resistance is useless. The
next thing I know I'm groggily hurling the ball into the far
corners of our bedroom while Leica scrambles to retrieve it
with acrobatic leaps (that have broken two lamps and a
vase).

This game that begins at dawn continues until exhaustion
and is played both indoors and out. There is absolutely no
variety to it but Leica plays it with a relentless joy, rushing
with wild barks to retrieve the ball and trotting back to have
it thrown again.

One spring day I was sitting on the edge of our pool
dangling my feet in the water when Leica appeared with
her inevitable ball and that "Tennis, anyone?" expression on
her face. I didn't feel like playing and told her to go bury a
bone. She looked at me as reproachfully as a cockroach that
had been swatted by Dr. Schweitzer. Then she dropped the
ball in the pool and watched it float toward the middle
while she barked furiously.

The pool was chilly, having just been filled, and I wasn't
anxious to go in, but to silence the barking I finally plunged
in and retrieved the ball for her. She joyously dropped it in
again and began to bark more furiously than ever. Although
she was only a puppy she made as much noise as a pack of
bloodhounds in full cry after an escapee from a chain gang.
Again I dived in and got the ball for her. Then it suddenly
struck me—this wasn't the way things were meant to be.
The *dog* had *me* doing the retrieving. It was Paar's Law
again.

There's a popular theory that if you don't put things in writing you'll stay out of trouble, but this is contradicted by the operation of Paar's Law. I am very careful about what I put in writing, and even avoid answering mail whenever possible. In fact, I still haven't answered my last subscription letter from the Literary Digest. Yet trouble still has a way of seeking me out, as I was reminded again not long ago.

It all started with a letter informing me that I had been given a square foot of land in Tennessee. I knew it was some kind of a promotional stunt, so I simply dropped the letter in the waste basket. However, the promoters were a persistent lot. At regular intervals I would get letters keeping me informed about "my property" in Tennessee. One would describe the area in glowing terms. A few months later another letter would tell of future plans for the region. I continued to just drop them in the waste basket. Finally, I got a notice that began:

"Since you are a landowner in Tennessee, will you kindly notify us when you will be available for jury duty."

It was Paar's Law working by remote control.

*THE FATHER OF THE YEAR!*

All my life I've had one distinction. I never won *anything*. In high school the senior class didn't vote me the one most likely to succeed—perhaps because I never succeeded in becoming a senior. I never won baseball's Most Valuable Player award. I was an also ran in the Pillsbury Bakeoff. I lost the Mr. Universe Contest by a bicep. The winner had one. Not only did I never win the Irish Sweepstakes; the man who sold me my ticket got arrested.

Even in show business I never won anything, and that's not easy. You can hardly turn around in that business without someone handing you a plaque for something, or giving you a testimonial dinner. Show people hand out awards at the drop of an option. Get four of them together and instead of starting a gin rummy game they'll vote somebody an award.

In movies I never won an Oscar because they didn't have a category I fitted. After five years in Hollywood I was still a new face. In television I never got an Emmy even though they had trouble getting people to accept them. After twenty-five years in show business all I had to hang in my den was a thank-you letter from Hugh Downs.

Then it happened! The National Fathers' Day Committee named me Television Father of the Year for 1964. I was flattered, of course, but a little surprised. It seemed to me that men like NBC newscaster Frank Blair, who has eight children, or Frank Fontaine of the Jackie Gleason Show, who has eleven, have done more for fatherhood than I have. After all, since the birth of Randy, fifteen years ago, I haven't been as active in fatherhood. Of course, doing the *Tonight Show*, which occupied me until 1 A.M. each weekday night, may have had something to do with my decline as a father. By the time I'd finished *that* I was too tired to say hello to my wife. In any event I was pleased to receive the award even though I feel I got it under false pretenses.

For one thing Miriam has had more to do with raising Randy than I have, although I suppose they can't name *her* TV Father of the Year. However, ever since Randy was born I've tried to share in her upbringing. Even when she was a baby we handled her bath just like doing the dishes: Miriam washed and I dried. Another thing that makes me feel guilty about winning an award as a father is that actually Randy raised me. Of course, she had advantages that I didn't have as a youngster.

Raising children is so different today. When I was a kid growing up in Jackson, Michigan, we got our exercise by walking to school. Today we have a $20,000 bus to haul our children to a $100,000 gymnasium to exercise. Some of the kids today can't even read—and that can lead to problems we grownups don't think of. Randy has a little friend, Nicolette Goulet, the daughter of singer Robert Goulet, who ran into one of the hazards of being unable to read not long ago. She was only five at the time and went out to lunch with her father at a restaurant. About midway in the lunch (it's *always* midway in the lunch) Nicolette announced she had to go to the ladies' room. Goulet asked the headwaiter where the ladies' room was and then dispatched Nicolette in that direction. She was back a few moments later.

"There are two doors there," she said bitterly, "and you know I can't read."

Fortunately Randy learned to read at an early age. She went to a progressive school which my friend Milt Kamen describes as one where they make you do what you want to. It has turned out very well. Instead of my helping Randy with her homework, she helps me with my income tax returns. I gave up trying to help with her homework after the fifth grade. Now when she asks something like, "Papa, does 25 equal X squared?" I say, "I'd rather not discuss it."

Although Randy is very good with figures, her sense of values hasn't yet caught up with her mathematics in some instances. Recently she asked me, "Papa, how much did Major Cooper's space flight cost?"

"I'm not sure," I said. "I think I read somewhere it was around $20,000,000 for the orbital flight."

"Holy cow!" she exclaimed. "They could have made another *Cleopatra* for that."

We wanted to give Randy practical training in the handling of money so we had her take what she earns from little chores, like baby sitting or doing the dishes, and helped her invest it in the stockmarket. We insisted she choose her own stocks as I wanted her to learn about investments herself and not take advantage of my experience and contacts. So, while I was losing $47,000 one year, on tips from experts like comedian George Jessel, Randy made a tidy profit in Hershey Chocolate stocks. I asked her what her system was and how she happened to choose Hershey Chocolate stock

instead of, say, AT&T or General Motors. "I love their chocolate almond bars," she said.

With her way with mathematics, Randy has developed a
unique way of measuring time and space—a sort of junior
grade Einstein theory of relativity. I discovered it when I
overheard her talking to girl friends about the colleges they
were visiting to inquire about admission. "From our drive
it's *Lawrence of Arabia*," I heard her say. Later I overheard,
"From here it's *Cleopatra* and a newsreel." I was baffled.
"What in the world is that code you're talking?" I asked.
"Debbie was asking how long it takes to drive to Welles-
ley," she explained. "*Cleopatra* is four hours and a newsreel
is ten minutes, and that's how long it takes," she explained.
"That's how we tell time. Vassar is only *Divorce Italian
Style* from here."

The language of kids has always perplexed and fascinated
me. Several hundred years ago King George II of England
believed that children, if left alone, would speak Hebrew.
To test this theory, two babies were put on an island with
a mute nurse. Then George II died and everybody forgot
about the two children . . . so no one knows what happened. The children I've met don't speak Hebrew (except
Buddy Hackett's children who were raised on an island
with *him*) but they speak *some* strange language.

Consider the Beatles. They've become an international
mania in defiance of all the laws of music, speech, and bar-
bering. Yet the kids love them. Their songs are gibberish
usually swallowed up in the caterwauling of their adoring
fans, and their haircuts and speech are equally as difficult
to comprehend. Here's a sample from Beatle John Lennon's book:

MADAM: I have a hallowed tooth that suffer me grately.

SIR: Sly down in that legchair Madam and open your gorble wide—your mouse is all but toothless.

MADAM: Alad! I have but eight tooth remaining.

That's how Beatle John Lennon writes, and they call him the "intellectual Beatle."

Although I plead guilty to having first inflicted the Beatles on America on my show, their appeal has always eluded me. However, with their youthful fans' hot-eyed enthusiasm, I have decided it is wise to keep my gorble shut or I might wind up with my mouse all but toothless. Also, Randy has tried to set me straight on their popularity. "Don't you see, Papa?" she said. "It's the Lawrence Welk backlash."

I suppose that's as good an explanation as any. To me, the popularity of a quartet of Liverpudlians (and that name seems to fit them) with sheep dog haircuts, offkey voices, and fans who express their rapture by pelting them with jellybeans, is a sorry portent for the future. Yet I spent a good deal of time with Randy watching the two political conventions in the 1964 Presidential campaigns. Like many people, I winced inwardly at the raucous demonstrations, the windy speeches for favorite sons who weren't serious candidates, and other traditional shenanigans of American politics. After watching one particularly silly session, Randy turned to me and said, "And adults think *we're* immature for liking the Beatles."

There's one problem about Randy as a literary subject: there's only one of her and she's a model young lady. She goes to church regularly, does her homework faithfully and gets good grades. She's a joy, but no help when it comes to writing a book. Now take Jean Kerr, my friend and West-chester neighbor. She has four sons and they're all impos-sible. At least to hear Jean tell it, although one of her boys has weighed in with a dissenting opinion. Her son Christo-pher capsuled her book about him and his brothers in these words, "While it is funny it is exaggerated to the point of being flat lies." Maybe she's right about them. It's a strain on the nerves of Jean and her drama-critic husband Wal-ter, but they've had balm for any psychic wounds inflicted by their unruly offspring. Jean's made a mint chronicling their antics. It's been great for her, but she'd better be care-ful about confiding her kids' problems to *me*. They'll turn up in my book and Jean will be left high and dry with noth-ing but her fat royalties from *Mary, Mary* and *Poor Richard*.

Jean told me that she and her clan returned recently from a shopping expedition to the Scarsdale Supermarket only to find two hundred dollars' worth of costume jewelry myste-riously tucked away amid the groceries they had purchased. At a loss to account for the jewelry, her husband Walter called the local police. An officer arrived and asked the as-sembled Kerrs, "Well, what happened?"

"I stole it," said Jean, dead-pan. "The Kerrs are notorious thieves."

"Quit kidding, Jean," her husband said. "This officer has to find out the facts." The Kerrs then related the facts of their shopping while the boys drifted in and out of the room. The officer finished writing his report and reached for his cap to leave. One of the boys had taken it!

Unlike the mischievous Kerr boys, Randy is a very good girl. She not only never gets into trouble but gets upset with me when I do. She was angry with me a few years ago when I got into a hassle with Ed Sullivan when he threatened to ban performers from his show if they appeared on mine. This widely headlined rhubarb broke out on St. Patrick's Day—which is an unfortunate time to get in an argument with an Irishman named Sullivan.

The dispute was finally settled but diplomatic relations between Ed and myself remained strained. Then one evening Miriam, Randy, Tom Cochran, and I went to the movie preview of *It's a Mad, Mad, Mad, Mad World*. Our tickets were one pair of seats down front and another pair farther back. I suggested that Randy and Tommy take the seats down front while we took the others. We watched them go down the aisle and when they sat down people in the audience began to laugh. Then I saw Randy speak to the man next to her and *they* both began laughing. "What's so funny?" I whispered to Miriam. "Oh, dear God," she said. "Randy is sitting next to Ed Sullivan."

She loved Ed and they had a wonderful time chatting together, but I felt guilty. It suddenly struck me I hadn't been close enough to her, and hadn't paid enough attention to her upbringing. She can't even keep track of my enemies.

Some time later Randy asked me one night if I felt I was a good Christian. "Well, as you know I'm not much of a churchgoer," I told her, "but I try to follow the precepts of Christianity. I try to observe the golden rule."

"Do you forgive your enemies?" she asked.

I thought a moment of some of the assortment of enemies I'd made in my long fighting career: Walter Winchell, Jimmy Hoffa, Dorothy Kilgallen. It seemed like a mighty unlovable group.

"I'm afraid I have a quick temper," I said, "but I'm always sorry afterward. I don't really bear a grudge against anyone."

"Then why don't you call Mr. Sullivan and say you're sorry?" Randy demanded. "And while you're talking with him could you ask for two tickets for the Beatles Sunday night?"

That Sunday night Randy had two of the best seats in the house, for the Beatles appearance on the *Ed Sullivan Show*, as a guest of Ed Sullivan.

Thanks to television, Randy has had the advantage of meeting a good many famous people, including the President of the United States. Because of my show on television, with its equal time provision, I have stressed to Randy the necessity of remaining publicly neutral in politics. The night that John F. Kennedy, then campaigning for the Presidency, appeared on the program, Miriam and Randy sat with him backstage while he waited to go on. When I came offstage after the show, I found Randy wearing a large "JFK for President" button.

"You're not being very neutral," I chided her in mock seriousness. "Mr. Nixon may demand equal space for his button."

"Don't blame her," Mr. Kennedy laughed. "I pinned it on her."

Randy was charmed by Mr. Kennedy and deeply shocked and saddened by his assassination. Some time later, when Miriam and I were going to have dinner with the Robert Kennedys, Randy was excited to be included. Before going out, I briefed Randy in my best pseudo-Emily Post etiquette style. "Papa has known Mr. Kennedy since he was counsel for a senate committee," I explained. "You've probably even heard me call him Bobby on the phone. However, he's now the Attorney General, and the proper way to address him is Mr. Attorney General."

My briefing seemed to sink in. Randy's manners were impeccable, as she chatted animatedly with Mr. Kennedy at dinner, and she always politely addressed him as Mr. Attorney General. She seemed so proper and grown-up it was easy to forget she was really still a child. However, she reminded me.

"Mr. Attorney General," she said, very formally. "I have two shrimps left. Would you like to try them?"

Richard Nixon also appeared on the program during the 1960 Presidential campaign, and we got to know Mr. and Mrs. Nixon and their attractive teen-age daughters Tricia and Julie.

Later we were guests of Huntington Hartford at his fabulous Ocean Club on Paradise Island in the Bahamas at the same time the Nixons were there. Mr. Nixon had just lost a hotly contested election for the California governorship and was there to recover from the grueling campaign. I must say that the Ocean Club is a good place to recover from *anything*—except a hangover. They seem to flourish there. Paradise Island was formerly called Hog Island but Hartford renamed it after he disposed of the hogs and paved it with money. He didn't pave it with money, really, but it might have been cheaper. He poured over $30,000,000 into turning the former hog ramble into a tropical Eden. It has a magnificent manor house, elegant restaurant and colorful terraced gardens with enough statuary to start a medium-sized cemetery. It also sports such splendiferous trinkets as a medieval cloister, imported stone by stone from

France, a huge pool and a golf course with the whole Atlantic Ocean as a water hazard. I told Hartford that the island and his hospitality were a far cry from a few years before when Jonathan Winters and I had swum ashore from a boat to explore the island. "We were chased off by some natives waving rakes," I recalled. "We had to swim back to the boat." Now the only guests wallowing in all the luxury were the Hartfords, the Nixons, and ourselves.

We found both the former Vice-President and his wife Pat drained by the hard campaign and close defeat, following so closely on the heels of his loss in the Presidential campaign, but they were outwardly cheerful. Mr. Nixon seemed much warmer, more relaxed and humorous than the rather stiff image he had projected in the Presidential TV debates and in the California campaign where he angrily castigated the press. He told me with rueful humor of some of the ups and downs of the tough Presidential campaign which his wife Pat had shared with him. On one occasion, he said, he made a speech in Chicago warning Republicans against the temptation to "stand pat on what we have done." One newspaper headlined the speech: CAN'T STAND PAT, NIXON SAYS. I reminded him that because of my program, and because both he and Mr. Kennedy were good friends, I had to remain politically neutral. I said I felt like the old lady who marked her ballot, "God bless 'em both."

On Friday night I wanted to see my program which had been taped the previous Sunday in New York. I had noticed one house on the island with a big antenna capable of receiving programs from the States. I introduced myself to the owner, a man who designs golf courses, and asked if I could come over that night and watch my show. "Of course," he said. "You'll be welcome." When I told the Nixons we were going to watch the show they said they would enjoy seeing it too so I took the liberty of inviting them along.

I think our host was a little startled when I knocked on the door and he saw I had additional guests. And he seemed a little *more* startled when I said, "I'd like you to meet Mr. and Mrs. Richard Nixon." The Nixons were a bit surprised, *too*, when we turned on the show and the featured guests were Senator and Mrs. Ted Kennedy of Massachusetts. Even by flying a thousand miles, and taking refuge on an island, the former Vice-President couldn't escape the Kennedys.

Although Mr. and Mrs. Nixon were pleasant and philosophical, their two daughters were taking their father's defeat hard. Tricia, the older of the girls, is the more serious, and she seemed especially downcast by her father's loss. Julie, the younger sister is funny and more outgoing, but even she seemed visibly affected by her father's disappointment. I felt I'd like to do something to cheer the girls up and suggested that I take them into the town of Nassau ten minutes away across the water, for a night on the town. Mr. Nixon said it would be fine for the girls, but that he and Mrs. Nixon wouldn't go along because they still were exhausted and they didn't want to go where there would be crowds of people or reporters.

"I'll take good care of the kids," I promised. "I think they'll get a kick out of those wild night clubs. They're old enough."

We piled the Nixon girls and Randy in a motorboat and raced across the water to the old town of Nassau. There we got a taxi and asked to be taken to the colorful native quarter which they call "over the hill." The place was full of

rickety night clubs and the night air alive with the rhythm
of bongo drums. We picked one particularly garish-looking
night club that was jammed with American tourists, local
British and Bahamians. The music was raucous and the
dancing uninhibited. Some of the native dancing girls had
very little on but a few colored ribbons. I was a little embar-
rassed when I noticed that Randy seemed to be studying
them intently. "Look, Pop," she said joyously. "The Bronx-
ville school colors."

After we had watched for a while a native drummer recognized me and flashed a big grin. The next thing I knew he
winked at me and grabbed Tricia and began dancing. Tricia
is blonde and the drummer obviously thought she was
Randy. He began to twist and suddenly Tricia, who had
seemed so reserved, was doing the wildest twist I'd ever
seen. Then they did the limbo—the dance where you go
under a pole bending backward, and the pole is lowered
closer and closer to the floor as the dance progresses. When
the dancing ended the manager appeared with a big statue
and crowned Tricia the twist-limbo queen of the Bahamas.
It was apparent the crowd, who had been watching fascinated, thought she was Randy.

"Your name?" he asked.

"Tricia Nixon."

The MC looked at me with a puzzled expression but I
just smiled and shrugged.

"Where are you from?" he asked.

"Los Angeles," Tricia said.

"Are you the daughter of . . . ?" the emcee said, and
couldn't finish the sentence. It had suddenly dawned on
him the girl the drummer had been doing a wild twist
with was the daughter of the former Vice-President.

At any rate we all had a wonderful time and I didn't get the Nixon girls back until one in the morning. Both Mr. and Mrs. Nixon had retired. The next morning the former Vice-President saw the trophy and asked, "What happened last night?" "Mr. Paar will explain," Tricia said not very helpfully. I felt like some sixteen-year-old lad who had kept his daughter out too late.

"Well, Mr. Nixon, we went over the hill," I explained, beginning to feel guilty. "There was this big night club and there were about a thousand people there, and Tricia danced with the drummer. The people thought it was Randy but it was Tricia and she won that trophy as the limbo and twist queen of the Bahamas, and holy cow, I'm sorry we got back so late."

"*And?*" he said, fixing me with the stern gaze with which he once shriveled Alger Hiss in the witness chair. I tried to meet his steely gaze, since I felt we hadn't done anything wrong, but I was so flustered I was looking him straight in the knee. I couldn't tell whether he was genuinely angry or just pulling my leg.

"To tell you the truth, Mr. Nixon," I said, "if you'd unwound in the campaign, the way Tricia did last night, you'd be President today."

*TALK, TALK, TALK*

Jimmy Durante once took his father, an immigrant Italian barber, to see a long and gloomy play by Eugene O'Neill. Afterward Jimmy asked his father what he thought of the marathon drama. "Talk, talk, talk," said the elder Durante. "Alla time talk, talk, talk."

Looking back, that capsule critique seems to pretty well sum up my own career on television. For nearly ten years now I have been presiding over television programs the chief ingredient of which has been talk . . . unrehearsed, uninhibited and, at times, unintelligible. During that time I have bandied ad libs with some of the most strenuous and witty conversationalists of our times, and a few of the most crashing bores.

If I've made any contribution to the medium (other than bringing strife into the living room) I like to think it's been in making conversation respectable again. When I started on NBC's *Tonight Show* in July of 1957, conversation was almost unknown on television. TV was filled with the sound of bongo drums, bird calls, tap dancers, and xylophones. It was the golden age of noise. Ed Sullivan had the nearest thing to conversation; he was pointing at performers. The night he pointed at Harpo Marx in the audience and Harpo waved back it was the closest thing to conversation the medium had seen.

Off television, conversation wasn't doing very well either. Dr. Ray Birdwhistell of Temple University figured out that the average person spent only twenty-five minutes a day in articulated conversation. The rest of the time, he reported, people communicated by grimacing, smiling, frowning, raising an eyebrow, tugging an earlobe, nodding, or shrugging. All that grimacing, eyebrow raising, and shrugging seemed terribly tiring to me, which was another reason I liked conversation.

On the *Tonight Show* I began with the simple premise that the public would enjoy good, literate, and lively conversation as much or more than jugglers or dancing girls. I felt that people would as soon listen to Oscar Levant, Bea Lillie, Robert Morley, or Alex King talk as listen to a seal play *The Stars and Stripes Forever* on a horn. I thought people would be more interested in Zsa Zsa Gabor's conversation than in her cleavage. (You can't be right about *everything*.)

Generally, though, apparently I was right. The freewheeling conversation klatches became the main ingredient of the *Tonight Show* and later of my own program. Sometimes the guests were witty and sometimes I felt, as Marya Mannes once groaned, "like a deaf mute in a field of hog callers." However, by and large the talk was usually spirited and seldom dull. Soon talk shows were all the thing and even interruptions were popular. Arthur Godfrey spent a whole week talking to Jackie Gleason. Of course the conversation covered a big subject—it was about Gleason. Edward R. Murrow had a program where he talked to people all over the globe. And David Susskind talked to everyone including Nikita Khrushchev, which was a mistake. It turned out that when Khrushchev said "I'll bury you," he meant Susskind.

Oscar Levant is one of the most brilliant conversationalists I have encountered in a long and talkative career. He is a genius's genius. "If he did not exist," playwright S. N. Behrman said, "he could not be imagined." Oscar shoots from the lip and his verbal bullets usually hit the target. He can skewer anyone, including himself, with one barbed line. He suggested that Elizabeth Taylor win an award as The *Other* Woman of the Year. He defined ballet as the fairies' baseball, and said that sleeping with your wife is like striking out the pitcher. When Marilyn Monroe divorced Joe DiMaggio Oscar said, "Oh, well, no man can excel at *two* national pastimes." He described Zsa Zsa Gabor as a one-woman telethon without a dime going to charity. He once defined a newsreel as "a series of catastrophes ending with a fashion show." When a conductor criticized his piano technique, Oscar snapped, "If you don't behave I'll follow your beat." Once he spoke of dancing with Elsa Maxwell. "With some difficulty," he said, "I swept her off *my* feet."

Levant suffers from a host of maladies, real and fancied, and having him as a guest on the show is like being trapped in an oxygen tent with an angry wasp. Once before appearing on my show he asked to be made up lying down. When I went into the make-up room to have my chin dimple buffed I thought I'd stumbled into a wake. When Oscar comes on stage he weaves on like a drunk trying to find the rest room. He gropes his way to a chair and slumps in it twitching, scowling, and clutching his heart. "It might fall out," he once told me. For every pearl that comes from his mouth a pill goes in. One night he told me he had been thrown out of a mental institution for depressing the other patients. While there, he said, he was taken on an outing to Disneyland. "It was horrible," he groaned. "I prefer my own hallucinations." Another time he described his condition as too late for sweets and too soon for flowers. I mentioned a famous actress he knows. "I'm two nervous breakdowns up on her," he said, "and she's two suicide attempts up on me."

Oscar seems such a shambles that his appearance on our program usually brings on some scolding by critics and viewers. Once when we repeated a show featuring Oscar, Gordon McLendon, a Texan who owns a half-dozen radio stations (don't *all* Texans?) took to the air to denounce NBC and me for having him on when he was in such a shaky condition. "We strongly urge," McLendon editorialized, "that you miss Jack Paar's unforgivable repeat of the Oscar Levant obituary, particularly if you have a weak stomach."

Well, I have a small rebuttal for the nosey Texan. For one thing, a sick Levant makes more sense than a well McLendon. For another, Levant isn't as sick as he appears. This is not to say that Oscar is consciously acting when he comes on twitching, holding his heart and talking about his nervous breakdowns. He's just achieved the full flower of a widespread American trait: hypochondria. Oscar is the Bernarr McFadden of hypochondria. It isn't so much that he is sicker than other people as that he has a deeper appreciation of his ailments. He wants to look as bad as he thinks he feels. One night I went to dinner with Oscar and his pretty wife June after he had appeared on the show looking like a zombie. Oscar carved his steak as steadily as Ben Casey performing a lobotomy and put away a dinner that would have given a lumberjack heartburn.

One other thing. Oscar likes to appear on television. As Groucho Marx said of him, an ounce of attention is worth a pound of cure. Sick or well, Levant likes to talk. And, oddly enough, he likes to be paid for it.

McLendon's advice to NBC and me not to repeat the show with Oscar fell on deaf ears. (I always wear earmuffs during a McLendon broadcast.) The program drew an even larger audience the second time, and much favorable mail. "It was so good to see Mr. Levant again," one lady wrote. "He looked so much better on his second appearance."

S. N. Behrman has mentioned the "spiked embrace" of Levant's friendship, and I have a few scars to show for it myself. To paraphrase Will Rogers, Oscar has never met a man he didn't *dis*like. So barbed is his tongue that he himself has said that Los Angeles is going to erect a statue of him with a fig leaf over its mouth. Even friendship is no protection from his mordant wit. He was a close friend of composer George Gershwin yet he speared him with more than one acid line. "If you had it to do over again," he asked him, "would you fall in love with yourself again?" When Gershwin died a composer Levant knew composed an elegy in his honor. He proudly played it for Oscar.

"What do you think of it?" he asked anxiously.

"Maybe it would have been better," Oscar said, "if you had died and Gershwin had written the elegy."

"All you have is amiability," Oscar once told me, "and you're in danger of losing that." Another time I remarked to Oscar that a humorist is just a comic who scratches. "No," he said. "A humorist is someone like you who has four writers and then ad libs."

Levant is equally unsparing of himself. "The secret of my marriage," he once told me, "is that neither one of us can

stand me." Despite their domestic spats, which both Oscar
and his wife June air publicly on television, she is fiercely
loyal to him. Once she said that she wished I "would stop
calling Oscar nutty on TV." "If we took it to court," Oscar
mused, "we'd have a hard time disproving it."

For all his problems with health, wife, and family, Levant
never fails to brighten the show with his prickly wit. "My
behavior has been impeccable," he announced on one show.
"I've been unconscious for six months. Beneath this flabby
exterior lies an enormous lack of character."

I asked what he thought of Elizabeth Taylor. "I think she
should get a divorce and settle down," he said. "They say
Richard Burton is out to prove his masculinity. What a wonderful way to prove it."

He spoke of a Frank Sinatra movie. "It was so terrible I
went right out and made a citizen's arrest of the cashier." He
added that he had a theory on the kidnaping of Frank Sinatra, Jr. "It was done by music critics," he fanged.

For all his ailments and hypochondria, Oscar stumbles
serenely along, dropping sallies as he goes. There is even
talk that Warner Brothers' is going to film the story of his
life. "Do you know who's going to play my part?" he asked
me. "Rosalind Russell!"

England has some of the greatest wits and conversationalists, and they have provided my show with many of its
merriest moments. Most of them are brilliantly versatile.
Noël Coward is a writer, composer, and performer. Robert
Morley is a playwright and a great actor. Peter Ustinov,
who was raised in England and had his first success there,
writes, directs, and stars in his own plays and motion pictures, and writes novels as well. All of them have one thing

in common: they are, above all, fascinating conversationalists. It must be something in the air—perhaps fog. I love the understatement of the British and the clipped cadence of their speech. They sound just like us—but with the volume turned down.

I once cabled Robert Morley in London asking if he knew Malcolm Muggeridge's address. He promptly cabled back, "Yes." I suppose that one-word reply might be taken for typical British understatement, but there is little that is typical or understated about Morley. In fact, he is a passionate disciple of *over*statement, full of the most preposterous notions which he has a gift of making somehow seem plausible. He loves to debunk sacred cows and nothing is safe when Robert starts to talk. "I don't believe anyone learns anything from experience except caution," he says. Certainly caution is something Morley has avoided like the plague. "The real trouble with the world is exercise," he told me one night. "The greatest single disaster to befall man was the invention of the ball."

"The ball?" I said incredulously.

"I have never in my life struck a ball in anger," he declared. "It's most unnatural and wicked to hit a ball. The first thing you do with a ball is give it to a child. And he throws it away, which is the proper thing to do with a ball."

Morley's targets include everything from schoolteachers to the theater, and he delights in biting the hand that feeds him. When I have him on the show I feel as insecure as a zoo keeper gingerly poking pieces of meat through the bars to a tiger. "Schoolteachers are wicked people who teach children what they don't want to learn," he told me. "Children—how wonderful they are at four . . . how dreadful at fourteen. Only one answer—schoolmasters."

Morley also has a very low estimate of the theater, especially playwrights of which he is one. "I always keep a playwright out of the theater at rehearsal," he told me. "After they've seen my performance they stay out of their own accord."

He said that people in England don't go to matinees. "Then why do you have them?" I asked. "It keeps the actors sober for the evening performance," was his reply.

I once asked Robert whom he thought were the wittiest conversationalists. "If you name them they stop talking," he said. "They're so afraid they'll destroy their reputation they clam up. The best thing to say about your enemies is that they are good conversationalists. It gets back to them and they shut up."

Another of the great English wits and conversationalists is Noël Coward. For years I have admired Coward's stiletto style with a squelch. Once he was approached by a reporter for the *London Star*. "Mr. Coward, would you like to say something to the *Star*," he was asked. "Certainly," Noël replied. "Twinkle."

Another time he visited veteran actor Clifton Webb in Hollywood and found him still in mourning for his mother who had died some time before. "You must pull yourself together, Clifton," Coward said. "It's not unnatural, you know, to be orphaned at the age of seventy-one."

I told Coward once that I thought the lyrics to his *Mad Dogs and Englishmen* were some of the most brilliant ever written. He told me that Churchill and Roosevelt had met in England after the Atlantic Charter meeting and had a long dispute over the correct words to the song. Later Sir Winston met Coward and told him of the argument. "Well,

Mr. Prime Minister," said Noël, "President Roosevelt was right and you were wrong."

Churchill pondered for a moment and then grunted, "England can take it."

I had to interrupt our conversation on the air for a commercial. "I never thought when I watched *Cavalcade* in a theater in Jackson, Michigan," I said, "that some day I'd be selling Bromo Seltzer in front of Noël Coward. Democracy may have gone too far."

"Oh, I think it does overstep sometimes," Coward smiled.

When the filmed commercial came on it was Elsa Maxwell, an old friend of Coward's, extolling the merits of the headache remedy. When it ended I asked, "When you first knew Elsa, did you ever think she'd go that far?"

"Yes," said Noël, in a world-weary voice.

Coward reminisced fascinatingly on the program about his long career in the theater. He recalled playing in his *Tonight at 8:30* in England. The scene, he said, was a comfortable old living room with a big fireplace and a mantel laden with bric-a-brac. "Alan Webb and Joyce Carey were doing a love scene before the fireplace," he said. "Meantime a young fellow with a walk-on part was wandering around backstage killing time. He noticed a little wooden peg in the back of the scenery and idly yanked it out. There was a thundering crash and screams of horror. The whole fireplace collapsed on stage, burying the lovers in shattered bric-a-brac. The little peg, of course, had fastened the fireplace to the side of the set. And just at that moment Gertrude Lawrence made her entrance."

"What in the world did she do?" I asked.

"She just looked in horror at the lovers lying amid the

wreckage," Noël said. "Then she said, 'It is an old house, but *very* sweet.'"

Another great talker, one of the great raconteurs of the world, is Peter Ustinov, the bearded, roly-poly one-man gang of show business. Both as an artist and a man, Peter combines more varied ingredients than a bouillabaisse. He is of Russian, French, Italian and Armenian descent. He speaks a half-dozen languages and is funny in all of them. He is also a show business cartel. He writes, directs, and stars in plays and movies. He is a short story writer and novelist. It is as a conversationalist and raconteur, however, that I enjoy him most. His talk is always stimulating, whether it's a long story, with Peter playing half a dozen characters in as many dialects, or just a pointed observation, such as, "People in England who get to the top are those having no qualifications for detaining them at the bottom."

Peter got to the top in a hurry, after an unpromising start. The son of a German diplomat of Russian descent, he was raised in England. He never made much of a mark in school. "Peter shows great originality," a teacher wrote his parents, "which must be curbed at all costs." Fortunately, the school wasn't able to curb it. At eighteen he made his debut in a London theater in a sketch he wrote himself. Since that time he has been writing, acting, and directing in the theater, television, and motion pictures. He does much of his work on his yacht on the Riviera. "It will sleep six people who know each other very well," he says, "or one prude."

Peter told me one night of playing in his own comedy *Photo Finish* in London. At a matinee latecomers were still straggling in when he was startled to hear a lady's voice from the audience counting.

"One . . . two . . . three . . ." she counted, in a loud, clear voice.

"The suspense got worse as the counting continued," Peter said. "The other actors and I began to forget our lines in our fascination with this disconcerting performance in the audience."

"Six . . . seven . . . eight . . ." the count continued.

"There was complete confusion on the stage," Peter said. "We were going crazy out of curiosity. What was happening? we wondered. Finally the lady got to ten. She rose in her seat, waved toward the back of the house, and said in a loud voice, "Yoo-hoo . . . Penelope—here I am in the tenth row!"

Once Ustinov attended a meeting of British and Russian playwrights. Two writers discovered that a play by each had been done in the other's country. It was suggested writers from both countries meet regularly to discuss such matters of mutual interest. Someone pointed out the Soviet Union would not permit such meetings. "They permit sports teams to meet," Ustinov observed. "We could organize writers' football teams and meet on the playing field."

"No," a Russian told the plump playwright. "You and I are both so heavy we would be the goalies."

Since he has traveled so extensively, many of Ustinov's stories have to do with Europe. He particularly loves to tell stories illustrating the Italian character. He told one night of a man arrested for defiling the walls in an Italian election. He had written: "Long live everybody!"

The same spirit was reflected in another Italian election story. Peter went to a political rally in Rome where three candidates spoke. All had fiery and diametrically opposed views, yet the crowd applauded all with equal fervor. Peter asked a man why they applauded all with enthusiasm, when they had such opposed views. "We've got to treat them as guests," the Italian explained. "They came a long way."

Peter's attitude toward life is tolerant and philosophical, yet he detests generals, even Italian generals. "They are fascinating cases of arrested development," he says. "After all, at five we all wanted to be generals." He tells a story of a newspaper correspondent observing Italian war maneuvers. Everything went wrong. Tanks were bumping into each other and the whole thing was a comedy of errors. The correspondent remarked on the confusion. "I, too, get depressed at this," the general sighed. "But remember, the enemy has generals, too."

Another time Ustinov went to Horcher's, a famous restaurant in Madrid. He was greeted effusively by the headwaiter, who recognized him as a film star, and shown to the finest table. The headwaiter hovered over Ustinov, smothering him with service, and particularly recommending a salad with a special dressing. Ustinov agreeably ordered the salad. In the zeal of mixing the salad with the proper flourishes, the headwaiter spilled some dressing on Peter's necktie. The man was covered with confusion but Peter accepted the accident good-naturedly. All apologies, the headwaiter said if Peter would give him the tie he would take it to the kitchen and remove the stain. Peter gave him the tie and he disappeared into the kitchen on a wave of muttered regrets. The doors had scarcely closed behind him when the restaurant owner entered. He eyed the rumpled, tieless Ustinov with horror. Going quickly to his table, he announced in a voice dripping with disdain, "I'm sorry, sir, but dining without a tie is not permitted at Horcher's. We will have to ask you to leave."

# THAT'S SHOW BIZ

They say there's no business like show business, and I think it's just as well. For all its occasional rewards, the entertainment business is booby-trapped with surprises. In fact, the very expression, "Well, that's show biz," seems to cover almost any contingency from a ruptured spleen to your wife's running away with her Arthur Murray dancing instructor.

When I arrived in New York from Hollywood in the spring of 1953 I was unemployed, discouraged, and broke. Today I am employed, optimistic and owe $1,900,000. (I borrowed it to buy a television station in Maine.) In the past owing that much money would scare me, but my business manager tells me I should be delighted. "How many people can borrow that kind of money?" he asked. "That's a sign you've arrived. You're a star!"

"If it weren't for the honor attached," I suggested meekly, "I'd just as soon I didn't owe all that money."

That seems to be one of the facets of stardom: little things like $1,900,000 debts are always bobbing up to surprise you. When I was a kid starting out as a radio announcer in places

like Jackson, Michigan, Youngstown, Ohio, Cleveland, Pitts-
burgh, and Buffalo, I used to daydream about how nice it
would be to be a big star. Actually, I had a rather modest
form of stardom in mind. I wondered if someday I might be
as famous as Tony Wons. I dreamed of signing autographs,
driving a Duesenberg, living at the Garden of Allah and
dates with Maureen O'Sullivan who looked so fetching in
those Tarzan pictures. Well, I did become a star, my agent
keeps telling me, but it didn't quite work out the way I
thought it would. Now they no longer make Duesenbergs,
the Garden of Allah has been torn down, and Maureen
O'Sullivan has climbed down out of the trees long enough
to have seven children. And now signing autographs makes
me nervous. Originally I enjoyed signing autographs, especially for kids, even though my signature looks like an
appendix scar on a ticklish patient. Eventually, though, autograph signing began to pall. One night a teen-aged boy
asked for my autograph in an elevator at NBC. "You've always been my idol, Mr. Paar," he said. "I've always wanted
to follow in your footsteps." I was really quite touched. "You
mean you'd like to have your own TV show?" I asked.
"Naw," the boy said. "I want to go into the Army and marry a
girl from Pennsylvania, just like you did."

Another time a lady came up to me in a New York restaurant brandishing a menu for me to sign. "I loved you on the
*Tonight Show*," she said. "A young man like Johnny Carson
can never replace an old man like you."

Little things like that do a lot to buck up your morale.
The time I finally lost what remained of my enthusiasm for
autograph signing, though, was when a sweet-faced lady
stopped me in a corridor at NBC. While I was signing an
autograph for her, she smilingly slipped me a summons.

Such unnerving experiences with fans are not at all uncommon, other performers have told me. Ethel Merman was in a Chicago night club when she was accosted by a woman who asked, "Aren't you Ethel Merman?" "Yes, I am," the singer acknowledged. "Well," said the woman, "you don't look it."

Sam Levenson, who appears frequently on television, both live and on tape, told me he once attended a funeral in Brooklyn. At the cemetery a woman asked him if he was Sam Levenson. Levenson said he was. "Gee," the woman said, "I never expected to see you here live."

Once I did a filmed stunt for *Candid Camera* at a parking lot in New Jersey. I was wearing a parking attendant's uniform and cap and dark glasses to disguise my identity. A woman with two small children left her car with me to park while she went shopping. When she returned, burdened down with bundles and towing the two children, I was all set with one of Allen Funt's diabolical practical jokes and the hidden cameras were rolling. The woman handed me the parking ticket for her car. "I'm sorry," I told her, "but I can't get your car started. Also you must have run over some glass. All four tires are flat."

We hoped to provoke some funny response, but the stunt backfired. The harried woman simply dropped her bundles and dissolved in tears. Her genuine distress was more than I could stand. I yanked off my dark glasses, smiled reassuringly, and said, "I'm Jack Paar."

"Oh, that's too bad," she sobbed, "but what about my car?"

One type of fan I have never quite understood is the one who tells you he never watches the show and then asks for an autograph for his nephew. Always a nephew. "It

seems," Alfred Hitchcock sighed, "that there are more
nephews than people." Lately I've noticed that some of the
more waspish members of the show business fraternity have
been striking back at fans who are rude. One such lady accosted Oscar Levant in a hotel elevator. "You don't remember me, do you?" she said, accusingly.

"No," admitted Oscar. "Fortunately I'm suffering from
amnesia."

Noël Coward also has a good retort for people who greet
him with, "You don't remember me, do you?" Coward always replies, "Of course I do. How's Muriel?" "There's something about that name Muriel," Coward told me. "They
never ask again."

A fan once stopped Groucho Marx and asked him if
the Marx brothers were really brothers. "Certainly," said
Groucho. "All but two of us, who are sisters. Which two,
we've never been able to find out."

Actress Joan Collins was once in the ladies' room at Lindy's restaurant when a woman told her she looked like Joan
Collins. "I *am* Joan Collins," the actress said. "Well, what are
*you* doing in the ladies' room at Lindy's?" the woman asked.

"Where would you suggest I go?" Miss Collins said. "The
*men's* room?"

Nearly as annoying as the fans who insult you outright
are those who do it unconsciously by mistaking you for
someone else. This is a common occurrence with entertainers and I've been mistaken for everyone from Van Johnson
to Lyndon Johnson. (The man who mistook me for Van
Johnson just asked me to sign my name, but the lady who
mistook me for Lyndon Johnson asked me to sign the Civil
Rights bill.)

This confusion is usually harmless enough, except to an

actor's ego, but it could lead to complications. Garry Moore is known by his real name of Garrison Morfit in Rye, New York, where he lives. One morning his wife was setting out shopping when she found her car had a flat tire. Taking Garry's car she drove to a service station and asked the attendant to go to her house and change her tire.

When he arrived at the Morfit house, Garry answered the door in pajamas. The startled men asked, "Is this . . . er . . . the Morfit residence?" Garry assured him that it was and the man fixed the tire.

Later a friend of Garry's told him he had gone into the service station for gas and the attendant had told him about the call at the Morfits'.

"And guess who answered the door in his pajamas?" the attendant asked. *"Dave Garroway."*

Noël Coward likewise once found himself entangled in an amusing case of confused identity. He went into a Western Union office to send a gag cable to some friends in England. He wrote it out, signed it "Mayor La Guardia," and handed it to the girl behind the counter. "I'm sorry, sir," she said. "We cannot accept messages signed with another person's name."

Coward then rewrote the cable and signed his own name. "But I told you, sir, that you can't sign another person's name," the girl reiterated.

"But I *am* Noël Coward," the playwright said.

"Oh, in that case, Mr. Coward," the clerk said, "you *can* sign 'Mayor La Guardia.'"

Not so lucky, in a somewhat similar situation, was TV actor Brett Halsey. Halsey flew to San Francisco to buy a painting. Carrying it under his arm he went to an airline counter to get a ticket back to Hollywood.

"Oh, Mr. Halsey," the girl at the counter gushed, "I love you on TV. Could I have your autograph?"

Halsey signed graciously. The girl then weighed the painting and his other luggage and told him he was over his weight allowance.

"May I write a check?" the actor asked.

"Only if you have some identification," the girl replied.

Of course, if there is one thing more irritating to most performers than being recognized on the street by people, it's *not* being recognized.

This happened once to film star Gregory Peck. One night he and a friend went to a fancy restaurant where customers were waiting. The maitre d' did not recognize Peck. "I'm sorry, gentlemen," he said, "you'll have to wait in line." Peck's friend asked the actor, "Greg, why don't you tell him who you are." Peck smiled. "If I have to tell him who I am," he said, "then I'm *not*."

Although I usually flee from autograph seekers, I'll confess to having been annoyed on a couple of occasions when someone failed to recognize me. This happened once when I called our local, friendly, *wealthy* neighborhood TV repair service. After they had carefully checked my credentials, they agreed to grant me an appointment to discuss the problem with one of their representatives over coffee and brandy. The representative proved to have all the finesse of a skilled diplomat—Comrade Molotov. He examined our TV set as though he were looking for a case of leprosy.

"Do you know what's wrong with it?" I asked.

"No," he said, "but it will cost eighty-six dollars to fix."

I forget why he said it would cost so much. I think he said they would have to rebuild the set from the aerial down. Or maybe it was from the plug out. Anyway it was expensive. Moreover he kept addressing me as "Mac."

I mentioned the set in our bedroom was also acting up. "Could you look at it, too, while you're here?" I asked.

"I'm sorry, Mac," he said. "That will have to be a separate trip."

By this time I was beginning to get irritated, particularly with that "Mac."

"You could go out the front door and come in again," I suggested. "Or you could just stay here and fix it and I could drive around the neighborhood and put some mileage on your truck. That would cost just as much but would speed things up."

"Let's see what we can do with this one first, Mac," he said. "Just grab one end and we'll pull it out where I can get at it."

By this time I was really annoyed. Not only was he overcharging me, while I did half the work, but I was getting awfully tired of that "Mac." I was trying to think of some impolite way to tell him my name was not Mac but Jack Paar, and that I wasn't a volunteer assistant television repair man, I had my own show. Finally one of those happy coincidences happened, or so I thought for a moment. While he was tuning the set he turned to Channel 4 and an NBC promotional announcement for my show came on, with a shot of me and an announcer saying, "Be sure to watch the *Jack Paar Show* Fridays at 10 P.M. Eastern time."

The repairman gave no sign that he recognized that the man on the screen and the one he was ordering around and calling "Mac" were one and the same. I decided to make one last try. "Do you ever watch that show?" I asked.

"Naw," the man snorted. "I just fix TV sets. There's no law that says I hafta look at 'em. Here, give me a hand again, willya, Mac?"

Another time I had an equally deflating experience with a cab driver. One morning I had to fly to Portland, Maine, for a meeting at my television station. I got a taxi from my home and pulled out a copy of *Time* magazine to read en route to La Guardia Airport. There are several highways by which you can reach La Guardia, and after a while I looked up from my magazine to notice we were going some back way through quiet residential streets.

"Aren't you going to take the freeway?" I asked.

"This is a short cut I know," the driver said. "It will get us there faster and won't cost any more."

Lulled by this assurance, I buried myself again in my magazine. Suddenly the cab made an abrupt turn and we pulled into the driveway of a modest bungalow on a side street. "Hey, Margaret," the driver bellowed. "Lookit who I got in the cab." With this a big mongrel dog bounded off the porch barking furiously and acting as though he would like to rend me limb from limb. "Hey, Margaret," the man yelled again. "Come look who I got out here."

While the dog continued barking wildly and slavering to get at me, a frowsy-looking woman came out on the porch, wiping her hands on her apron, and peering at me suspiciously.

"I give up," she said. "So who is it?"

"Jack Paar!" the driver cried triumphantly.

"No wonder I didn't recognize him," the woman said. "You know I don't follow baseball."